OXFORD MODERN LANGUAGES
AND LITERATURE MONOGRAPHS

Editorial Committee

Borges and Kafka

Sons and Writers

SARAH ROGER

OXFORD
UNIVERSITY PRESS

OXFORD

UNIVERSITY PRESS

Great Clarendon Street, Oxford, OX2 6DP,
United Kingdom

Oxford University Press is a department of the University of Oxford.
It furthers the University's objective of excellence in research, scholarship,
and education by publishing worldwide. Oxford is a registered trade mark of
Oxford University Press in the UK and in certain other countries

© Sarah Roger 2017

The moral rights of the author have been asserted

First Edition published in 2017

Impression: 1

Published in the United States of America by Oxford University Press
198 Madison Avenue, New York, NY 10016, United States of America

British Library Cataloguing in Publication Data
Data available

Library of Congress Control Number: 2016943229

ISBN 978–0–19–874615–7

Printed in Great Britain by
Clays Ltd, St Ives plc

For my parents

Copyright Acknowledgements

Acknowledgements

Many people deserve credit for helping with the research and writing that culminates in this book. Foremost, my thanks are owed to Professor Edwin Williamson and Dr Clive Griffin at the University of Oxford, who supervised my master's and doctoral research. Their guidance has made me the scholar I am today.

I owe thanks to Professor Robin Fiddian and Professor John King, who offered many fruitful suggestions as examiners of my doctoral dissertation, from which this book has grown. I would also like to thank the reviewers who read my manuscript for Oxford University Press: Professor Harriet Turner, Dr Joyce Crick, and Professor Robin Fiddian. Many thanks as well to Dr Emily Troscianko and Jennifer Strachan for their careful editing and Dr Alice Brooke for her help, both as a scholar and as a friend.

For funding the doctoral and postdoctoral research that underlies this work, I am grateful for a scholarship from the University of Oxford's Clarendon Fund, a studentship from The Queen's College Oxford, a grant from Abbey Santander for research in Argentina, and a Junior Research Fellowship from St Edmund Hall Oxford. My thanks as well to the Institute for Advanced Studies at the University of Edinburgh for a quiet place to work in the final stages of editing.

This book would not have been possible without the permission of copyright holders, and I thank the Borges estate for generously allowing me to reproduce source material. For their guidance and hard work, I also owe thanks to Ellie Collins, Rachel Platt, Fiona Tatham, Nishantini Amir, Dawn Ingram, Danie Woodbridge, Katharine Hellier, and the editing and production team at Oxford University Press.

Lastly, my thanks to those who have endured my attempts to relate everything in the universe to Borges and Kafka: my aunt Robin Roger (whose knowledge as a psychotherapist and writer helped me understand Borges's relationship with his father), my partner Robert Siddaway, and my parents Howard and Jackie Roger.

Contents

A Note on Editions, Translations, and Titles

Throughout this book, quotations are provided in their original languages and in English translation. For Borges, the Spanish quotations come from modern, complete, scholarly editions of his works, for which publication details are provided in the footnotes and the bibliography. For Kafka, where possible, the German quotations come from the *Gesammelte Schriften* published by Schocken in 1935 (volumes one through four) and by Heinrich Mercy Sohn in 1936–7 (volumes five and six). Although the editions of Kafka published in the 1930s are not commonly used for scholarly research, these volumes—with reconstructions and edits made by Max Brod—were the ones that Borges would most likely have read. Publication details for these works are provided in the footnotes and the bibliography; citations (but not the quotations, which may vary by a few words) are also provided for the locations of the same material in modern, scholarly editions. At the first mention of each text, the year provided in parentheses denotes the first year of publication by any source, and not the year in which the work was written.

Translations are taken from published editions wherever possible to allow readers of English to locate full versions of the texts if desired. In the case of Kafka, the English quotations are from translations by Willa and Edwin Muir where possible, because Borges wrote about reading their translations (although he also read Kafka in the original German). Where a translation is provided alongside an original, the translator is given as the source for the quotation in the footnote. Where no mention of a translator appears, I was unable to locate a published translation and have provided my own. For titles, a translation is provided the first time a work is mentioned in each chapter.

A brief word on nomenclature and spelling: Kafka's 'Die Verwandlung' [The Metamorphosis] is regarded throughout as a long short story, rather than as a novel. Therefore its title is placed in quotation marks rather than italicized. Borges's translation of the story, when discussed as a work of interest in and of itself, is referred to as 'La metamorfosis'. Borges's collection of translations, which takes its name from its title story, is referred to as *La metamorfosis*. Additionally, of the two titles for Kafka's 1927 novel, *Der Verschollene* [*The Man Who Disappeared*] and *Amerika* [*America*], the title used here is *Amerika* because that was the one Borges preferred for his criticism. For spelling, where there is a discrepancy in the German between the more commonly used spelling of a term and the spelling as used in the editions edited by Brod to which Borges had access, Brod's spelling is preferred. For example, *Der Prozeß* [*The Trial*] is used in preference to *Der Proceß*. For English, spelling is in keeping with the choices made by the Muirs in their translations of Kafka: for example, 'Oklahoma' in preference to Brod's (and Kafka's) 'Oklahama'.

1

Biographical Predecessors and Literary Precursors

1938 was a significant year in Jorge Luis Borges's development, a year during which three events took place that catalysed a shift in his writing. First, his father Jorge Guillermo Borges died on 24 February, ending an almost forty-year relationship of shared literary interests and aspirations. Just prior to his death, Borges *père* (Jorge Guillermo) asked Borges *fils* (Jorge Luis) to compensate for his shortcomings as an author by rewriting his poorly received novel, *El caudillo* [*The Chieftain*] (1921). Second, Borges translated and published a collection of nine stories by Franz Kafka under the title *La metamorfosis* [*The Metamorphosis*]. Third, in December 1938 Borges contracted blood poisoning after running into an open window—an incident that led to his hospitalization and his creation of 'Pierre Menard, autor del *Quijote*' [Pierre Menard, Author of the *Quixote*] (1939), a story Borges identified as a turning point in his writing:

> I thought that if I tried to write a review now and failed, I'd be all through intellectually but that if I tried something I had never done before and failed at that it wouldn't be so bad and might even prepare me for the final revelation. I decided I would try to write a story. The result was 'Pierre Menard, Author of *Don Quixote*'.[1]

Critics such as Gene Bell-Villada and Edna Aizenberg have identified 1938 as a decisive year with respect to Borges's transition from writing poetry to writing prose fiction and with respect to the influence of Kafka, while Edwin Williamson was the first to point out that these key events coincided with Borges *père*'s death.[2]

---

[1] Jorge Luis Borges, 'An Autobiographical Essay', *The Aleph and Other Stories: 1933–1969*, trans. and ed. Norman Thomas di Giovanni (London: Jonathan Cape, 1968), pp. 203–60 (p. 243).

[2] Gene Bell-Villada, *Borges and his Fiction: A Guide to his Mind and Art*, 2nd ed. (Austin: U of Texas P, 1999), pp. 36–7; Edna Aizenberg, 'Kafka, Borges and Contemporary Latin-American

This study provides a detailed investigation of Borges *fils*'s development as an author in the light of Kafka's influence and Borges *père*'s death, events that marked a turning point in Borges *fils*'s career, but which endured in subsequent decades and which explain some of his aims as a writer. Although a number of shorter studies (mostly articles) have been written on aspects of Borges's engagement with Kafka, this is the first comprehensive assessment of Borges's interpretation of Kafka and the nature and extent of Kafka's influence on Borges's stories. In exploring the connection between Borges and one of his major literary interlocutors, it follows the model set by similar productive readings, such as Humberto Núñez-Faraco's *Borges and Dante: Echoes of a Literary Friendship* (2006) and Patricia Novillo-Corvalán's *Borges and Joyce: An Infinite Conversation* (2011).

1.1 READING AND BIOGRAPHY

When writing about Kafka in a capsule biography and in the prologues to the Spanish editions of *América* [*America*] and *La metamorfosis*, Borges contextualized his reading with details from Kafka's historical, artistic, and familial background:

> 1883, 1924. Esas dos fechas delimitan la vida de Franz Kafka. Nadie puede ignorar que incluyen acontecimientos famosos: la primera guerra europea, la invasión de Bélgica, las derrotas y las victorias, el bloqueo de los imperios centrales por la flota británica, los años de hambre, la revolución rusa, que fue al principio una generosa esperanza y es ahora el zarismo, el derrumbamiento, el tratado de Brest-Litovsk y el tratado de Versalles, que engendraría la Segunda Guerra. Incluye asimismo los hechos íntimos que registra la biografía de Max Brod: la desavenencia con el padre, la soledad, los estudios jurídicos, los horarios de una oficina, la profusión de manuscritos, la tuberculosis. También, las vastas aventuras barrocas de la literatura: el expresionismo alemán, las hazañas verbales de Johannes Becher, de Yeats y de James Joyce. El destino de Kafka fue transmutar las circunstancias y las agonías en fábulas.

> [1883, 1924—the two years that frame the life of Franz Kafka. Nobody can ignore the notable events contained within them: the first European war, the invasion of Belgium, the defeats and the victories, the blockade of the central imperial powers by the British fleet, the years of hunger, the Russian Revolution, that initially flourishing hope that is now Tsarism, the collapse, the Brest-Litovsk treaty, and the treaty of Versailles leading to the Second World War. They also include the personal events recorded in Max Brod's

Fiction', *Newsletter of the Kafka Society of America* 6.1–2 (1982): 4–13 (p. 8); Edwin Williamson, *Borges, A Life* (London: Viking, 2004), p. 235.

biography: Kafka's rift with his father, his solitude, law studies, hours spent working in an office, the proliferation of manuscripts, and his tuberculosis. There were also the baroque forays into literature: German expressionism and the verbal feats of Johannes Becher, Yeats and James Joyce.

Kafka's destiny was to transform circumstances and agonies into fables.][3]

In 1937, Borges suggested that 'Los hechos de la vida de este autor no proponen otro misterio que el de su no indagada relación con la obra extraordinaria' [The events of this author's life propose no other mystery than their unexplored connection with his extraordinary work].[4] Borges made this comment in the same year that Kafka's friend and executor, Max Brod, published his biography of Kafka. Borges and Brod are among those who have argued that Kafka's writing contains a 'hidden core of ramified personal allusions'.[5]

As with Kafka, it is possible to read Borges's writing both with and without reference to his biography. Critics such as Daniel Balderston in *Out of Context: Historical Reference and the Representation of Reality in Borges* (1993) and Bell-Villada in *Borges and his Fiction: A Guide to his Mind and Art* (1999) present Borges's personal experiences as integral to their interpretations. Some biographies—particularly Emir Rodríguez Monegal's *Jorge Luis Borges: A Literary Biography* (1978) and Williamson's *Borges, A Life* (2004)—take this further by using biography to illuminate Borges's stories. However, there are many insightful studies of Borges that look at aspects of his writing separate from his biography, among them Juan Nuño's *La filosofía de Borges* (1986) and Floyd Merrell's *Unthinking Thinking: Jorge Luis Borges, Mathematics, and the New Physics* (1991), which focus more closely on the abstract concepts underpinning Borges's work. While both perspectives can be equally productive, this monograph takes a biographical approach to reading Borges. It is based on the model of Borges's own reading of Kafka, which draws on aspects of Kafka's life to explain his work. As such, it is worth briefly exploring Borges's under-standing of the relationship between biography and text.

The history of critics separating author from text can be traced to T. S. Eliot's 1919 essay, 'Tradition and the Individual Talent', which is a point of origin for Borges's essay on literary context, 'Kafka y sus precursores'

---

[3] Jorge Luis Borges, 'Franz Kafka: *América*', *Biblioteca personal: Prólogos*, 1988, *Obras completas*, Vol. 4 (Buenos Aires: Emecé, 1996), p. 454.

[4] Jorge Luis Borges, 'Franz Kafka: Biografía sintética', *Textos cautivos*, 1986, *Obras completas*, Vol. 4 (Buenos Aires: Emecé, 1996), p. 326.

[5] Charles Neider, *The Frozen Sea: A Study of Franz Kafka* (New York: Russell & Russell, 1962), p. 73; for an example of Kafka criticism that actively disengages from biography, see James Hawes, *Excavating Kafka* (London: Quercus, 2008).

[Kafka and His Precursors] (1951). In brief, Eliot proposed that poets write from within a literary tradition. Their work adds to and modifies but is also the product of the tradition that precedes it. To be part of this tradition, poets must write from within the context of poetry and not from personal experience, while readers must assess the poetry itself, and not the poet who produced it:

> To divert interest from the poet to the poetry is a laudable aim: for it would conduce to a juster estimation of actual poetry, good and bad. There are many people who appreciate the expression of sincere emotion in verse, and there is a smaller number of people who can appreciate technical excellence. But very few know when there is expression of *significant* emotion, emotion which has its life in the poem and not in the history of the poet. The emotion of art is impersonal.[6]

Eliot argued that good poets should strive to preserve this principle of impersonality, since 'the more perfect the artist, the more completely separate in him will be the man who suffers and the mind which creates'. Tradition and context define a poet's work, while personal experience is comparatively insignificant, and 'the poet cannot reach this impersonality without surrendering himself wholly to the work to be done'.[7]

Eliot is associated with New Criticism, a movement that rejected the (American and academic) tendency to read texts historically and philologically in favour of viewing them as self-sustaining and closed. New Critics disputed the belief that personal information about the poet could explain a literary work. In 'The Intentional Fallacy' (1954), W. K. Wimsatt and Monroe C. Beardsley argued that 'there is a danger of confusing personal and poetic studies', so while literary biography is 'a legitimate and attractive study in itself', it cannot yield the same depth of understanding with the same credibility as reading for syntax and internal information.[8] Based on this, they disapproved of using anything outside of the text to analyse literary works. Using Samuel Taylor Coleridge's 'Kubla Khan' (1816) as an example, they asserted 'There were certainly other combinations, other poems, worse or better, that might have been written by men who had read Bartram and Purchas and Bruce and Milton';

---

[6] T. S. Eliot, 'Tradition and the Individual Talent', *The Sacred Wood: Essays on Poetry and Criticism*, 2nd ed. (London: Methuen, 1928), pp. 47–59 (p. 59), original emphasis.

[7] Ibid., p. 54, 59; for more on Borges's response to Eliot's 'Tradition and the Individual Talent', see Sarah Roger, 'Critics and Their Precursors: Theories of Influence in T. S. Eliot, Jorge Luis Borges, and Harold Bloom', *Bloomsbury Adaptations*, eds. E.H. Wright and Paul Edwards (Newcastle: Cambridge Scholars, 2014), pp. 2–15.

[8] W. K. Wimsatt and Monroe C. Beardsley, 'The Intentional Fallacy', 1974, *Praising It New: The Best of the New Criticism*, ed. Garrick Davis (Athens: Swallow-Ohio UP, 2008), pp. 102–16 (p. 108).

Coleridge did not write 'Kubla Khan' because of 'what he had read or otherwise experienced'.[9] Coleridge was not destined to write the poem as a result of his experiences, and therefore readers cannot draw on Coleridge's past as the guide to understanding it.

Eliot, Wimsatt, Beardsley, and the other New Critics were not the only theorists who drew a boundary between author and text across which meaning cannot travel. Russian Formalists also disregarded the possibility of using details from an author's life as the basis for textual analysis. In 'What Is Poetry?' (1934), Roman Jakobson said, 'Poeticity is present when the word is felt as a word and not a mere representation of the object being named or an outburst of emotion, when words and their composition, their meaning, their external and internal form acquire a weight and value of their own instead of referring indifferently to reality.'[10] In other words, poetry exists in a space where meaning is not directly or solely tied to reality. Later, Structuralists denied that there could be a knowable relationship between author and text, since readers can never untangle an author's intention due to the slippery nature of language. Roland Barthes explained this in 'La mort de l'auteur' [The Death of the Author] (1967): 'sa main, détachée de toute voix, portée par un pur geste d'inscription (et non d'expression), trace un champ sans origine—ou qui, du moins, n'a d'autre origine que le langage lui-même, c'est-à-dire cela même qui sans cesse remet en cause toute origine' [the hand, cut off from any voice, borne by a pure gesture of inscription (and not of expression), traces a field without origin—or which, at least, has no other origin than language itself, language which ceaselessly calls into question all origins]; as a result, the text becomes 'un espace à dimensions multiples, où se marient et se contestent des écritures variées, dont aucune n'est originelle' [a multi-dimensional space in which a variety of writings, none of them original, blend and clash].[11] According to Barthes, texts are inherently intertextual, and 'il y a un lieu où cette multiplicité se rassemble, et ce lieu, ce n'est pas l'auteur, comme on l'a dit jusqu'à présent, c'est le lecteur' [there is one place where this multiplicity is focused and that place is the reader, not, as was hitherto said, the author].[12] It is the reader who gives a work its meaning, not the author.

---

[9] Ibid., p. 109.

[10] Roman Jakobson, 'What Is Poetry?', 1934, *Semiotics of Art: Prague School Contributions*, trans. Michael Heim, eds. Ladislav Matejka and Irwin R. Titunik (Cambridge: MIT, 1976), pp. 164–75 (p. 174).

[11] Roland Barthes, 'La mort de l'auteur', 1967, *Le bruissement de la langue* (Paris: Seuil, 1984), pp. 61–7 (pp. 64–5); Stephen Heath, trans. and ed., 'The Death of the Author', *Image Music Text* (London: Fontana, 1977), pp. 142–8 (p. 146).

[12] Barthes, 'La mort de l'auteur', p. 66; Heath, trans., 'The Death of the Author', p. 148.

In contrast to the views of Eliot, Wimsatt and Beardsley, Jakobson, and Barthes, some scholars contemporary to the New Critics believed in using personal information about the author for literary analysis. One such critic was Leslie Fiedler, whose 1952 article 'Archetype and Signature: A Study of the Relationship between Biography and Poetry' anticipated and partly refuted Wimsatt and Beardsley *avant la lettre*. Fiedler referred to what Wimsatt and Beardsley later called the intentional fallacy as biographical 'idiocy': the misuse of personal information about an author in the quest to understand a text.[13] Fiedler argued for a measured approach to employing details from an author's life in reading the author's works: 'The poet's life is the focusing glass through which pass the determinants of the shape of his work: the tradition available to him, his understanding of "kinds," the impact of special experiences (travel, love etc.). But the poet's life is more than a burning-glass; with his work, it makes up his total meaning.' The author's personal experience—including what the author has read and the tradition to which the author responds—is part of a text's total meaning. Therefore to understand the 'life [the poet] writes', the reader must understand 'the life he lives'.[14] Fiedler's idea that the author's life can be used as a focusing glass to help clarify meaning is similar to the view this study takes of the relationship between Borges's writing and his reading of Kafka: Borges's personal and literary interest in Kafka is a prism that refracts new meaning onto Borges's stories.

Although Borges did not openly engage with the question of whether an author's biography should be enlisted to understand an author's work, his view on the matter can be discerned through his use of biography, particularly (in this case) his references to Kafka's life. Of the views discussed here, Borges's approach is most closely related to Fiedler's, since Borges believed Kafka's writing to be the product of his personal experiences. This does not mean, however, that an uncomplicated link can be drawn between Borges's ideas about writing and his ideas about biography, not least with respect to his own work. Borges's writing is known for its ironic twists and negations, and his views are famously unstable when it comes to the relationship between author and text. In support of this, consider the assertion made by Borges's narrator in 'Pierre Menard, autor del *Quijote*', when he says that any author could have written Miguel de Cervantes's acclaimed novel. It is possible to believe that Borges shared his narrator's view that Menard's version of

---

[13] Leslie A. Fiedler, 'Archetype and Signature: A Study of the Relationship Between Biography and Poetry', *The Sewanee Review* 60.2 (1952): 253–73, *JSTOR*, Web, 28 Oct. 2009 (p. 258).

[14] Ibid., p. 260.

the novel is better than Cervantes's, but by contrast, it is also possible to trust that, unlike his arrogant narrator, Borges believed that Cervantes's masterpiece was unique to its original (and only) author.

In *Biography and the Question of Literature in France* (2007), Ann Jefferson identifies a connection between 'Pierre Menard, autor del *Quijote*' and the justification for employing an author's context to determine the meaning of a text. She reads Borges's story with an eye to how Menard's version changes Cervantes's original, and she subsequently uses Borges's narrator's ironic praise of Menard's partial version of *Don Quijote* to consider how biographical context can be used to interpret a literary work:

> Borges's fable 'Pierre Menard, Author of the *Quixote*' illustrates how differently the same text . . . will be read, depending on its authorial attribution and implied biographical origin. Dated at the beginning of the seventeenth century and read as the work of Cervantes, the text is one thing; but taken as the work of Pierre Menard, a French writer from the turn of the twentieth century, its general purport, its argument, and even its style are totally transformed, even though the words on the page remain the same. The change of author, and of historical, geographical, and cultural context produces an entirely different conception of the undertaking that is assumed to inform the work. In short, read as the expression of an authorial attitude, the work must be treated as a quite different entity according to its biographical attribution and cease to be a single, self-identical object.[15]

Context and details from an author's other writing can be essential in understanding a literary work, a fact demonstrated by the two meanings of *Don Quijote* that are produced when read with consideration of Cervantes's and Menard's histories. Jefferson looks beyond the debate over whether Menard could have written *Don Quijote* anew (an ultimately insoluble problem) to ask, more practically, whether a text is influenced by its author's context. For her, *Don Quijote* is not 'a single, self-identical object' but rather is the product of its author's historical and personal circumstances, as are all books. A text is influenced by the context in which it was written, and readers cannot overlook this in their interpretations.

Jefferson's book is one instance of the growing enthusiasm for biographical literary analysis in recent years. Michael Benton corroborates her view in *Literary Biography: An Introduction* (2009). Benton says that these sorts of approaches serve as a return to the text and its author for those 'who find the contemporary preoccupation with theory to be personally

---

[15] Ann Jefferson, *Biography and the Question of Literature in France* (Oxford: Oxford UP, 2007), p. 6.

undernourishing and critically unenlightening'.[16] For Benton, biography fills the gaps left by literary theory. It emphasizes the relationship between author, historical context, personal experience, and meaning. In his book, Benton undertakes readings that use internal and external biographical material to show how biographical details, including what an author has read, may help explain what an author has written.

Although Benton limits himself to authors writing in English, the ideas he proposes are applicable to Borges. Details from Borges's life clarify aspects of his writing that cannot be accessed in any other way. To understand how this works, consider two analyses of 'El Congreso' [The Congress] (1971). In '"El Congreso" in the Works of J. L. Borges' (1987), Peter Standish proposes that the Congress's secretary, Nora Erfjord, is a veiled reference to the Congress of Erfurt:

> I find that *fjord*, English *ford*, and its German equivalent *Furt* all share the same root, and moreover in Old Norse. While Erfjord is Borges' creation, Erfurt is a city and a region, to the east of the city of Gotha, in the present day German Democratic Republic; it is known for the fact that in September of 1808 it saw the 'Congress of Erfurt', in which Napoleon confronted the Russian Emperor (without success). Of the leadership of Napoleon one need say nothing; it only remains to point out that the Russian Tsar was another Alexander. If this were not enough, a second congress of international importance, 'The Erfurt Union', was held in 1850, to discuss the constitution of a Germany to be dominated by Prussia. Doubtless Borges was quite aware of all this, as also of the fact that Anacharsis Cloots had Prussian origins![17]

Meanwhile, Williamson proposes a biographical approach to the same detail in *Borges, A Life*: 'Nora Erfjord is clearly modelled on Norah Lange, who was herself of Norwegian descent on both sides of her family and whose mother's maiden name was Erfjord.'[18] The suggestion that Nora Erfjord's name alludes to Borges's former girlfriend, Norah Lange, is simpler and therefore more plausible than the link between Erfjord and Prussian politics. This is not to say that a biographical approach is the best or the only way to read Borges's writing or that Standish's analysis does not contribute to an understanding of the story. Rather, it demonstrates how details from Borges's life can be used to help explain his writing.

---

[16] Michael Benton, *Literary Biography: An Introduction* (Oxford: Wiley-Blackwell, 2009), p. 1.

[17] Peter Standish, '"El Congreso" in the Works of J. L. Borges', *Hispanic Review* 55.3 (1987): 347–59, *JSTOR*, Web, 7 Nov. 2009 (p. 352).

[18] Williamson, *Borges, A Life*, p. 248.

This analysis follows on from Fiedler, Benton, and Williamson by examining Borges's prose fiction and his commentaries on Kafka to see how Borges's writing is illuminated by applying to it the ideas he identified and admired in his reading of Kafka. Its goal is to demonstrate how Borges developed into a short story writer in response to Borges *père*'s expectations of and aspirations for his son—a change that was motivated, in part, by Borges's reading of Kafka, whose work showed Borges how the father–son relationship could be a productive source for fiction. In brief, this study investigates Borges *père*'s and Kafka's roles as Borges *fils*'s literary precursors.

To understand Borges's relationship with Borges *père* and Kafka, it is necessary to look to Borges's theory on precursors, which he detailed in 'Kafka y sus precursores'. The origins of this essay can be traced to Eliot's 'Tradition and the Individual Talent', where (among other things) Eliot proposed that literary tradition could be belatedly created by a later author or identified by the reader, so that 'the past should be altered by the present as much as the present is directed by the past'.[19] Borges extended this idea by arguing that 'El hecho es que cada escritor *crea* a sus precursores. Su labor modifica nuestra concepción del pasado, como ha de modificar el futuro' [The fact is that each writer *creates* his precursors. His work modifies our conception of the past, as it will modify the future].[20] Borges's belief is that a later author's writing highlights elements in the work of an earlier author, influencing the reader's understanding of the earlier author's texts and the tradition connecting the two. Borges identified aspects of Kafka's writing in works by Zeno of Elea, Søren Kierkegaard, Robert Browning, León Bloy, and Lord Dunsany; while it is possible that Kafka had read some of their works, it is almost certain that he was not acquainted with them all.

With its focus on the reader, Borges's theory of influence is the most productive approach for understanding his relationship with Borges *père* and the connection this relationship had to Kafka's role as Borges *fils*'s literary precursor. It is more useful than either of the two main theories of literary influence: Kristeva's theory of intertextuality and Bloom's theory of the anxiety of influence. Kristeva's intertextuality refers to a range of ideas that are linked by a web of connections. It leaves the text open to endless slide, where readers add new levels of meaning to those that are

---

[19] Eliot, 'Tradition and the Individual Talent', p. 50.

[20] Jorge Luis Borges, 'Kafka y sus precursores', *Otras inquisiciones*, 1952, *Obras completas*, Vol. 2 (Buenos Aires: Emecé, 1996), pp. 88–90 (pp. 89–90), original emphasis; Eliot Weinberger, trans., 'Kafka and His Precursors', *Selected Non-Fictions* (New York: Viking, 1999), pp. 363–5 (p. 365), original emphasis.

already provided by the author. While intertextuality is a potentially fruitful approach for reading an author with as many precursors as Borges, it is not productive for isolating the particular influence of Borges *père* and Kafka. By contrast, Bloom's more specific theory is too narrow to apply to the relationship between an author, his familial predecessor, and his literary precursor. In *The Anxiety of Influence* (1973), Bloom describes a six-stage process in which authors recognize, turn away (or swerve) from, and eventually return to the influence of an earlier author. He likens the early stages of this process to the Oedipus complex, where the poet (the son in the literary, Oedipal relationship) desires to kill his precursor (the literary father) in order to form a relationship with the muse (the literary mother). The poet swerves away from his precursor in order to establish his independence as a writer, but he eventually realizes that he will never fully rid himself of his precursor's influence. By doing so, the poet comes into his own as a writer.

In *The Anxiety of Influence*, Bloom cites Borges as an inspiration for his theory, albeit a source from which he differentiates himself:

> I want to distinguish the phenomenon [of the anxiety of influence] from the witty insight of Borges, that artists *create* their precursors, as for instance the Kafka of Borges creates the Browning of Borges. I mean something more drastic and (presumably) absurd, which is the triumph of having so stationed the precursor, in one's own work, that particular passages in *his* work seem to be not presages of one's own advent, but rather to be indebted to one's own achievement, and even (necessarily) to be lessened by one's greater splendor.[21]

For Bloom, the earlier writer is indebted to the later one because of the greatness that the later writer brings to bear on the earlier writer's work. While Bloom's extension of 'Kafka y sus precursores' correctly suggests that without Borges's greatness Borges *père* would not still be read, the same logic does not apply to Borges's interpretation of and response to Kafka. The scholarly attention given to Kafka's writing is not dependent on Borges. Further, the influences of Borges *père* and Kafka were connected for Borges, since Borges's response to Kafka was linked to his understanding of Kafka's portrayal of the father–son relationship. Consequently, Bloom's theory, which focuses on the influence of a single precursor, can only be a point of inspiration, suggesting the possibility that the relationship between an author and his precursor can resemble the one between a son and his father.

---

[21] Harold Bloom, *The Anxiety of Influence: A Theory of Poetry*, 2nd ed. (Oxford: Oxford UP, 1997), p. 141, original emphasis.

Borges's own theory of influence, as explained in 'Kafka y sus precursores', invites readers to consider how the works of earlier authors are brought to life in a way that would not be possible if they were read independently of a later author. Using it as a model, Kafka's and Borges *père*'s works can be understood in the light of Borges *fils*'s writing, while Borges *fils*'s writing can be illuminated by a reading of Kafka and Borges *père* in turn. By reading with these influences in mind, Borges's familial predecessor (Borges *père*) and Borges's literary precursor (Kafka) appear to have jointly and collectively influenced Borges's work.

Chapter two looks at Borges *fils*'s relationship with Borges *père*, and it analyses Borges *père*'s writing to see how he served as a literary precursor for Borges *fils*. Chapter three connects the father–son relationship with Borges's interest in Kafka by examining Borges's critical writing on Kafka. Chapter four applies Borges's ideas about Kafka's writing to two short stories in which Borges said he was trying to emulate Kafka: 'La lotería en Babilonia' [The Lottery in Babylon] and 'La biblioteca de Babel' [The Library of Babel] (both 1941). Chapter five extends this approach to a broader selection of Borges's short stories. Chapter six looks at Borges's 'El Congreso' to see how he returned to Kafka's influence late in his career while also turning away from Kafka toward other influences—particularly that of Gilbert Keith Chesterton. Chapter seven offers an analysis of 'Borges y yo' [Borges and I] (1957) as a way of showing how reading (and writing in the style of) Kafka contributed to Borges's understanding of what it meant to be an author.

Before continuing, however, a brief word about terminology. Both Borges and Kafka have had their names turned into adjectives. 'Borgesian' and 'Kafkaesque' mean in the manner of Borges and Kafka respectively, with all of the connotations of the stories they wrote. However, Kafka's presence as a cultural figure is so strong that Kafkaesque has come to mean something more than just pertaining to or in the style of Kafka. The term is now used to mean '(of a situation, atmosphere, etc.) impenetrably oppressive, nightmarish, in a manner characteristic of the fictional world of Franz Kafka'.[22] With this definition in mind, 'Kafkaesque' is used throughout to refer to the nightmarish, bizarre, and mystifying. When referring to something as being written in the manner of Kafka, such as when a story is fragmented or lacks a conclusion, Borges's preferred term of 'Kafkian' is used.

---

[22] 'Kafkaesque', *Oxford English Reference Dictionary*, eds. Judy Pearsall and Bill Trumble, (Oxford: Oxford UP, 2002).

2

Borges *Père* and Borges *Fils*

In Borges's 1967 interview with Jean de Milleret, Borges *père*'s death and Borges *fils*'s blood poisoning accident served as an introduction to a discussion about the father–son relationship:

J. M.—Mais l'année 1938 va marquer, par deux traits décisifs, un tournant capital dans votre vie: d'une part, la mort de votre père; d'autre part, l'accident de Noël 1938. Quelle a été la répercussion sur vous—sentimentale, spirituelle, psychique—de la mort de votre père?

J. L. B.—Ah! très grande. D'abord...évidemment, un père pour son fils...Et il était toujours là, avec moi, non?

J. M.—C'est en vous qu'il avait mis toutes ses espérances et il pensait réaliser par vous son rêve d'être un écrivain célèbre, ce qu'il avait à peine esquissé avec son roman '*El caudillo*'.

J. L. B.—Oui, il était essentiellement homme de lettres, et il avait tant lu.

J. M.—Je vais vous faire une confidence qui va choquer votre modestie maladive. Votre mère, qui m'a parlé très souvent de la passion exclusive qu'elle avait pour votre père, m'a dit un jour: 'Mon mari était un homme très intelligent, aussi intelligent que Georgie, mais à lui, il lui manquait le génie de son fils.'

J. L. B.—Mon génie! Evidemment, c'est un hyperbole, non? une tendresse.

J. M.—Avec sa mort disparaissait le conseiller affectueux de tous les jours, mais aussi l'appui matériel qui vous avait débarrassé jusqu'alors de tout souci pécuniaire...

[J.M.—But the year 1938 can be defined by two decisive events in your life: first, there was your father's death, and then the accident you had at Christmas in 1938. What was the impact—emotional, spiritual, mental—that your father's death had on you?

J.L.B.—Ah, very great. Of course...obviously, a father to his son...and of course he was always there for me.

J.M—He had put all of his hopes in you, and he thought you would be able to fulfil his dream of being a famous writer, which he had only made a brief foray into in writing his novel, *El caudillo*.

J.L.B.—Yes, he was essentially always a man of letters, and he was such a reader.

J.M.—I will tell you a secret that will shock your excessive sense of modesty. Your mother, who frequently spoke to me about her unbounded affection for your father, said to me one day, 'My husband was a very intelligent man, as intelligent as Georgie, but he lacked his son's genius.'

J.L.B.—My genius! Obviously that is somewhat of an exaggeration, no? Kind words.

J.M.—With your father's death you lost your faithful advisor, but also the financial support that had sustained you . . .][1]

On de Milleret's prompting, Borges confirmed that his father's death profoundly affected him, but he downplayed the impact by asserting that his feelings were not noteworthy: his was the natural response of a son to the death of his father. In an effort to circumvent Borges's evasiveness, de Milleret mentioned Borges *père*'s expectation that Borges *fils* write in a way in which his father could not, connecting Borges *père*'s death to Borges *fils*'s career as an author. The portrayal of Borges that de Milleret presented was that of an author whose career was fostered by an affectionate father, literary adviser, and generous benefactor. While Borges would not corroborate this view, over the course of decades of interviews and personal writings he revealed that their relationship was a positive one.

This chapter determines how Borges *fils*'s interaction with Borges *père* shaped his development as an author in order to later show how Borges *fils*'s relationship with Borges *père* influenced Borges *fils*'s reading of Kafka. Borges *fils* saw Kafka's writing as the product of his relationship with his father. Therefore to understand Borges *fils*'s writing about and in response to Kafka, it helps to understand his relationship with his literary and familial predecessor, Borges *père*.

2.1 FATHER AND SON

In the 1955 prologue to *Evaristo Carriego* (1930), Borges reminisced about his father's library: 'Yo creí, durante años, haberme criado en un suburbio de Buenos Aires, un suburbio de calles aventuradas y ocasos visibles. Lo cierto es que me crié en un jardín, detrás de una verja con lanzas, y en una biblioteca de ilimitados libros ingleses' [For many years, I believed that I had grown up in a suburb of Buenos Aires, a suburb with

---

[1] Jean de Milleret, *Entretiens avec Jorge Luis Borges* (Paris: Pierre Belfond, 1967), pp. 66–7.

dangerous streets and conspicuous sunsets. The truth is that I grew up in a garden, behind a spiked wrought-iron fence, and in a library with count-less English books].[2] Similarly, in the 1968 'An Autobiographical Essay' he commented, 'If I were asked to name the chief event in my life, I should say my father's library. In fact, I sometimes think I have never strayed outside that library.'[3] Alongside time spent in his father's library, Borges *fils* remembered trips with Borges *père* to the national library where he read the *Encyclopædia Britannica*, and he recalled his father's conversations with literary friends, among them Macedonio Fernández and Evaristo Carriego.

A love of literature was not the only thing Borges learned from his father. Borges also considered his philosophical education, particularly his childhood lessons in metaphysics, to be an important part of his inheritance:

> He also, without my being aware of it, gave me my first lessons in philosophy. When I was still quite young, he showed me, with the aid of a chessboard, the paradoxes of Zeno—Achilles and the tortoise, the unmoving flight of the arrow, the impossibility of motion. Later, without mentioning Berkeley's name, he did his best to teach me the rudiments of idealism.[4]

The philosophical seeds that Borges *père* planted during these tutorials grew into some of Borges's best-known works. Without idealism there would be no 'Tlön, Uqbar, Orbis Tertius' (1940), and without Zeno's paradoxes there would be no 'La biblioteca de Babel' [The Library of Babel].

In Borges's portrayal, his education was restricted, more or less, to two experiences: reading books in his father's library and learning philosophy from his father. His was a childhood that prepared him for his career as an author. Even Borges subscribed to this teleological view: 'Nunca ignoré que mi destino sería literario. Siempre estaba leyendo y escribiendo. La biblioteca de mi padre me parecía gratamente infinita.... Ahora com-prendo que *mi padre despertó y fomentó esa vocación*' [I always knew that my destiny would be a literary one. I was always reading and writing. My father's library seemed pleasingly infinite to me ... I now understand that *my father awakened and nurtured that calling*].[5] Borges became an author out of a combination of destiny, expectation, and family influence (as well as natural aptitude and personal desire), a perspective that the writers of

---

[2] Jorge Luis Borges, Prologue, *Evaristo Carriego*, 1930, *Obras completas*, Vol. 1 (Buenos Aires: Emecé, 1996), p. 101.

[3] Jorge Luis Borges, 'An Autobiographical Essay', *The Aleph and Other Stories: 1933–1969*, trans. and ed. Norman Thomas di Giovanni (London: Jonathan Cape, 1968), pp. 203–60 (p. 209).

[4] Ibid., p. 207.

[5] Jorge Luis Borges, *Jorge Luis Borges: A/Z* (Madrid: Siruela, 1988), p. 86, emphasis added.

biographies and memoirs share. For example, according to Volodia Teitelboim, 'No expresó esa voluntad por escrito; pero en la familia se la
interpretó como un mandato implícito: el hijo debía realizar el fracasado
sueño paterno' [While he did not express that desire in writing, there was a
tacit understanding in the family that the son would fulfil his father's
failed dream], while according to Borges's friend Estela Canto, 'Desde su
infancia Georgie fue destinado a ser escritor, del mismo modo que los
padres decidían entonces que sus hijos iban a ser médicos, ingenieros o
abogados. Jorge [Guillermo] Borges... educó a su hijo para ser literato.
Este fue el primero de los mandatos que recibió Georgie' [Georgie was
destined to be a writer since he was a young child, in the same way that
parents in those days decided that their children would be doctors,
engineers or lawyers. Jorge Guillermo Borges... brought up his son to
be a man of letters. This was the first of the mandates that Georgie received
from his father].[6] Whether these views developed out of something Borges
said or whether they were speculative, Borges's choice of vocation gives
the impression of having been an attempt to fulfil an order passed down by
his father.

Like Borges *père*, Borges *mère* was similarly influential in her son's
career. However, while Borges suggested that he felt his writing to be a
familial obligation, his biographers have argued that Leonor's influence
came into its own only after Borges was established as an author, during
the years he was reliant on her assistance as his amanuensis:

> Some of his autobiographical texts talk freely about Mother, but they reveal
> little that is relevant to his childhood years. He mentions the help he received
> from her after his father's death and after his own blindness made it very
> difficult for him to read and write. About his own father, on the contrary, he
> is always explicit and precise. Even when he is confronted with an inter-
> viewer, like Jean de Milleret, who is determined to subject him to a bit of
> simplified Freudianism, Borges is adamant. Again and again he dodges a
> question about his mother's supposedly dominant personality and attributes
> everything to his father's strong will. When he is asked, rather directly, if he
> thinks that his was 'an oppressive mother', he answers that it was his father
> who was a decisive influence on his life because it was through him that he
> learned English and had access to a vast library.[7]

Williamson corroborates this view, suggesting that Leonor's expectations
for her son extended only to a desire for him to restore the family's fallen

---

[6] Volodia Teitelboim, *Los dos Borges: Vida, sueños, enigmas* (México, DF: Hermes,
1996), p. 20; Estela Canto, *Borges a contraluz* (Madrid: Espasa Calpe, 1989), p. 54.
[7] Emir Rodríguez Monegal, *Jorge Luis Borges: A Literary Biography* (New York:
E. P. Dutton, 1978), p. 21.

social standing. This wish features in Borges's stories with themes about honour and betrayal, which are not usually the same as those that exhibit Kafka's influence.[8] Further, Borges *mère*'s overt involvement in Borges *fils*'s literary career was restricted to the later years, when there 'was a general impression among Borges's friends that it was Doña Leonor who was working behind the scenes to promote her son's career, and this would have been entirely consistent with her strong personality and lofty social aspirations'.[9] Borges *mère* helped Borges achieve international acclaim, but her role in his development as a writer—her help with the acquisition of the techniques and themes for which he would become well known—was minimal. Because of this, and because Borges did not credit Borges *mère* with influencing his literary development, her impact on his work is put to one side for the purpose of this study.

On the whole, Borges presented authorship as a family obligation, supported by both of his parents but stemming predominantly from his father's aspirations: 'From the time I was a boy, when blindness came to him, it was tacitly understood that I had to fulfil the literary destiny that circumstances had denied my father. This was something that was taken for granted (and such things are far more important than things that are merely said). I was expected to be a writer.'[10] However, it is possible that this view existed only in Borges's mind. Borges *mère* said that Borges announced that he wanted to be a writer at the age of 6; in her version of the story, it was Borges's decision to become an author, not his father's. Navigating between the possibility that Borges *père* was the one who wanted Borges *fils* to become an author and the possibility that Borges chose the vocation for himself, Rodríguez Monegal writes,

> Which of the two versions is closer to reality? It is difficult to know. Perhaps one day, when he was six, Georgie stated solemnly to Father: 'I want to be a writer.' This statement (transformed by Mother's recollection into an 'anecdote') does not exclude the other version: a flat statement about what Father took for granted about Georgie's future. The emphasis is on his duty: fate as something inherited. By accepting the destiny of writer as a kind of paternal bequest, Georgie accepts the fact that he is a son.[11]

What matters is that Borges—as an adult—believed that his father wanted him to be a writer and that as a child he thought he knew this to be so.

---

[8] Edwin Williamson, 'Borges in Context: The Autobiographical Dimension', *The Cambridge Companion to Jorge Luis Borges*, ed. Edwin Williamson (Cambridge: Cambridge UP, 2013), pp. 201–25 (p. 202).

[9] Edwin Williamson, *Borges, A Life* (London: Viking, 2004), p. 329.

[10] Borges, 'An Autobiographical Essay', p. 211.

[11] Rodríguez Monegal, *Jorge Luis Borges: A Literary Biography*, p. 81.

Based on this, it is possible to read Borges's stories in the light of the idea that his interest in reading and his vocation were passed down from father to son.

Despite this familial pressure, father and son had a positive relationship, and by the time Borges *fils* grew into a young adult, his bond with his father had changed from one of student and teacher into a balanced friendship. With reference to the mid-1920s, Borges commented, 'These years were quite happy ones because they stood for many friendships. There were those of Norah Lange, Macedonio [Fernández], [Sergio] Piñero, and my father.'[12] In 'Los amigos' [The Friends] (1972), Borges referred to his father as first and foremost among his friends: 'La más íntima de las pasiones argentinas es la amistad; yo pienso mucho en mis amigos. El primero es mi padre' [The deepest of Argentine passions is friendship; I think about my friends a great deal. The first among them is my father].[13] Willis Barnstone has corroborated this view:

> I heard only unrepressed praise [for Borges *père*], even reverence, from Borges's lips. He expressed sympathy for his father's blindness, praise for his counsel and wisdom—frequently. Whatever Oedipal weapons may have been lurking in the inner labyrinth, such knives never floated into the daylight. His public posture gave one clear sign: his father was the one non-military male ancestor he spoke about and the sole ancestor he wished to emulate.[14]

During the 1910s and 1920s, Borges *père* treated Borges as a literary equal, asking for help with his writing. By circumstance or by design, he was reliant on his son's assistance, a need most notable in his request for help with *El caudillo* [*The Chieftain*]: 'My father was writing his novel, which harked back to old times during the civil war of the 1870s in his native Entre Ríos. I recall giving him some quite bad metaphors, borrowed from the German expressionists, which he accepted out of resignation.'[15] Borges helped his father revise *El caudillo*, and he also assisted with the publicity and distribution of the book. Borges even arranged for it to be reviewed by his friend Roberto Ortelli, the same individual he trusted to sell copies of *Fervor de Buenos Aires* [*Fervour of Buenos Aires*] (1923) while he was abroad in Geneva. Ortelli's review was remarkably kind:

> ¡Qué pureza de lenguaje! ¡Qué dominio del valor de las palabras y de las frases!... Tenemos la convicción de que hay en el autor de *El Caudillo*, un

---

[12] Borges, 'An Autobiographical Essay', p. 235.

[13] Jorge Luis Borges, 'Los amigos', *Textos recobrados (1956–1986)* (Buenos Aires: Emecé, 2003), pp. 162–6 (p. 162).

[14] Willis Barnstone, *With Borges on an Ordinary Evening in Buenos Aires: A Memoir* (Urbana: U of Illinois, 2000), p. 123.

[15] Borges, 'An Autobiographical Essay', p. 219.

poeta, un filósofo y un novelista, los tres dotados de una claridad que es patrimonio de los cerebros que han llegado a una madurez [en] la que se poseen las cualidades espirituales perfectamente definidas.

[What purity of language! What mastery of the power of words and phrases! . . . We believe that in the author of *El Caudillo* we have a poet, a philosopher and a novelist, each with the clarity that is the legacy of mature minds, one that possesses perfectly defined spiritual qualities.][16]

Despite this compliment from Ortelli, Borges *père*'s novel only received a lukewarm reception: '[Borges *père*] had hoped to succeed as a writer, but his novel, *El Caudillo*, had made no impact at all in Buenos Aires.'[17]

When Borges *fils* was establishing himself as an avant-garde poet in Spain, Borges *père* was also reliant on his son's help to have his writing published. Borges *père*'s first translation of Edward FitzGerald's *Rubáiyát of Omar Khayyám* (FitzGerald's version 1859; Borges *père*'s version 1920) appeared opposite one of Borges *fils*'s own pieces in a 1920 issue of the Seville journal *Gran guignol* [*sic*]. Borges *père*'s later and longer translation (1924–5) was accompanied by an introduction written by Borges *fils* praising both Edward FitzGerald and Borges *père*, and it was published in *Proa*, a magazine founded by Borges *fils*.

In some respects, it seems as though Borges's relationship with his father in this period was one-sided. Borges *père* asked his son for assistance, but Borges *fils* said his father refused to help him in return: 'My father never interfered. He wanted me to commit all my own mistakes, and once said, "Children educate their parents, not the other way around"', and also 'I wanted to show my manuscripts to my father, but he told me he didn't believe in advice and that I must work my way all by myself through trial and error.'[18] In reality, however, their support was bidirectional even if it was not comparable. While Borges *fils* helped his father with writing and publishing, Borges *père* aided his son financially, which allowed Borges *fils* to concentrate on his poetry. Although essential at the time, some critics see this financial assistance as both help and hindrance: 'Borges received complete tolerance and active encouragement from his parents. Domestically, he was not practical . . . and at this stage [in 1921] showed no ambition whatsoever to cope by himself. Jorge and Leonor were his keepers and, in effect, his pay-masters', and 'Although Father had always supported (if not thoroughly invented) his vocation . . . Georgie probably

[16] Roberto Ortelli, 'Letras argentinas: *El Caudillo*, novela por Jorge Borges', *Nosotros* 17.166 (1923): 403–7 (p. 407).

[17] Williamson, *Borges, A Life*, p. 105.

[18] Borges, 'An Autobiographical Essay', p. 211, 218.

felt that he was taking advantage of his father.'[19] Borges *père's* financial support of Borges *fils's* career gave the impression that it was something in which his father had invested.

Based on all of this, Borges *fils's* relationship with Borges *père* as a fellow writer can be seen in both a positive and a negative light. According to Jason Wilson,

> Much has been made of Borges's parricidal tendencies, his sense of being a nobody, his father's ghost, and more psychoanalytical speculations. However, I see this father as a literary encourager, much as Edmund Gosse's and V. S. Naipaul's fathers were to them.[20]

Meanwhile, Rodríguez Monegal has argued,

> Although Borges' attempts to soften the harsh judgment (Father had failed as a writer) by remembering his 'nice' sonnets, it is obvious that on that matter he shares Mother's opinion. It is also obvious that his own literary destiny was molded by that failure. Somehow, he had to fulfil Father's project; he had to *vindicate* him. This was his main task in life.[21]

The idea that Borges had to clear his father's name or absolve him of his literary sins is too strong an interpretation, but it is also too charitable to suggest that Borges *père's* role was limited to that of literary encourager. What is certainly true—and where Wilson and Rodríguez Monegal agree—is that Borges's development as an author was linked to his relationship with his father.

2.2 DEATH AND NEAR DEATH

Borges *père* died in 1938 after a series of ailments starting in 1935. Around the time that Borges *père* first fell ill, Borges *fils* established his financial independence from his father by taking a job as a librarian. However, his literary relationship with his father did not end just because he was able to pay his own way. On his deathbed, Borges *père* ensured their continued connection by asking his son to 'rewrite the novel [*El caudillo*] in a straightforward way, with all the fine writing and purple patches left out'—the fine writing presumably referring (at least partially) to the

---

[19] James Woodall, *The Man in the Mirror of the Book: A Life of Jorge Luis Borges* (London: Hodder and Stoughton, 1996), p. 49; Rodríguez Monegal, *Jorge Luis Borges: A Literary Biography*, p. 225.

[20] Jason Wilson, *Jorge Luis Borges* (London: Reaktion, 2006), p. 25.

[21] Rodríguez Monegal, *Jorge Luis Borges: A Literary Biography*, p. 81, emphasis added.

metaphors Borges *fils* offered to Borges *père*.[22] The impact of this request resonated throughout Borges's career.

When discussing the events of 1938 in 'An Autobiographical Essay', Borges connected his father's death with his own near-death experience. He described the two episodes in one sentence: 'One morning, my mother rang me up and I asked for leave to go home, arriving just in time to see my father die. He had undergone a long agony and was very impatient for his death. It was on Christmas Eve of 1938—the same year my father died—that I had a severe accident.'[23] The accident Borges is referring to is the one in which he contracted blood poisoning after running up a flight of stairs and cutting his head on a freshly painted casement window that had been left open to dry. The subsequent septicaemic infection left him hospitalized for over a month, and while recovering, Borges wrote 'Pierre Menard, autor del *Quijote*' [Pierre Menard, Author of the *Quixote*]. This started a productive vein of prose fiction writing that lead to the publication of *Ficciones* [*Fictions*] (1944) and *El Aleph* [*The Aleph*] (1949).

Views of this incident vary greatly: for some biographers and critics, Borges *fils*'s accident was no more than an accident, while for others there was an unconscious connection between it and Borges *père*'s death. This latter possibility has been explored in a number of psychoanalytic studies of Borges by critics and analysts such as Didier Anzieu, Luis Kancyper, and Julio Woscoboinik. In straying into speculations on Borges's interior life these analyses are sometimes implausible, yet they still warrant a mention because they set the stage for a more measured biographical approach.

With reference to the psychoanalytic possibilities inherent in the events of 1938, Woscoboinik writes,

> Los psicoanalistas accidentólogos suelen enfatizar que las posibilidades de accidentes se acrecientan frente a situaciones de cambio. ¿Cómo podríamos comprender esta herida, este accidente que se complica con una septicemia, a pocos meses de la muerte del padre?
>
> ¿Es simplemente la expresión de su ansiedad frente al encuentro con una mujer?
>
> ¿Sería esta herida como una auto-circuncisión que le permite el ingreso a la vida adulta y autónoma? Y en esta dirección, este corte—en la frente—¿podría ser interpretado como un simbólico desplazamiento de otro corte, que no se dió en su momento, por ausencia del padre como función?
>
> Lo cierto es que 'alguna cosa, como dice Doña Leonor, cambió dentro de su cerebro'.
>
> [Psychoanalysts who specialize in accidents usually emphasize the fact that the probability of accidents increases in situations of change. How else could

---

[22] Borges, 'An Autobiographical Essay', pp. 219–20.   [23] Ibid., p. 242.

we understand this injury, this accident that led to the complication of septicemia, a few months after the death of the father?

Is it just the expression of his anxiety before meeting with a woman?

Might this injury be like a self-circumcision that allows him to access an adult, autonomous life? And, pursuing this line of thought, can this cut on the forehead be interpreted as a symbolic displacement of another cut, one that did not occur at the appropriate time, on account of the absence of the father as paternal function?

What is certain is that 'something', as doña Leonor says, 'changed inside his brain.']²⁴

In *The Psychopathology of Everyday Life* (1941), Sigmund Freud proposed that although some events may appear to be accidents, they are actually the product of unconscious desires. Examples of this include verbal slips of the tongue and bungled actions.²⁵ According to Woscoboinik, Borges's head injury was one such unconscious, motivated occurrence meant to sever him from his recently deceased father.

Similarly, Rodríguez Monegal has suggested that Borges *fils* unconsciously orchestrated the accident out of grief over Borges *père*'s death. He has argued that the injury was a symbolic suicide in response to the pressure Borges felt to fulfil his father's literary expectations:

> The accident dramatized Borges' guilt over Father's death and his deep, totally unconscious need to be set free at last from Father's tutelage. From a symbolic point of view, the accident represented both a death (by suicide) and a rebirth. After the accident Borges emerged as a different writer, a writer this time engendered by himself. . . .
>
> This new Borges would go further than Father had ever planned or even dreamed about. In attempting symbolically to kill himself, Borges was actually killing the self that was only Father's reflection. He assumed a new identity through the mythical experience of death and rebirth.²⁶

When viewed symbolically, Borges's injury separated him from his father and enabled him to take up the mantle of literary and personal independence that he was denied during his father's lifetime. Rodríguez Monegal offers supporting evidence for this on the basis that the Borges who wrote 'Pierre Menard, autor del *Quijote*' was different to the Borges who existed before.

²⁴ Julio Woscoboinik, *El secreto de Borges: Indagación psicoanalítica de su obra* (Buenos Aires: Trieb, 1988), p. 52; Dora C. Pozzi, trans., *The Secret of Borges: A Psychoanalytic Inquiry Into His Work* (Lanham: UP of America, 1998), pp. 30–1.

²⁵ Sigmund Freud, *The Psychopathology of Everyday Life*, 1901, *The Basic Writings of Sigmund Freud*, trans. and ed. A. A. Gill (New York: Random House, 1938), pp. 35–178 (p. 69, 129).

²⁶ Rodríguez Monegal, *Jorge Luis Borges: A Literary Biography*, p. 326.

There is another way of looking at this incident, both biographically and psychoanalytically, which may be more plausible and more productive for understanding the stories Borges wrote around this time. Borges *fils*'s accident can be seen to be just an accident (likely the product of his poor eyesight and nerves due to the fact that he was going to collect a woman), and it, along with Borges *père*'s death, can be treated as a part of a continuum of events rather than as two isolated instances. Instead of viewing 'Pierre Menard, autor del *Quijote*' as a response to Borges *père*'s death and Borges *fils*'s accident, and therefore seeing Borges's move to prose fiction as a stark change, the story can be placed in the context of a longer transitional period for Borges's writing that can be traced as far back as 'Hombre de la esquina rosada' [Streetcorner Man] (1933) and the pseudo-factual tales in *Historia universal de la infamia* [*A Universal History of Iniquity*] (1935). The transition may have also been the product of Borges's reading from around this time: 'At the time of his father's final illness, Borges was engaged in translating a selection of Kafka's stories for the Editorial Losada and it was Kafka who would provide him with the means of exploring further the ambivalent relations with his father and the ghost of their ancestral hero.'[27] When all of these factors are combined, it seems unlikely that Borges's break from his father was enacted with one symbolic cut. Over the course of the many years of his father's illness, Borges seems to have undergone a gradual process of self-realization that correlated with his increasing confidence and capabilities as a storyteller.

2.3 BORGES *PÈRE*, AUTHOR

Even if Borges *père*'s writing is noteworthy only in hindsight and only because of Borges's subsequent success, the relationship between Borges *père* and Borges *fils* can still be understood as a literary one between a precursor and a subsequent author, as revealed by Borges *père*'s writing. The earliest known piece of his work is his law school thesis, *Hipoteca naval* [*The Mortgaging of Ships*] (1879); the remainder of his printed legacy includes (*i*) a cycle of poems called 'Momentos' [Moments] from 1913, (*ii*) a poem based on Song of Songs titled 'El cantar de los cantares' [The Song of Songs] from 1920, (*iii*) two translations of Edward FitzGerald's *Rubáiyát of Omar Khayyám* from 1920 and 1924 (*see* Appendix II for reproductions of Borges *père*'s poetry), (*iv*) his self-published novel, *El caudillo*, from 1921, and (*v*) *La senda* [*The Path*], a philosophical

---

[27] Williamson, *Borges, A Life*, p. 235.

manuscript from 1917, which has recently been rediscovered. A number of his other pieces have been lost or destroyed, including a play called *Hacia la nada* [*Towards Nothingness*] about a father's disappointment in his son, short stories collected under the title *El jardín de la cúpula de oro* [*The Garden of the Golden Dome*], and a collection of poems.

Borges *père*'s writing can be loosely categorized as *modernista*. The modernista movement took place between the 1880s and the 1920s, which makes it contemporary to the period of Borges *père*'s known work, and its goal was to establish a distinctive Spanish American literary style. Drawing inspiration from Parnassianism and French symbolism, modernismo was characterized by highly stylized works that spurned the world in which the authors lived. Modernista texts often portrayed an intellectual writer who sought to escape the material world through the rejection of bourgeois values, instead choosing to pursue spiritual and cultural renewal and a cosmic sense of harmony. When achieved, this liberation is represented by images of the exotic Orient and the fulfilment of erotic longing.

Elements of modernismo appear throughout Borges *père*'s writing, starting with his earliest (existing) creative work, 'Momentos', a cycle of three numbered sonnets. In the first sonnet, the poet mourns the loss of his lover. In the second sonnet, the poet reflects on how everything fades, even happy memories, and he wonders whether he ever really felt anything for his now-absent lover. In the third sonnet, the poet concludes that time will erase everything, and he bids a final farewell to his lover. This sense of loss is worked into the language of the poem, which contrasts past-tense descriptions of the former lover with present-tense descriptions of the poet's actions. The lover 'Enmudeciste' [fell mute], and the poet recalls 'el beso que no halló tus labios' [the kiss that never found your lips]—with the preterite verbs emphasizing the irrecoverable past—while he muses about the nature of time and memory:[28]

> Toda Vida es trunca.
> Las horas dan, lo que las horas quitan
>
> [All Life is cut short.
> The hours give, and the hours take away.][29]

The passage of time does not bring renewal. Spring turns to winter, but no mention is made of it returning to spring again; rather than a cycle of seasonal rebirth, there is only death.

---

[28] Jorge Guillermo Borges, 'Momentos', *Nosotros* 7.18 (1913): 147–8 (l. 1, 41).
[29] Ibid., ll. 15–16.

To conjure the presence of his former lover, the poet employs modernista images of unceasing fountains, gardens, flowers, the seasons, and
moonlight, but his efforts are to no avail. Even the nature imagery reminds
the poet that his lover is not there. He notes that 'la noche . . . no tuvo
azahares' [the night . . . had no orange blossoms]; orange blossoms are
traditionally associated with brides.[30] The poet responds to this loss by
writing poetry. He defiantly fills the space left by his lover's 'hosco
silencio' [harsh silence] with his verse:

> Yo, no puedo olvidar, ni callar puedo
> porque el Dolor es lengua que no calla
> nunca, nunca.
>
> [I cannot forget, nor can I be silent
> because Pain is a language that cannot be silenced
> never, never.][31]

Even though 'todo es mudanza' [everything is shifting], love and suffering
are permanent, and by capturing these emotions the poet tries to set his
work beyond the bounds of time. The poetic voice becomes the antidote
to the pain of a lover spurned:

> Por eso sobre el ledo
> ritmo del verso mi dolor restalla
>
> [And so my pain cracks like a whip
> over the happy rhythm of the verse][32]

The poet gains a sense of permanence by transforming his suffering into art.

Although the poems of 'Momentos' are predominantly modernista,
they also anticipated Borges *fils*'s early, similarly dramatic, lovelorn poetry.
Throughout his career, Borges's poetry exhibited a fascination with the
idea that change is inevitable and the past is irretrievable, ideas he also
played with in essays such as 'Nueva refutación del tiempo' [A New
Refutation of Time] (1944) and stories such as 'El Aleph' [The Aleph]
(1945). Like 'Momentos', much of Borges's poetry was also about the act
of writing poetry, but this trait is not exclusive to father and son.

The only other surviving piece of Borges *père*'s original poetry is 'El
cantar de los cantares', published in Spain in *Gran guignol* [*sic*], a journal
to which the younger Borges was also a contributor. From the title, the
inspiration for the poem is clear: it is a gloss on the Song of Songs,
condensing to 550 words the original's 2,500 words (in both Spanish
and English, the languages in which Borges *père* may have read the text).

---

[30] Ibid., l. 40.   [31] Ibid., ll. 2, 5–7.   [32] Ibid., ll. 7–8.

This practice of rewriting is part of the biblical text's history, which itself was assembled from pre-existing works, and it is also a technique common among modernistas, who embraced the idea of making a new text out of an old one. Although 'El cantar de los cantares' is not a translation, it follows the same narrative as the original, celebrating the love between two individuals. It describes the sense of suffering they endure when apart, but only as a counterpoint to their joy in being together. Borges *père* focused on the male lover's praising of his beloved, omitting descriptions given by the female in biblical text.

Throughout 'El cantar de los cantares', Borges *père* borrowed liberally but selectively from other versions of the Song of Songs. He focused on nature imagery—particularly references to animals, fruits, flowers, and landscapes—rather than on geographical landmarks, perhaps to render the poem more familiar to his contemporaries. Within the nature imagery, he emphasized orchards and harvests: 'el gajo roto al peso de la fruta' [the branch broken beneath the weight of the fruit], and

> ¿Qué verde falda, qué región dorada
> de trigo y pleno sol[?]
>
> [What green slope, what golden region
> of wheat and sunshine?][33]

The bough heavy with apples is an image for the wealth of the land and for the Garden of Eden (an association invoked by Borges *père* in lines six and fifty-three), while the wheat represents the fertility of both the land and the beloved. This fecundity is also expressed by the use of mirroring, which multiplies images and gives the poem a feeling of plenitude. Sounds and words are repeated within a single line—'Bésame con el beso de tu boca' [Kiss me with the kiss of your mouth]—and also across lines:

> sobre tus hombros perfumado manto,
> sobre tus hombros y desnudos senos
>
> [around your shoulders a perfumed mantle,
> around your shoulders and bare breasts][34]

Borges *père*'s 'El cantar de los cantares' takes sex as its focus, paring down the original to a selection of encounters between the poet and his beloved that culminate with the concluding declaration:

> ¡Oh torre de marfil! ¡Oh llama de oro
> que en esplendor de luz anuncia el día!

---

[33] Jorge Guillermo Borges, 'El cantar de los cantares', *Gran guignol* 1.2 (1920): 5–7 (ll. 60, 68–9).
[34] Ibid., ll. 12, 19–20.

[Oh ivory tower! Oh golden flame
that heralds the day in the splendour of light!][35]

The exclamation marks and the repetition of the word 'Oh' suggests that the lovers are joined in an erotic union, or that the poet is imagining a time when they were or will be. This does not mean, however, that the poem is only about sex. The joy of the lovers' union is heightened by the sorrow the poet feels when they are apart. The suffering of being in love is plainly stated in section two, 'Este es el pesar de los pesares' [This is the sorrow of sorrows].[36] The poet may be 'enfermo y triste' [sick and sad], but his pain is assuaged by the possibility of reunion with his beloved.[37] This contrasts with 'Momentos', where the lover's absence produces suffering and alerts the poet to the meaninglessness of creation. In 'El cantar de los cantares', the lover's fertility invites creation, and her presence motivates the poet to write.

Modernistas believed that writing about sex could be a way of writing about writing: 'The ideal female with whom the poet must join to attain the much pursued perfect vision is often linked with the poetic language and the product of their union described in sensuous and seductive terms. Creation, whether poetic, personal, or cosmic, is conceived as sexual.'[38] 'El cantar de los cantares' fits this mould. It combines the poet's recollections of his beloved's physicality with his desire to declare his affections for her in verse. From the beloved's 'aliento' [breath] comes 'la canción nupcial' [the wedding song], and when he raises her dress, he is inspired to sing.[39] When she is gone, there is only silence, but when she is present, she revives the song 'del perdido Edén' [of a lost Eden].[40] The otherwise mute poet is reinvigorated by the beloved, which places 'El cantar de los cantares' in opposition to 'Momentos', where writing is a response to the poet's suffering and the lover's absence. Biographically, there is evidence for this difference. Borges *père* wrote 'El cantar de los cantares' while the family was abroad in Majorca, a period in which he 'rediscovered with his wife Leonor the kind of passion he had been seeking when he left Buenos Aires in 1914'.[41] By contrast, when he published 'Momentos', he was struggling with his writing, had failing eyesight, and was lacking passion in his marriage.

Borges *père*'s third remaining work is a Spanish version of FitzGerald's translation of the eleventh-century Persian poems of the *Rubáiyát of Omar Khayyám*. His decision to translate a Persian text was in line with the

---

[35] Ibid., ll. 82–4.   [36] Ibid., l. 9.   [37] Ibid., l. 67.

[38] Cathy L. Jrade, 'Modernist Poetry', *The Cambridge History of Latin American Literature*, eds. Roberto González-Echevarría and Enrique Pupo-Walker (Cambridge: Cambridge UP, 2008), pp. 7–68, *Cambridge Histories Online*, Web, 18 Oct. 2010 (p. 21).

[39] Jorge Guillermo Borges, 'El cantar de los cantares', ll. 13, 26–8.

[40] Ibid., ll. 48–9, 53.   [41] Williamson, *Borges, A Life*, p. 69.

modernistas' interest in Middle Eastern and Oriental subject matter as well as their penchant for rewriting. Modernistas 'presuppose that most, if not all, of human knowledge has already been codified and collected in a single place: in other words, modernista writing presupposes the existence of a Library' from which authors can borrow to generate their works.[42] Borges *père* did precisely this, making his own poems out of the Song of Songs and FitzGerald's translation.

There are two versions of Borges *père*'s translation of the *Rubáiyát of Omar Khayyám,* one from 1920 and the other from 1924–5. Both consist of stanzas from FitzGerald's Persian to English translation, which have been retranslated by Borges *père* into Spanish. Neither FitzGerald nor Borges *père* kept the stanzas in the original order. When translating from Persian, FitzGerald moved Khayyám's words around, and he divided stanzas, reassembling them according to his aesthetic and thematic interests.[43] Borges *père* did the same. He chose a selection of FitzGerald's 114 quatrains and rearranged them to make his own unified poems: one of eight quatrains and another of sixty-three. In both he combined the quatrains in a way that reinterpreted the *Rubáiyát of Omar Khayyám.*

Some of Borges *père*'s stanzas are good approximations of FitzGerald's, such as FitzGerald's forty-sixth quatrain and Borges *père*'s rendering of it, which preserves both image and meaning:

> El Mundo es sólo el cuadro iluminado
> que arroja la Linterna del Juglar
> cuya vela es el Sol, y nuestras Vidas,
> Sombras que vienen, Sombras que se van.

> [The World is but a picture that is illuminated
> with light cast by a Minstrel's Lantern
> Whose candle is the Sun, and our Lives,
> Are Shadows that come, Shadows that will go.][44]

> For in and out, above, about, below,
> 'Tis nothing but a Magic Shadow-show,
> Play'd in a Box whose Candle is the Sun,
> Round which we Phantom Figures come and go.[45]

---

[42] Aníbal González, *A Companion to Spanish American Modernismo* (Woodbridge: Tamesis, 2007), p. 10.

[43] Daniel Karlin, Introduction, *Rubáiyát of Omar Khayyám* (Oxford: Oxford UP, 2009), pp. xi–xlviii (p. xxxviii).

[44] Jorge Guillermo Borges, 'Del poema de Omar Jaiyám', *Gran guignol* 1.1 (1920): 8, quat. I.

[45] Edward FitzGerald, *Rubáiyát of Omar Khayyám,* ed. Daniel Karlin (Oxford: Oxford UP, 2009), quat. XLVI.

Borges *père*'s version is more pedestrian than FitzGerald's: the world that FitzGerald alludes to in his first line is named by Borges *père* for precisely what it is. Otherwise, his translation is faithful and even poetic. Not all of Borges *père*'s stanzas are as accurate, and some are not even present in the original. For example, there is no equivalent in FitzGerald's version of the final quatrain from Borges *père*'s shorter translation:

> ¡Oh dicha de mi amor! yo estaré quieto,
> tendido en tierra de una larga Paz,
> durmiendo el sueño que no tiene sueños,
> ni aurora, ni inquietud, ni despertar.
>
> [Oh my love's fortune! I will lie still,
> on the ground of a long Peace,
> slumbering a sleep that has neither dreams,
> nor dawn, nor restlessness, nor waking.][46]

Borges *père* invented this last quatrain to facilitate his narrative, rounding out his poem with a goodbye from the poet who goes to his final sleep without his lover—an ending similar to the one that closes 'Momentos'. In general, Borges *père* selected quatrains that employ a subset of FitzGerald's themes and images to produce a text with a narrower focus and a greater sense of unity. His shorter version in 'Del poema de Omar Jaiyám' emphasizes a lover who is barely present in FitzGerald's version, and it concludes with the impossibility of romantic fulfilment—a theme favoured by Borges *père* but not present in FitzGerald's collection, which focused on living for the moment.

Aside from his second, longer translation of FitzGerald's *Rubáiyát of Omar Khayyám* (published in 1924 but perhaps written alongside the shorter translation in 1920), Borges *père*'s last surviving publication was his 1921 novel *El caudillo*. The novel's primary plot is about the titular caudillo, Don Andrés Tavares, who has to choose between supporting Domingo Sarmiento's Unitarians and Ricardo López Jordán's Federalists—a version of the Argentine conflict between civilization and barbarism. Tavares's decision is aided by an Italian immigrant known as El Gringo who convinces him to build a bridge across a river that separates his estancia from a neighbouring one. El Gringo advocates a modernized Argentina 'con sus casas y sus calles, sus plazas y jardines, la ciudad que debió partir al encuentro del futuro' [with its houses and streets, squares and gardens, a city that ought to set forth to meet the future] rather than one carved up into strongholds of private estancias such as those from

---

[46] Jorge Guillermo Borges, 'Del poema de Omar Jaiyám', quat. VIII.

Tavares's time.[47] Tempted by the vision of the future that El Gringo proposes, Tavares meets with the Unitarian Governor and pledges to help defeat the Federalists. He changes his mind, however, when the bridge he has built on El Gringo's advice enables a romance between the neighbour's unsuitable son and Tavares's daughter, Marisabel. Family takes precedence over the national agenda. Meanwhile, a storm floods the river and causes El Gringo's bridge to collapse as though it were a 'ciudad de naipes' [city of cards], sweeping away his vision of civilization with it.[48] El Gringo drowns in the flood (perhaps a suicide, although this is never made clear) and the old order is reinstated. The proposed modernization is defeated by the innate barbarism of the pampas.

El caudillo's subplot concerns the neighbouring property owner's son, Carlos Dubois, who has a love affair with Marisabel. Dubois is a *porteño* who has neglected his law school studies while courting an unsuitable local girl named Lina. As punishment, Dubois's father sends him to his estancia, hoping that the hard work on the ranch and time away from Lina will mend Dubois's ways. Dubois takes refuge from his punishment in his philosophy books—particularly those on eternal return, a favourite of Borges *père*—which earns him a reputation among the locals as lazy and weak. Marisabel is the only person on the pampas who admires his stories about Paris and his philosophical musings; her father, by contrast, shares Dubois *père*'s critical view of his son. Tavares intimidates Dubois to encourage him to return to the city, and when he discovers Marisabel and Dubois's affair he has Dubois killed. Although Dubois twice seeks freedom through romance, father figures intervene. First, he is subject to a paternal edict from his biological father who stops his courtship with Lina; second, Tavares, who acts as a surrogate father by taking Dubois in and showing him how to run his estancia, murders Dubois to end his affair with Marisabel.

Dubois's wishes are thwarted, both practically and philosophically. Romance denies him the refuge he seeks from the authority of the father, and his belief in eternal return denies him the autonomy or uniqueness for which he yearns:

—Lo que sería curioso, observó Dubois, siguiendo el hilo de sus propios pensamientos, es saber si alguna vez hemos recorrido juntos este mismo camino, hemos pensado lo que hoy pensamos y dicho las mismas palabras....

—Escuchen, insistió Dubois, si los elementos que forman el mundo son los mismos y son contados, el azar, el Dios o los dioses que los manejan, a la larga

---

[47] Jorge Guillermo Borges, *El caudillo*, 1921 (Buenos Aires: Academia Argentina de Letras, 1989), p. 118.
[48] Ibid.

tendrían que combinarlos de la misma manera. Un paquete de cartas, por ejemplo, tiene un número limitado de combinaciones, forzosamente deberán repetirse si disponemos del tiempo y la paciencia necesaria. ¿Por qué hemos de sorprendernos si la partida actual en que entramos ustedes, yo y todas las circunstancias que nos rodean se ha jugado ya muchas veces? Quizás nos encontraremos en el sendero infinito del tiempo y de aquí muchos millones de años yo como ahora discuta con ustedes.

[—It would be strange, observed Dubois, following the thread of his own thoughts, to know whether we had ever travelled this same road together, thought the same things that we are thinking now, and said the same words. . . .

—Listen, insisted Dubois, if the elements that make up the world are the same and if they are limited, chance, God or the gods who control them, will eventually have to combine them in the same way. A pack of cards, for example, has a limited number of combinations, which will necessarily be repeated if we have the time and patience. Why should we be surprised if the current game in which we, you, me and all of the circumstances around us, are a part has been played out many times already? Perhaps we will meet on the infinite path of time, many millions of years in the future, and find ourselves discussing the same things we are now.][49]

Dubois's philosophical musings find their counterpoint in Marisabel's mystical belief that the universe—and each of its inhabitants—is unique. In a conversation with Dubois, she presents her ideas as an argument against eternal return:

—Eso es un absurdo, dijo Marisabel. ¿Cómo se le ocurre semejante cosa? Esta es la primera vez que se inaugura el puente y el vestido que llevo es nuevo, ¿le gusta? . . .

—Me gusta, es muy bonito y le sienta a maravilla, pero también me gusta mi teoría que no es mía, pues ya se le ha ocurrido a muchas personas serias que la pensaron bien.

—Hay muchos locos, yo no le veo pies ni cabeza. . . . Eso es tan absurdo, insistió Marisabel, que no lo creo. . . . Ya le he dicho que mi vestido es nuevo, sepa que lo corté y lo cosí con mis propias manos y usted siendo porteño es muy poco galante, apenas me ha dicho que es bonito, y eso porque se lo he preguntado.

[—That's absurd, said Marisabel. Where do you get such ideas? This is the first time the bridge has been inaugurated, and I'm wearing a new dress. Do you like it?

—I like it, it is very pretty, and it looks wonderful on you, but I also like my theory, which isn't really mine, because it has already occurred to many important people who thought it was plausible.

---

[49] Ibid., p. 89, 90.

—There are many crazy people out there, and I can't make head or tail of your theory.... It is so absurd that I cannot believe it, insisted Marisabel. I have already told you that my dress is new. You should know that I cut and sewed it with my own hands. For a Porteño, you are not much of a gentleman; you've hardly said it is pretty, and even then it was only because I asked you.][50]

The narrator suggests that Marisabel's belief that everything is unique is 'una falla mística' [a mystical flaw], yet it is not necessarily a fault. It leaves her open to a sense of fulfilment that Dubois desperately desires but cannot access within his own philosophical system.[51]

Although he is initially sceptical of Marisabel's ideas, Dubois is won over by a mystical or spiritual experience that occurs when he is joined with Marisabel in sexual congress towards the end of the novel:

Lina, Marisabel y las mujeres que en otro tiempo deseara o poseyera nada significaban, habían cesado de existir. Qué tonto fue fijando la atención en el color de los ojos, en el tono de los cabellos, en las letras de los nombres, en raza, idioma o ademanes. Hallóse transformado, estaba libre, perfectamente libre de toda orientación determinada, de toda vana disputa, era sólo el hombre invadido y arrollado por la pasión única de la hombría. Lina, Marisabel y todas cuantas deseara o poseyera, nada le importaban, había cesado de amarlas o quizás las amaba a todas. Su cuerpo sólo existía tenso en la busca de la mujer que se esconde detrás de todas las mujeres cuando la careta multiforme desaparece.

[Lina, Marisabel and the women whom at one time or another he had desired or possessed no longer mattered and had ceased to exist. How foolish to have focused his attention on the colour of their eyes, the shade of their hair, the letters in their names, their race, language, or gestures. He found himself transformed, he was free, completely free of any fixed bearings, of every vain dispute; he was simply a man invaded and overwhelmed by the singular passion of manhood. Lina, Marisabel, and all those women whom he might desire or possess, none of them mattered, he had ceased to love them, or perhaps he loved them all. His body only existed taut in the search for the woman hiding behind all women when the multifarious mask falls away.][52]

In this moment, Lina and Marisabel merge and dissolve to provide Dubois with a Platonic sense of oneness. This experience conflicts with Marisabel's idea that everything is unique, but more strikingly it undermines Dubois's belief that everything will repeat someday. In their union, Dubois discovers the existence of an essential, archetypal oneness that joins everything in the universe in a mystical whole. Instead of repetition or individuality, he finds that a shared spirit lies behind their identities.

[50] Ibid., p. 89, 90, 91.   [51] Ibid., p. 59.   [52] Ibid., p. 148.

This view of the cosmos allows Dubois to break free from the meaningless repetitions of eternal return, and he merges with Marisabel to
achieve spiritual fulfilment through sex. Similar concepts appear in Borges
père's other writing. In 'Momentos', the poet despairs because he has lost
his love, and the changeable nature of the universe means he will never
regain the once-treasured relationship. In 'El cantar de los cantares', the
poet rejoices in his union with his lover; in the original Song of Songs, this
celebration represents a poetic union between art and artist, and it also
represents a union between the individual and God.

Despite his revelation, Dubois's experience of spiritual fulfilment is
temporary. After Dubois and Marisabel make love, he writes a letter to
Tavares where he proposes marriage to Marisabel out of a sense of
obligation. He recognizes that through his relationship with Marisabel,
he has betrayed Tavares's expectations of him. He has also betrayed his
father's wish that he will change while on the estancia, and he has betrayed
his engagement to Lina. Dubois tries to set all of this right with his
proposal. His letter is never received, however, and Tavares has Dubois
murdered, reinstating the patriarchal authority and destroying the sense of
oneness that Dubois and Marisabel shared.

For the few critics who have read Borges *père*'s novel, *El caudillo* seems
to foreshadow Borges *fils*'s writing. James Woodall writes, 'Georgie did
eventually set some of his own much shorter, more genuinely brutal and
provocative tales in the same landscape, period and martial ambience as *El
caudillo*'s', presumably referring to Borges's gaucho stories.[53] Similarly,
Rodríguez Monegal acknowledges that in 'El muerto' [The Dead Man]
(1946), 'The caudillo Otálora is really a more sinister version of Tavares,
with some sado-masochistic elements added. He pretends to be overwhelmed by the young man and even humiliated by him, because from
the very beginning he has planned a deadly revenge. Like Tavares, he is
deaf to compassion.'[54] He also points out that the knife fight in Borges's
'El Sur' [The South] was 'anticipated by Carlos' [Dubois's] final confron-
tation with the caudillo's henchman'.[55] Underlying these similarities is a
theme that fascinated both father and son:

> There is in both writers a preoccupation, almost an obsession, with a certain
> kind of confrontation: between powerful, primitive men and weak, educated
> men. Father was (like his son) an intellectual who learned to make his living
> through the practice of law and the teaching of psychology. But his own
> father had been a colonel, a man of action. In Father's situation one can

---

[53] Woodall, *The Man in the Mirror of the Book*, p. 45.
[54] Rodríguez Monegal, *Jorge Luis Borges: A Literary Biography*, p. 83.
[55] Ibid.

already recognize the conflict between arms and letters that Georgie would have to face later. It is easy to recognize in the protagonist of *El caudillo*, in that half-European Carlos, an alter ego of the author. In many respects, they were similar. But what is really important is that in trying to portray his own predicament Father was also concerned with understanding the caudillo's psychology. In confronting Carlos with the caudillo, Father was exploring one of his private obsessions: the feeling of inadequacy he felt in contrasting his fate with that of his own father.[56]

This idea of the weak son's inadequacy compared to his powerful father features in Borges *fils*'s interpretation of Kafka. It also appears later in Borges's own work, which combines elements from both Kafka and Borges *père*. As chapter three will show, Borges *fils* saw Kafka's writing partly as a son's response to his relationship with his father. It is for this reason that Borges *fils*'s relationship with Borges *père* (as both a son and a writer) is relevant to an understanding of Borges's interpretation of and response to Kafka.

[56] Ibid.

3

Reading, Translating, and Writing about Kafka

Over the course of many years of reading Kafka's work and writing about it, Borges came to see Kafka as the greatest author of the modern age. He saw in Kafka a model for navigating the father–son relationship in writing, while also identifying Kafka's stories as timeless, agnostic parables. Borges eventually borrowed themes and techniques that he admired in Kafka for some of his most successful stories. To understand Borges's use of the Kafkian in his own writing, this chapter provides a history of Borges's reading of, translations of, and writing about Kafka. It outlines the features Borges admired in Kafka, as well as those that he neglected to acknowledge but which still resonate with his work.

3.1 BORGES READS KAFKA

In 'Un sueño eterno: Palabras grabadas en el centenario de Kafka' [An Eternal Dream: Words Recorded on Kafka's Centenary] (1983), Borges recalled his first experience of reading Kafka:

> Mi primer recuerdo de Kafka es del año 1916, cuando decidí aprender el idioma alemán. Antes lo había intentado con el ruso, pero fracasé. El alemán me resultó mucho más sencillo y la tarea fue grata. Tenía un diccionario alemán-inglés y al cabo de unos meses no sé si lograba entender lo que leía, pero sí podía gozar de la poesía de algunos autores. Fue entonces cuando leí el primer libro de Kafka que, aunque no lo recuerdo ahora exactamente, creo que se llamaba *Once cuentos*.

> [My first memory of Kafka is from 1916, when I decided to learn German. I had previously tried to learn Russian, but failed. German turned out to be much easier for me, and it was a pleasant experience. I had a German–English dictionary and after a few months—although I don't know whether I was able to fully understand what I was reading—I was able to enjoy the poems of a few authors. It was then that I read Kafka's first book which,

although I can no longer remember exactly, I think was called *Eleven Stories*.][1]

In the prologue to *El buitre* [*The Vulture*] (1979), Borges remembered this event differently, tracing his first reading of Kafka to a journal that he read in 1917:

> No olvidaré mi primera lectura de Kafka en cierta publicación profesionalmente moderna de 1917. Sus redactores—que no siempre carecían de talento—se habían consagrado a inventar la falta de puntuación, la falta de mayúsculas, la falta de rimas, la alarmante simulación de metáforas, el abuso de palabras compuestas y otras tareas propias de aquella juventud y acaso todas las juventudes. Entre tanto estrépito impreso, un apólogo que llevaba la firma de Franz Kafka me pareció, a pesar de mi docilidad de joven lector, inexplicablemente insípido. Al cabo de los años me atrevo a confesar mi imperdonable insensibilidad literaria; pasé frente a la revelación y no me di cuenta.

> [I will never forget my first reading of Kafka in a certain professionally modern publication in 1917. Its editors—who didn't always lack talent—were dedicated to the abolition of punctuation, the abolition of capital letters, the abolition of rhyme, the alarming simulation of metaphor, the abuse of compound words, and other tasks appropriate to youth at the time and perhaps to youth at any time. Amidst this clatter of type, an apologue signed by one Franz Kafka seemed to my young reader's docility inexplicably insipid. After all these years, I dare to confess my unpardonable literary insensibility: I saw a revelation and didn't notice it.][2]

Borges named two possible sources for this early reading: the German journals *Die Aktion* and *Sturm*.[3] Unsurprisingly, since Borges recalled these details more than sixty-five years later, his recollections were inaccurate. Neither journal contained anything written by Kafka in 1916 (the year Borges said he read *Once cuentos*), 1917 (the year Borges said he read *Die Aktion* and *Sturm*), or the surrounding years. Although Borges is unclear on when he first encountered Kafka's works, he is certain that he was unimpressed when he first read them. As the second quotation above plainly states, it was only years later, when he began to write short stories of his own, that Borges decided that Kafka was a great author.

Even though Kafka did not publish anything in *Die Aktion* in 1916 or 1917, it is possible that he and Borges were readers of the same magazine,

---

[1] Jorge Luis Borges, 'Un sueño eterno: Palabras grabadas en el centenario de Kafka', *Textos recobrados (1956–1986)* (Buenos Aires: Emecé, 2003), pp. 237–9 (p. 237).

[2] Jorge Luis Borges, Prologue, *El buitre* (Buenos Aires: La Ciudad, 1979), pp. 7–11 (pp. 8–9); Eliot Weinberger, trans., 'Franz Kafka, *The Vulture*', *Selected Non-Fictions* (New York: Viking, 1999), pp. 501–3 (p. 502).

[3] Jorge Luis Borges, 'Borges sur Kafka', *Change International* 3 (1985): 44–5 (p. 45).

and therefore were influenced by the same ideas. In 1913, *Die Aktion* published a selection of writings by the psychoanalyst Otto Gross, including 'Zur Überwindung der kulturellen Krise' [On Overcoming the Cultural Crisis], in which Gross argued that '"the revolutionary of today" should not aim merely to combat the father; he has to take a stand against the principle of power itself, the *patriarchal right*'.[4] Gross's argument for overthrowing the patriarchy may have left an impression on Kafka; in discussing Kafka's 'Brief an den vater' [Letter to His Father], Jennifer E. Michaels has suggested that 'Kafka expresses his criticism of his father... in Grossian... terms, since he focuses on the tyranny of authoritarian fathers and their psychological destruction of their sons'.[5] Subsequently, Borges may have also read Gross's writing in *Die Aktion* (albeit in a back issue, since he did not move to Geneva until 1914) and he might later have made a connection between Gross and Kafka.

In order to understand the influence Kafka had on Borges, we need to know which of Kafka's works Borges read. There are two ways to determine this. One approach is to draw up a list of the Kafka volumes Borges owned and the stories contained in them. Borges mentioned using the Schocken *Gesammelte Schriften* [*Collected Works*] (1935 and 1936–7) for his translations of Kafka; these two volumes contain Brod's edited and reconstructed versions of eighty of Kafka's stories and fragments and four critical texts, all of which Borges could have read as early as 1937.[6] Borges also had a copy of Kafka's *Hochzeitsvorbereitungen auf dem Lande* [*Wedding Preparations in the Country*] (1953), which he received as a birthday present from Adolfo Bioy Casares the year it was published.[7] Owning these works (or using them for his translations), however, does not necessarily mean that Borges read them in full. It is also likely that he read some works by Kafka in volumes he did not own, and he may have owned more volumes than just those named above.

A second, more reliable approach is to assemble a list of the Kafka texts that Borges mentioned in his writing (*see* Appendix I). If Borges read Kafka starting in 1916 or 1917, he was a very early reader of Kafka, whose work was published starting in 1908 in journals and from 1912 in books.

---

[4] Reiner Stach, *Kafka: The Years of Insight*, trans. Shelley Frisch (Princeton: Princeton UP, 2013), p. 304, original emphasis.

[5] Jennifer E. Michaels, 'Psychoanalysis, Literature and Sociology', *Sexual Revolutions: Psychoanalysis, History and the Father*, ed. Gottfried Heuer (London: Routledge, 2011), pp. 155–67 (p. 164).

[6] Margaret Byrd Boegman, 'Paradox Gained: Kafka's Reception in English from 1930 to 1949 and his Influence on the Early Fiction of Borges, Beckett, and Nabokov' (unpublished doctoral dissertation, U of California, Los Angeles, 1977), p. 210.

[7] Adolfo Bioy Casares, *Borges* (Buenos Aires: Destino, 2006), p. 85.

By 1938 Borges had read all three of Kafka's novels—*Amerika/Der Verschollene* [*America/The Man Who Disappeared*] (1927), *Der Prozeß* [*The Trial*] (1925), and *Das Schloß* [*The Castle*] (1926)—and forty-one of the eighty-nine stories by Kafka that were published in Borges's lifetime. By 1967, he had read the edited stories and fragments that Brod drew from the wealth of unpublished material in the eight notebooks known as the Oktavhefte, which Kafka kept between 1916 and 1918; included in these fragments were the aphorisms that Brod had published under the title 'Betrachtungen über Sünde, Hoffnung, Leid und den wahren Weg' [Reflections on Sin, Suffering, Hope, and the True Way] (1931). By 1967, Borges had also read the story fragments collected in *Hochzeitsvorbereitungen auf dem Lande* (1953), and Brod's *Franz Kafka: eine Biographie* [*The Biography of Franz Kafka*] (1937). Borges also read Kafka in English, reviewing Willa and Edwin Muir's translation of *The Trial*.

3.2 BORGES TRANSLATES KAFKA

As part of his reading, Borges published translations of eighteen texts (or fragments of texts) by Kafka between 1938 and 1967. The earliest of these publications was 'Ante la ley', a translation of Kafka's 'Vor dem Gesetz' [Before the Law], and it appeared in *El hogar* on 27 May 1938. Nearly half of Borges's Kafka translations were done in collaboration: four with Bioy Casares, one with Bioy Casares and Silvina Ocampo, and two with Margarita Guerrero. These joint translations were for anthologies that Borges was co-editing: *Cuentos breves y extraordinarios* [*Brief and Extraordinary Stories*] (1955), *Libro del cielo y del infierno* [*A Book of Heaven and Hell*] (1960), *El libro de los seres imaginarios* [*The Book of Imaginary Beings*] (1967), and *Libro de sueños* [*A Book of Dreams*] (1976). The translations done by Borges on his own were for stand-alone Spanish volumes of Kafka's writing: *La metamorfosis* [*The Metamorphosis*] (published with Losada in Buenos Aires in 1938) and *El buitre* (published with La ciudad in Buenos Aires in 1979).

Just because Borges's name appears on a translation does not guarantee that he read the story, since there is always the possibility that the translation was not Borges's own work. Fernando Sorrentino has argued that Borges was not responsible for three of the translations included in *La metamorfosis*—those of 'Ein Hungerkünstler' [A Hunger Artist, Un artista del hambre] (1922), 'Die Verwandlung' [The Metamorphosis, La metamorfosis] (1915), and 'Erstes Leid' [First Sorrow, Un artista del trapecio] (1922). According to Sorrentino, the language and syntax in these translations diverges significantly from Borges's own, and had Borges done the translations he would have deviated more frequently from the originals. Indeed, an earlier, anonymous translation of 'La metamorfosis' appeared in a 1925 edition of *Revista de Occidente* and was identical to the one published under Borges's name, which suggests that the translation was somebody else's work.[8] Sorrentino says that Borges was aware of these translations and allowed the misattribution to be made. Yet, although it is possible that Borges did not author any of the Kafka translations that bear his name, all those aside from the few singled out by Sorrentino are treated here as Borges's work.

Borges's work as a translator (and not just with respect to Kafka) has been analysed at length by Efraín Kristal in *Invisible Work: Borges and Translation* (2002) and by Sergio Waisman in *Borges and Translation: The Irreverence of the Periphery* (2005). Kristal is particularly insightful in his assessment of Borges's translation practice:

> (1) Borges's most common practice as a translator was to remove what he once called the 'padding' of a work: words and passages that seem redundant, superfluous, or inconsequential. (2) He removed textual distractions. This stratagem involves cutting part of the content of a literary work that might distract attention from another aspect Borges would prefer to highlight. (3) Borges often added a major or minor nuance not in the original: changing a title, for instance. (4) Borges sometimes rewrote a work in light of another, as when he inscribes a post-Nietzschean sensibility to his translations of Angelus Silesius. (5) He sometimes includes a literal translation of a work in one of his own works.[9]

As he did with the Kafka translations that he allowed to be falsely attributed to him, Borges took a liberal approach to translating by accounting for flexibility of ownership. He accepted credit for translations he did not produce, and he was known to attribute his own translations to others. For example, there is speculation that the Spanish edition of William Faulkner's *The Wild Palms* (1939), published under Borges *mère*'s name, was actually Borges *fils*'s work. Additionally, Borges's flexible approach to translation allowed for the possibility that a translation did not need to be accurate to be good. In essays on translation theory, such as 'Las

---

[8] Fernando Sorrentino, 'El kafkiano caso de la *Verwandlung* que Borges jamás tradujo', *Especulo: Revista de estudios literarios* 10 (1998): np. Web, 20 Nov. 2009; for an in-depth analysis of the Spanish translation of 'Die Verwandlung' attributed to Borges, see Rebecca de Wald, 'Possible Worlds: Textual Equality in Jorge Luis Borges's (Pseudo) Translations of Virginia Woolf and Franz Kafka' (unpublished doctoral dissertation, U of Glasgow, 2015), np. (chapter five).

[9] Efraín Kristal, *Invisible Work: Borges and Translation* (Nashville: Vanderbilt UP, 2002), p. 87.

versiones homéricas' [The Homeric Versions] (1932) and 'Sobre el *Vathek* de William Beckford' [On William Beckford's *Vathek*] (1943), Borges made comments to the effect that it was possible that readers might prefer a less accurate translation to a more accurate one. In some cases, a less accurate translation could be so much better that it would appear as though 'El original es infiel a la traducción' [The original is unfaithful to the translation].[10] These views may explain why Borges was willing to be credited with Kafka translations that were not his, and why he took such a liberal approach in some of his translations of Kafka.

A number of the traits Kristal identifies as common to Borges's translations are present in his Spanish versions of Kafka. For example, Borges occasionally omitted portions of Kafka's texts to highlight others. In Borges's 'Josefina la cantora o el pueblo de los ratones' [Josephine the Singer, or the Mouse Folk; Josefine, die Sängerin oder Das Volk der Mäuse], Borges cut 'a long sentence in which Kafka's narrator explains how working could adversely affect her voice, and thus her song', with the effect that the story becomes less about Josephine's singing and more about her obligation to work.[11] Borges also added nuances to Kafka by altering his titles. He turned 'Erstes Leid' into the more straightforward 'Un artista del trapecio' [A Trapeze Artist], perhaps to draw a parallel between it and Kafka's other story about a circus performer, 'Ein Hungerkünstler'. The two stories were printed successively in Borges's *La metamorfosis*. Similarly, Borges and Guerrero changed the name of 'Die Sorge des Hausvaters' [The Cares of a Family Man] (1919) to 'Odradek' to warrant its inclusion in *El libro de los seres imaginarios*. The brief tale describes an encounter between a father and a fanciful creature resembling a spool of thread. Kafka's title focused on the experiences of the father, while Borges and Guerrero recast the story to make the creature the title character.

Although a word-for-word, comparative analysis of Borges's translations of Kafka is beyond the scope of this study, it is worth noting that— aside from interventions meant to shift a story's focus—Borges's translations generally tended to be literal, especially for longer works.[12] This is particularly true of Borges's Kafka translations, as Borges 'could not transfigure Kafka the way he transfigured most writers he translated. At his most daring, Borges was able to alter subtly... Kafka's innovative

---

[10] Jorge Luis Borges, 'Sobre el *Vathek* de William Beckford', *Otras inquisiciones*, 1952, *Obras completas*, Vol. 2 (Buenos Aires: Emecé, 1996), pp. 107–10 (p. 109); Eliot Weinberger, trans., 'On William Beckford's *Vathek*', *Selected Non-Fictions* (New York: Viking, 1999), pp. 236–9 (p. 239).

[11] Kristal, *Invisible Work: Borges and Translation*, p. 129.   [12] Ibid., p. 40.

ideas' through the occasional substitution of one word for another.[13] That
said, these occasional substitutions were enough for Borges to make some
notable interventions, as Rebecca de Wald acknowledges. She points to
Borges's translations of 'Ante la ley' as an example of his ability to change
meaning through a few subtle variations. By choosing words that have
ambiguities in Spanish as substitutions for clearer German counterparts,
Borges was able to emphasize the uncertainty inherent in the countryman's wait for admission to the law:

> [Borges's] different translations of 'jetzt' ('now') as both 'ahora' and 'ese día'
> at the beginning of the text seem to hint at the long waiting time the man
> from the country has to endure. This is further unsettled by the ominous and
> vague question whether the entry would be possible later, 'luego', which can
> also mean 'afterwards', though it will remain unclear what the man from the
> country has to wait for. Like a pseudotranslation, the term 'luego' embodies
> here the uncertainty of what was before and what will be after.[14]

Throughout 'Ante la ley', Borges shortened sentences and omitted subordinate clauses, with the effect of narrowing the story's focus to the power
struggle it described. Borges removed an entire sentence—'Wenn es dich
so lockt, versuche es doch, trotz meines Verbotes hineinzugehn' [If you are
so strongly tempted, try to get in without my permission]—thus eliminat-
ing the possibility that the countryman might enter despite the doorkeeper's
edict.[15] In doing so, he strengthened the hierarchy of which the doorkeeper
is but a part, while diminishing any autonomy the countryman may have.[16]

In one instance, Borges made an even more drastic intervention into
Kafka's writing. 'Cuatro reflexiones' [Four Reflections] is Borges and Bioy
Casares's translation of selections from Kafka's *Die Zürauer Aphorismen*
[*The Zürau Aphorisms*], also known by the title Brod gave to the aphor-
isms, 'Betrachtungen über Sünde, Hoffnung, Leid und den wahren Weg'
[Reflections on Sin, Suffering, Hope, and the True Way].[17] Originally,
Kafka's aphorisms were discrete and numbered, but Borges and Bioy
Casares reassembled a selection of four as continuous paragraphs, failing
to acknowledge the existence of the others. The four aphorisms that make
up their story are as follows:

[13] Ibid., p. 75.   [14] de Wald, 'Possible Worlds', np. (chapter five).
[15] Franz Kafka, 'Vor dem Gesetz', *Erzählungen und kleine Prosa, Gesammelte Schriften*,
Vol. 1 (Berlin: Schocken, 1935), pp. 144–6 (p. 144); also Franz Kafka, 'Vor dem Gesetz',
Drucke zu Lebzeiten (Frankfurt: S. Fischer; New York: Schocken, 1994), pp. 267–9
(p. 267); Willa Muir and Edwin Muir, trans., *The Trial, The Complete Novels* (London:
Vintage, 1999), pp. 11–128 (p. 120).
[16] de Wald, 'Possible Worlds', np. (chapter five).
[17] For an extended analysis of the relationship between Borges *fils*'s translations of Kafka
and Borges *père*'s translation of FitzGerald and more on 'Cuatro reflexiones', see Sarah
Roger, 'A Metamorphosis? Rewriting in Borges's Translations of Kafka', *Comparative
Critical Studies*, 8.1 (2011): 81–94.

Leoparden brechen in den Tempel ein und saufen die Opferkrüge leer; das wiederholt sich immer wieder; schließlich kann man es vorausberechnen, und es wird ein Teil der Zeremonie.

Die Krähen behaupten, eine einzige Krähe könnte den Himmel zerstören. Das ist zweifellos, beweist aber nichts gegen den Himmel, denn Himmel bedeuten [*sic*] eben: Unmöglichkeit von Krähen.

Noch spielen die Jagdhunde im Hof, aber das Wild entgeht ihnen nicht, so sehr es jetzt schon durch die Wälder jagt.

Es wurde ihnen die Wahl gestellt, Könige oder der Könige Kuriere zu werden. Nach Art der Kinder wollten alle Kuriere sein. Deshalb gibt es lauter Kuriere, sie jagen durch die Welt und rufen, da es keine Könige gibt, einander selbst die sinnlos gewordenen Meldungen zu. Gerne würden sie ihrem elenden Leben ein Ende machen, aber sie wagen es nicht wegen des Diensteides.

[Leopardos irrumpen en el templo y beben hasta la última gota los cálices del sacrificio; esto sucede muchas veces; finalmente, se cuenta con ello y forma parte de la ceremonia.

Los cuervos afirman que un solo cuervo podría destruir los cielos. Indudablemente, así es, pero el hecho no prueba nada contra los cielos, porque los cielos no significan otra cosa que la imposibilidad de los cuervos.

Los perros de caza están jugando en el patio, pero la liebre no escapará, por velozmente que ahora esté huyendo por el bosque.

Les dieron a elegir entre ser reyes o correos de los reyes. Como niños, todos eligieron ser correos. Y así ahora hay muchos correos, se afanan por el mundo y, como no quedan reyes, se gritan sus insensatos y anticuados mensajes. Con alivio darían fin a sus vidas miserables, pero no se atreven, por el juramento profesional.]

[Leopards break into the temple and drink all the sacrificial vessels dry; it keeps happening; in the end, it can be calculated in advance and is incorporated into the ritual (Aphorism 20).

The crows like to insist a single crow is enough to destroy heaven. This is incontestably true, but it says nothing about heaven, because heaven is another way of saying: the impossibility of crows (Aphorism 32).

The dogs are still playing in the yard, but the quarry will not escape them, never mind how fast it is running through the forest already (Aphorism 43).

They were offered the choice between being kings and being royal envoys. Like children, they all wanted to be envoys. This is why there are so many envoys chasing through the world, shouting—for the want of kings—the most idiotic messages to one another. They would willingly end their lives, but because of their oaths of duty, they don't dare to (Aphorism 47).][18]

---

[18] Franz Kafka, *Tagebücher und Briefe, Gesammelte Schriften*, Vol. 6 (Prague: Heinr. Mercy Sohn, 1937), p. 201, 202, 204, 205; also Franz Kafka, *Nachgelassene Schriften und Fragmente II* (New York: Schocken, 1992), p. 117, 120, 122, 123; Jorge Luis Borges and

Unlike the original—a 'text in which Kafka directly confronts theological themes'—Borges and Bioy Casares's translation emphasizes the illusion of power and the inevitability of defeat.[19] This is achieved by the manipulation of Kafka's aphorisms to highlight their insufferable hierarchies and their unreachable goals. Although Borges and Bioy Casares only subtly altered one of the aphorisms (by changing 'the quarry' to 'la liebre' [the hare]), their reordering of the texts affected the overall meaning. Kafka seems to have invited this flexibility: he wrote each aphorism on a separate sheet of paper, a format that allows the reader to construct a new work from juxtapositions of the text by shuffling the pages.

The aspects of Kafka that Borges and Bioy Casares brought to the fore in their translation also appeared in some of Borges's own Kafkian writing. It was through his translations of Kafka that Borges learned the 'Kafkaesque uses of such devices as the non sequitur, the logical gap, and the abandonment of premises and assumptions in the course of the narrative', and it seems likely that Borges's translations of Kafka influenced Borges's own attempts at writing in a Kafkian manner.[20]

3.3 BORGES WRITES ABOUT KAFKA

Although Borges published his first translation of Kafka in 1938, his first publication about Kafka, 'Las pesadillas y Franz Kafka' [Nightmares and Franz Kafka], appeared a few years earlier in 1935 (*see* the Annotated Bibliography for a complete list of Borges's writing about Kafka).[21] Over the course of fifty years, Borges published fifty-six non-fictional texts that mention Kafka, and he wrote another five in collaboration. Borges published more prologues to works by Kafka than to any other author except Herman Melville, and he often invoked Kafka's name to praise authors such as Bioy Casares, Cervantes, and Nathaniel Hawthorne.[22]

Adolfo Bioy Casares, trans., 'Cuatro reflexiones', *Cuentos breves y extraordinarios* (Buenos Aires: Losada, 1992), p. 146; Michael Hofmann, trans., *The Zürau Aphorisms* (London: Harvill Secker, 2006), p. 20, 32, 44, 48. Note that the English translation provided here is for the German version of the aphorisms and not the Spanish. Differences between the German and Spanish are highlighted in the analysis.

[19] Roberto Calasso, 'Veiled Splendor', *The Zürau Aphorisms* (London: Harvill Secker, 2006), pp. 109–34 (p. 119).

[20] Kristal, *Invisible Work*, p. 129.

[21] For more on the Argentine context for Borges's reading of Kafka, see Julieta Yelin, 'Kafka en Argentina', *Hispanic Review* 78.2 (2010): 251–73.

[22] Julio Chiappini, *Los prólogos de Borges* (Rosario: Zeus, 1991), pp. 37–8; Jorge Luis Borges, 'Adolfo Bioy Casares: *La invención de Morel*', *Prólogos con un prólogo de prólogos*, 1975, *Obras completas*, Vol. 4 (Buenos Aires: Emecé, 1996), pp. 25–7 (p. 26); Jorge Luis

The frequency of Borges's comments on Kafka is paralleled by their consistency: aside from confessing his misguided lack of interest in Kafka in his youth, Borges said only positive things about Kafka. Three times he referred to Kafka as the greatest writer of the modern age.[23]

Borges wrote about Kafka over the course of many years, and, as a result, his interpretation developed over time. The possibility that Kafka's works could support such a variety of interpretations was also embedded in Borges's understanding of Kafka. For example, Borges believed that Kafka's writing could hold multiple, conflicting meanings because it could be read as both allegorical and non-allegorical:

> Es harto fácil denigrar los cuentos de Kafka a juegos alegóricos. De acuerdo; pero la facilidad de esa reducción no debe hacernos olvidar que la gloria de Kafka se disminuye hasta lo invisible si la adoptamos. Franz Kafka, simbolista o alegorista, es un buen miembro de una serie tan antigua como las letras; Franz Kafka, padre de sueños desinteresados, de pesadillas sin otra razón que la de su encanto, logra una mejor soledad.
>
> [It is very easy to belittle Kafka's stories by calling them allegorical games. Perhaps, but despite the ease with which we can dismiss them as such, we should be mindful that if we adopt this view, Kafka's greatness will be reduced to nothingness. Franz Kafka, as a symbolist or allegorist, is a worthy member of a group of authors as old as writing itself; Franz Kafka, the father of disconnected dreams, of nightmares that exist for no other reason than to captivate, achieves a better solitude.][24]

Reading Kafka's stories one way makes him part of the canon and therefore (perhaps) ordinary, while reading them another makes him unique but places him outside of the canon. Yet, according to either interpretation, Kafka's works are still noteworthy. For Borges, the simultaneity of these interpretations is part of what made Kafka remarkable.

The coexistence of multiple meanings was one of the reasons why Borges admired Kafka. Even when viewing Kafka's stories just as allegories, Borges thought that they could be read in a number of different ways: 'la obra de Kafka no habrá caducado porque... será interpretada no

---

Borges, 'Nota sobre el Quijote', *Páginas de Jorge Luis Borges*, ed. Alicia Jurado (Buenos Aires: Celtia, 1982), pp. 175–7 (p. 176); Jorge Luis Borges, 'Nathaniel Hawthorne', *Otras inquisiciones*, 1952, *Obras completas*, Vol. 2 (Buenos Aires: Emecé, 1996), pp. 48–63 (p. 55).

[23] Jorge Luis Borges, 'Franz Kafka: *La metamorfosis*', *Prólogos con un prólogo de prólogos*, 1975, *Obras completas*, Vol. 4 (Buenos Aires: Emecé, 1996), pp. 97–9 (p. 97); Jorge Luis Borges, 'Franz Kafka: *América*', *Biblioteca personal: Prólogos*, 1988, *Obras completas*, Vol. 4 (Buenos Aires: Emecé, 1996), p. 454; Borges, 'Un sueño eterno', p. 238.

[24] Jorge Luis Borges, 'Las pesadillas y Franz Kafka', *Textos recobrados (1931–1955)* (Buenos Aires: Emecé, 2001), pp. 110–14 (p. 114).

socialmente, no políticamente, sino metafísicamente, y siempre tendremos otro problema, de quién rige el universo, qué rige el universo, y eso no lo sabremos nunca' [Kafka's work will always be relevant, because it can be interpreted not just socially or politically but also metaphysically. There will always be another issue, about who and what rules the universe, something we will never know].[25] Borges saw a tension between interpreting Kafka's stories as nightmares written for nightmares' sake, as allegories with meaning specific to their time and place, and as more general allegories depicting an individual's relationship with God. The simultaneity of these possible interpretations highlights a fact implicit in Kafka's stories: while they suggest multiple meanings, they deny access to any specific one.

Before continuing, some problematic terminology requires a brief mention. At various times, Borges referred to Kafka's stories as 'sueños', 'pesadillas', 'alegorías', 'parábolas', and 'fábulas' [dreams, nightmares, allegories, parables, and fables]. In doing so, Borges seemed to be dividing the tales into two categories: one consisting of dreams and nightmares, and another consisting of allegories, parables, and fables.[26] Reading Kafka's works one way, they can be seen as portraying imagined experiences. Reading them another way, they seem to offer experiences that represent or echo the real world. Borges believed that, when read in this second way (as allegories, parables, and fables), Kafka's stories could be seen to be just as relevant to any reader's context as they were to Kafka's. For example, even though Kafka could not have possibly anticipated it, Borges saw in Kafka's writing a representation of Borges's contemporaries' relationship with the oppressive state: 'Ahora estamos en un mundo de desconfianzas, se requiere continuamente papeles, tenemos que demostrar a cada momento quiénes somos, quiénes fueron nuestros padres, dónde hemos nacido; vivimos en este mundo espantoso y ese mundo fue prefigurado y simbolizado para siempre por Kafka' [We now live in a world of mistrust, where documentation is constantly required. We must at any time be able to demonstrate who we are, who our parents were, and where we were born. It is in this terrible world that we live, a world that was foreshadowed and forever symbolized by Kafka].[27] At the same time, Borges also

[25] Jorge Luis Borges, 'Jorge Luis Borges habla del mundo de Kafka', *La metamorfosis* (Paraná: Orión, 1982), pp. 5–28 (p. 26).

[26] Borges refers to Kafka's stories as 'sueños' in 'Un sueño eterno' (p. 237), as 'pesadillas' in 'Las pesadillas y Franz Kafka' (p. 114) and 'Franz Kafka: La metamorfosis' (p. 97), as 'alegorías' in 'Jorge Luis Borges habla del mundo de Kafka' (pp. 26–7), as 'parábolas' in '*El buitre*' (p. 8) and 'Sobre Chesterton' (p. 74), and as 'fábulas' in 'Un sueño eterno' (p. 237) and 'Franz Kafka: América' (p. 454).

[27] Borges, 'Jorge Luis Borges habla del mundo de Kafka', pp. 25–6.

thought it was possible to read Kafka's stories as representing all individuals' relationship with an unknowable, incomprehensible God: 'ahora la obra de Kafka es ante todo una alegoría del Estado, pero con el tiempo será una alegoría del universo, regido por un dios incognoscible, y ya que hablar de esa idea, de uno de los textos más ilustres del mundo, del libro de Job' [While Kafka's work is now primarily an allegory of the State, in time it will become an allegory of the universe governed by an unknowable God, along the same lines of one of the most celebrated texts in the world, the Book of Job].[28] For Borges, Kafka's stories were simultaneously temporally specific and timeless, containing hierarchies that managed to be both contemporary and everlasting, depending on how they were interpreted.

Curiously, in the above quotations, Borges's reading of Kafka runs counter to the more common interpretation. Ever since Brod's early interventions as Kafka's editor, Kafka's stories have been thought of as allegories of the individual's relationship with God. It is only since the outbreak of the Second World War that they have been read as an allegory of the state. When Borges placed these two interpretations in the opposite order, he seemed to be referring not to the order in which they arose, but rather to the order in which they will cease to be relevant. Borges believed that Kafka's stories would continue to represent the individual's relationship with God long after governments changed and political circumstances evolved to such a degree that his tales could no longer be read as being about the relationship between citizens and the state.

It is worth noting that, with respect to these multifaceted interpretations of Kafka, Borges sometimes used the terms fables, parables, and allegories. Even though these terms have more specific meanings, Borges tended to use them as synonyms. Of the three, the word that is the most accurate and the most useful is parable. A parable is commonly a story 'in which something is expressed in terms of something else' but can also be 'enigmatic, mystical, or dark'.[29] As parables, Kafka's stories are unique: while readers of parables have an 'expectation that the ending will show their coherence, their meaning and the appropriate moral... with Kafka such an ending is never reached'.[30] Borges admired this unreachable quality. He saw Kafka's stories as nightmarish and mysterious, alluding

---

[28] Ibid., pp. 26–7.

[29] 'Parable', *Shorter Oxford English Dictionary*, Vol. 2, 6th ed. (Oxford: Oxford UP, 2007).

[30] Roy Pascal, 'Kafka's Parables: Ways Out of the Dead End', *The World of Franz Kafka*, ed. J. P. Stern (London: Weidenfeld and Nicholson, 1980), pp. 112–19 (p. 113); for more on parable in Kafka, see Heinz Politzer, *Franz Kafka: Parable and Paradox* (Ithaca: Cornell UP, 1962).

only indistinctly to the individual's place in the universe or the individual's relationship with God. Kafka's stories, as read by Borges, could best be described as agnostic parables.

3.4 HISTORY AND BIOGRAPHY

Borges wrote twelve major texts about—or that make substantial reference to—Kafka. Eight draw heavily on biography: 'Biografía sintética: Franz Kafka' [Capsule Biography: Franz Kafka], 'Franz Kafka: *La metamorfosis*' [Franz Kafka, *The Metamorphosis*], the prologue to *El buitre*, 'Franz Kafka: A Centennial Celebration', 'Jorge Luis Borges habla del mundo de Kafka' [Jorge Luis Borges Talks About the World of Kafka], 'Una valoración de Kafka por Jorge Luis Borges' [An Appraisal of Kafka by Jorge Luis Borges], 'Un sueño eterno: Palabras grabadas en el centenario de Kafka', and 'Franz Kafka: *América*'.[31] In the three that address biography most fully, Borges arranged his analysis of Kafka's life into three sections: the historical period in which Kafka lived, the artistic context that influenced his writing, and the experiences from his personal life.[32]

Borges believed that Kafka's writing was shaped by the things that happened in his life, including the events taking place around him: 'La opresión de la guerra está en esos libros: esa opresión cuya característica atroz es la simulación de felicidad y de valeroso fervor que impone a los hombres' [The oppression of war is in those books: the oppression whose appalling feature is the feigning of happiness and courageous ardour that it imposes upon men].[33] Although Kafka never mentioned the war outright, Borges thought his texts conveyed the experience in a broader way by focusing on the universal experiences that it engendered, of which oppression and feigned courage are two examples.

Borges also saw in Kafka the ability to write works that, while they could be read as reflective of their specific time and place, could also be interpreted as being more general:

> A Kafka podemos leerlo y pensar que sus fábulas son tan antiguas como la historia, que esos sueños fueron soñados por hombres de otra época sin

---

[31] The remaining four texts, which do not make significant reference to biography, are 'Las pesadillas y Franz Kafka', ' *The Trial*, de Franz Kafka', 'Kafka y sus precursores', and 'Borges sur Kafka'.

[32] Jorge Luis Borges, 'Franz Kafka: Biografía sintética', *Textos cautivos*, 1986, *Obras completas*, Vol. 4 (Buenos Aires: Emecé, 1996), p. 326; Borges, 'Franz Kafka: *La metamorfosis*', p. 97; Borges, 'Franz Kafka: *América*', p. 454.

[33] Borges, 'Franz Kafka: *La metamorfosis*', p. 97.

necesidad de vincularlos a Alemania o a Arabia. El hecho de haber escrito un texto que transciende el momento en que se escribió, es notable. Se puede pensar que se redactó en Persia o en China y ahí está su valor.

[We can read the works of Kafka and imagine that his fables are as old as history, that they are dreams dreamt by men from another age, without needing to connect them to Germany or Arabia. The fact that he wrote a text that transcends the moment in which it was written is remarkable. One could imagine that the texts were written in Persia or China, and therein lies their value.]34

This absence of the explicit historical reference in Kafka's writing has a dual effect: on the one hand, his stories are easily generalizable and therefore can be read as parables; on the other hand, since his stories bear no specific relation to the events of the world, they can be read as dreams or nightmares. Borges also acknowledged Kafka's simultaneous state of being separate from yet also connected to other authors. While he pointed out that Kafka's work was the product of 'las vastas aventuras barrocas de la literatura: el expresionismo alemán, las hazañas verbales de Johannes Becher, de Yeats y de James Joyce' [baroque forays into literature: German expressionism and the verbal feats of Johannes Becher, Yeats and James Joyce], he also noted that Kafka's writing differed significantly from that of his contemporaries.35 For Borges, Kafka was both the product of his artistic age and an exception to it.

Borges suggested that Kafka's writing also proceeded from his personal experiences. In biographical statements about Kafka, Borges emphasized the importance of Kafka's relationship with his father, his failed relationships with women, and his unfulfilling job:

> Kafka nació en el barrio judío de la ciudad de Praga, en 1883. Era enfermizo y hosco: íntimamente no dejó nunca de menospreciarlo su padre y hasta 1922 lo tiranizó. (*De ese conflicto y de sus tenaces meditaciones sobre las misteriosas misericordias y las ilimitadas exigencias de la patria potestad, ha declarado él mismo que procede toda su obra.*) De su juventud sabemos dos cosas: un amor contrariado y el gusto de las novelas de viajes. Al egresar de la universidad, trabajó algún tiempo en una compañía de seguros. De esa tarea lo libró aciagamente la tuberculosis: con intervalos, Kafka pasó la segunda mitad de su vida en sanatorios del Tirol, de los Cárpatos y de los Erzgebirge.

> [Kafka was born in the Jewish neighbourhood of Prague, in 1883. He was sickly and sullen; his father never stopped secretly despising him and tyrannized him up until 1922. (*Kafka himself has said that all of his work, including his persistent meditations on the mysterious compassions and endless demands of the 'patria potestad' [parental authority] derived from this conflict.*) We know two things about his youth: he had an unhappy love life and a taste

---

34 Borges, 'Un sueño eterno', p. 237.   35 Borges, 'Franz Kafka: *América*', p. 454.

for books on adventure. On finishing university, he worked for a while in an
insurance company. He was fatefully delivered from this work by tuberculosis. Kafka spent the second half of his life in a succession of sanatoriums in
Tyrol, in the Carpathians and in the Ore Mountains.][36]

Borges thought that knowing Kafka's biography could help explain his work,
since he believed that Kafka's stories were derived from his experiences.

Although a biographical view is not universally held, this approach to
understanding Kafka by using his personal and historical context neither
originated with nor ended with Borges. Borges read Brod's 1937 *Franz Kafka:
eine Biographie* shortly before he wrote his own biographical analyses of
Kafka. Brod's book was the first to make sense of Kafka's literature through
his life and vice versa. Subsequently, more than two-dozen biographies have
been written about Kafka, and many biographers have proposed a view of
Kafka that is similar to Borges's. Biographers have tended to portray Kafka's
nightmarish stories as the product of his relationship with his tyrannical
father, his failed relationships with women, and his obligation to support
himself with a dull job. This interpretation is based, in part, on Kafka's 'Brief
an den Vater'.

This letter, in which Kafka both criticized and tried to make amends
with his father, has not been given a uniform reception from critics. For
example, some have proposed that the letter be read as a fictional construction:

> Max Brod felt he had to steel readers against its exaggerations and 'construc-
> tions' even before publishing the letter in its entirety; Klaus Wagenbach
> decried its value as a primary source; Heinz Politzer analysed it as highly
> refined prose and grouped it with the literary work; psychoanalytically
> oriented biographies have regarded it as 'symbolic parricide'.[37]

Meanwhile, others have argued that 'The notion that Kafka distorted the
actual events to suit his purpose and that the "Letter to His Father" cannot
be used as a biographical source is utterly misguided.'[38] Ronald Hayman
has suggested that the letter reveals the biographical basis for the themes in
Kafka's writing, and Jack Murray maintains that the oppressive authorities
in Kafka are a representation of Kafka's relationship with his father.[39] Both
Frederick J. Hoffman and Martin Greenberg believe that Kafka's relationship

---

[36] Borges, 'Franz Kafka: *La metamorfosis*', p. 97, emphasis added.
[37] Reiner Stach, *Kafka: The Decisive Years*, trans. Shelley Frisch (London: Harcourt, 2005), p. 294.
[38] Ibid., p. 296.
[39] Ronald Hayman, *K: A Biography of Kafka* (London: Weidenfeld and Nicolson, 1981), p. 272; Jack Murray, *The Landscapes of Alienation: Ideological Subversion in Kafka, Céline, and Onetti* (Stanford: Stanford UP, 1991), p. 87.

with his father is evident not just in the letter but throughout his writing.[40] Borges made the same argument in 1938—one of the earliest critics to do so.

3.5 FATHER AND SON, SUBORDINATION AND INFINITY

Borges cited the father–son relationship as the source for one of Kafka's key literary themes, which he called the 'patria potestad' [parental authority]. The 'patria potestad' represents more than just Kafka's relationship with his father. It encapsulates other levels of authority too: the phrase pulls together the authority of the father (*pater*), the fatherland (*patria*), patriarchy (as a social and religious structure), and the idea of 'patria potestad' (parental authority or legal guardianship) itself. In doing so, the 'patria potestad' comes to represent a nesting of authorities, where the rule of the father over the son is situated within the power of a state over its citizens, which, in turn, is situated within the control of the patriarchy (or God) over humankind. As Borges saw it, the mysterious compassions and unending demands in Kafka's writing are passed down from father, from country, and from a limitless patriarchy, which are all collected together as the unnamed 'patria potestad' or law (*see* note 36).

Borges expanded on this idea by connecting Kafka's portrayal of the father–son relationship with his portrayal of the relationship between God and Man, so that the latter is implicated in the former: 'Nadie ignora que Kafka no dejó nunca de sentirse misteriosamente culpable ante su padre, a la manera de Israel con su Dios' [Everyone knows that Kafka always felt mysteriously guilty toward his father, in the manner of Israel with its God].[41] These ideas about Kafka's guilt may have come from Brod's biography:

> Das ewige Mißverstehen zwischen Mensch und Gott reizt Kafka, diese Disproportion immer wieder im Bilde zweier Welten darzustellen, die einander nie, nie verstehen können—daher ist der unendliche Abstand zwischen dem stummen Tier und dem Menschen eines seiner Hauptthemen, in so vielen Tiergeschichten, die sein Werk nicht zufälligerweise enthält. Ebenso die trennende Wand zwischen Vater und Sohn. Auf allem,

---

[40] Frederick Hoffman, 'Escape From Father', *The Kafka Problem*, ed. Angel Flores (London: New Directions, 1946), pp. 214–46; Martin Greenberg, *The Terror of Art: Kafka and Modern Literature* (London: Andre Deutsch, 1971), p. 63.

[41] Borges, Prologue, *El buitre*, p. 9; Eliot Weinberger, trans., 'Franz Kafka, *The Vulture*', *Selected Non-Fictions*, p. 502.

was *Inkommensurabilität* ausdrückt, haftet der Blick dieses Dichters mit un-
endlichem Mitleids-Verständnis und bringt es mit dem verhängnisvollsten
größten aller Mißverständnisse, dem Versagen des Menschen vor Gott, in
einen stummen Zusammenhang.

[The eternal misunderstanding between God and man induces Kafka to
represent this disproportion again and again in the picture of two worlds
which can never, never understand one another—hence the infinite separ-
ation between dumb animals and men is one of his chief themes in the
numerous animal stories which his works contain, not by accident. The same
is true of the partition wall between Father and Son. This writer's gaze rests
with the endless pity of understanding on everything that expresses incom-
mensurability, and brings it into silent relation with the most fatal and
greatest of all misunderstandings, the failure of man in the sight of God.][42]

Like Brod, Borges believed that the feeling of guilt that featured in Kafka's
writing was the product of—and was portrayed by—the hierarchical
relationships of the 'patria potestad'.

It is worth noting that it may have been more than just a likeness of
mind that led to Brod's interpretation of Kafka finding a counterpart in
Borges. The editions of Kafka that Borges read were those that Brod had
published shortly after Kafka's death, and it is now widely accepted that
Brod shaped Kafka's writing with a heavy editorial hand. Brod organized
the unnumbered sections of *Der Prozeß* into chapters and he omitted parts
in order to turn the work into a coherent narrative; he reorganized the
content of *Der Verschollene* and retitled it *Amerika*; he appended titles to
fragments and published them as short stories. In doing so, Brod did more
than just sort Kafka's fragmentary writings into accessible narratives: he
also shaped the texts to reflect his interpretation of them. Brod's Kafka is
optimistic and at times religious or even prophetic, hence Brod's decision
to locate the redemptive chapter on the Nature Theatre of Oklahoma at
the end of *Amerika*. Brod's optimistic editing of Kafka was subsequently
magnified by the Muirs' translations, which Borges also read. The Muirs'
version of Kafka has been criticized for being 'too in sync with Max Brod's
Messianic vision of the texts (and with his resultant editing practices)' and
for 'read[ing] Kafka via an overly religious lens'.[43] It is this lens—the one
that treats Kafka's writing, in part, as an allegory of the relationship
between an individual and God—through which Borges subsequently
read Kafka.

---

[42] Max Brod, *Franz Kafka: eine Biographie*, 3rd ed. (Berlin: S. Fischer, 1954), p. 213,
original emphasis; G. Humphreys Roberts and Richard Winston, trans., *Franz Kafka:
A Biography*, 1937 (New York: Da Capo, 1995), p. 175.

[43] Michelle Woods, *Kafka Translated: How Translators Have Shaped Our Reading of
Kafka* (New York: Bloomsbury, 2014), p. 3, 72.

Kafka's works were not available in editions that were (mostly) free of Brod's interventions until the 1980s; by this point, Borges's opinions on Kafka were fully formed. It is unlikely (although not impossible) that Borges ever encountered Kafka in these more lightly edited editions. As such, for the purposes of this study, Borges's Kafka is taken to be the version of the author who was accessible courtesy of Brod. While this may not be the Kafka who is known to critics today, it is still a significant version. As Clayton Koelb points out,

> The Brod version of *Der Prozeß* is the one that was translated and read around the world, the one that influenced several generations of writers and readers, and indeed the one that changed the course of modern literary history. It is now an indisputable part of that history that no scholarly denunciation, no matter how loud and no matter how well documented, can expect to dislodge... Literary historians will always have to use the Brod editions of this and other major texts as the basis on which to understand the Kafka of the twentieth century.[44]

The Kafka of the twentieth century—the Kafka of Brod—is the Kafka of Borges. It is Brod's edited version of Kafka about whom Borges was writing and whose influence shines through in Borges's work.

In Borges's Brod-inflected version of Kafka, the 'patria potestad' embodies two of Kafka's central themes: 'Dos ideas—mejor dicho, dos obsesiones—rigen la obra de Franz Kafka. La subordinación es la primera de las dos; el infinito, la segunda' [Two ideas—or more exactly, two obsessions—rule Kafka's work: subordination and the infinite].[45] Together, subordination and infinity comprise the 'patria potestad', where the individual is subordinate to authorities that stretch beyond his comprehension. Twice Borges made the assertion that subordination and infinity underpin Kafka's writing, and he supported this view with examples of frustrations faced by the characters in *Der Prozeß* and *Das Schloß*:

> El héroe de la segunda novela, Josef K., progresivamente abrumado por un insensato proceso, no logra averiguar el delito de que lo acusan, ni siquiera enfrentarse con el invisible tribunal que debe juzgarlo; éste, sin juicio previo, acaba por hacerlo degollar. K., héroe de la tercera y última, es un agrimensor llamado a un castillo, que no logra jamás penetrar en él y que muere sin ser reconocido por las autoridades que lo gobiernan.

---

[44] Clayton Koelb, 'Critical Editions II: Will the Real Franz Kafka Please Stand Up?', *A Companion to the Works of Franz Kafka*, ed. James Rolleston (Rochester: Camden House, 2002), pp. 27–33 (p. 30).

[45] Borges, 'Franz Kafka: *La metamorfosis*', pp. 97–8; Borges, Prologue, *El buitre*, p. 9; Weinberger, trans., 'Franz Kafka, *The Vulture*', p. 502.

[The hero of his second novel, Josef K., is increasingly oppressed by a senseless trial. He is unable to find out what crime he is accused of, nor can he even confront the invisible court that is supposed to be judging him and which, forgoing any trial, ultimately orders his execution. K., the protagonist of the third and final of Kafka's novels, is a land surveyor who is summoned to a castle to which he never manages to gain entry, and dies without being acknowledged by the authorities who govern it.][46]

Although Borges was emphatic that subordination and infinity were Kafka's obsessions, he did not define the terms. Simply put, subordination is 'the arrangement of persons or things in a series of successively dependent ranks or degrees', but more specifically, it is 'the condition of being duly submissive to authority or discipline; submission or subjection to the rule of a superior officer or the government of a higher power'.[47] In Kafka's writing, this takes the form of a single individual who is under the control of endless powers. According to Borges, while subordination is only half of Kafka's concern, it also functions as an example of the other half (infinity), since Kafka's characters are subject to the orders of endless guards and countless judges: 'En casi todas sus ficciones hay jerarquías y esas jerarquías son infinitas' [In almost all of his stories there are hierarchies, and those hierarchies are infinite].[48] Infinity is an abstract concept that Kafka portrays by way of the hierarchical authorities to which his characters are subordinate.

In the prologue to *El buitre*, Borges connects the God–Man relationship (which is implicit in his understanding of the 'patria potestad') with his view that Kafka's stories can be read as parables:

Cabría definir su labor como una parábola o una serie de parábolas, cuyo tema es la relación moral del individuo con la divinidad y con su incomprensible universo. A pesar de su ambiente contemporáneo, está menos cerca de lo que se ha dado en llamar literatura moderna que del Libro de Job. Presupone una conciencia religiosa y ante todo judía; su imitación formal en otros contextos carece de sentido. Kafka veía su obra como un acto de fe y no quería que ésta desalentara a los hombres.

[One could define his work as a parable or a series of parables whose theme is the moral relation of the individual with God and with His incomprehensible universe. Despite this contemporary ambience, Kafka is closer to the Book of Job than to what has been called 'modern literature'. His work is based on a religious, and particularly Jewish, consciousness; its imitation in

---

[46] Borges, 'Franz Kafka: *La metamorfosis*', p. 98.
[47] 'Subordination', *Oxford English Dictionary Online* (Oxford UP, 2009), Web, 10 Oct. 2009.
[48] Borges, 'Franz Kafka: *La metamorfosis*', p. 98.

other contexts becomes meaningless. Kafka saw his work as an act of faith, and he did not want to be discouraging to mankind.][49]

For Borges, Kafka's parables are about the impossibility of understanding either divinity or the universe. Even with the help of parables, the universe will always remain incomprehensible in and to Kafka. Borges emphasized this by referring to Kafka's stories as a modern version of the Book of Job, which Borges saw (*i*) as a depiction of stoicism, (*ii*) as a commentary on the origins of suffering, and (*iii*) as a meditation on 'lo inescrutable de Dios y del universo' [the inscrutability of God and the universe].[50] Of these three interpretations, Borges thought the final one was the most important. He saw the Book of Job as being about 'ese enigma que es el universo' [the enigma that is the universe].[51] The Book of Job ends with the explanation that God's authority is limitless and his ways are incomprehensible, a conclusion that aligns with Borges's view that Kafka's writing is fundamentally about the individual's guilt towards God and the individual's relationship with the infinite universe.

Borges drew a direct link between Kafka and the Book of Job in three texts: the prologue to *El buitre*, 'Jorge Luis Borges habla del mundo de Kafka', and 'Borges sur Kafka', where he said,

> Mais je pense qu'il serait très intéressant de faire un travail sur l'œuvre de Kafka et le *Livre de Job*: ce livre que Frantz considérait comme la plus haute cîme de la littérature. A la fin, vous vous en souvenez, la voix de Dieu parle. Mais [il] ne daigne pas s'expliquer. Il condamne ceux qui l'ont justifié, ceux qui l'ont blâmé, et il se compare, cela est très étrange, au Léviathan et à Behemoth. C'est-à-dire à des monstres inconcevables. Peut-être y a-t-il quelque rapport entre l'œuvre de Kafka et ces choses-là.

> [But I think it would be very interesting to do a study of Kafka's works and the Book of Job: the book that Franz considered the highest pinnacle of literature. At the end, you remember, it was the voice of God speaking. But he does not deign to explain himself. He condemns those who justified him or who condemned him, and he compares himself, which is very strange, to Leviathan and Behemoth, to those unimaginable monsters. Perhaps there is some sort of connection between Kafka's work and those things.][52]

[49] Borges, Prologue, *El buitre*, p. 8; Weinberger, trans., 'Franz Kafka, *The Vulture*', p. 501.

[50] Jorge Luis Borges, 'El Libro de Job', *Conferencias de Jorge Luis Borges en el Instituto de Intercambio Cultural y Científico Argentino-Israelí* (Np.: Instituto de Intercambio Cultural y Científico Argentino-Israelí, 1967), pp. 5–16 (p. 16); Edna Aizenberg, trans., 'The Book of Job', *Borges and His Successors: The Borgesian Impact on Literature and the Arts* (Columbia: U of Missouri P, 1990), pp. 267–75 (p. 275).

[51] Borges, 'El Libro de Job', p. 16; Aizenberg, trans., 'The Book of Job', p. 275.

[52] Borges, 'Borges sur Kafka', p. 45.

Kafka's writing and the Book of Job are both about the relationship between Man and God. Like Kafka's parables, the biblical text ends by concealing a secret rather than revealing one: Job learns that God's mysterious ways are not for humans to know. The Book of Job 'pass[es] back and forth from the particular case of Job to the general condition of mankind', which makes it a model for the hierarchy Borges identified in Kafka.[53] On one level, it is about a specific individual's relationship with a particular authority, while on another level it is about the more general relationship between Man and God.

Borges may have been inspired by Brod, who made a similar connection between the Book of Job and Kafka:

> Seit dem biblischen Buche Hiob ist nicht so wild mit Gott gehadert worden wie in Kafkas 'Prozeß' und 'Schloß' oder in seiner 'Strafkolonie', in der die Gerechtigkeit im Bilde einer mit raffinierter Grausamkeit ersonnenen, unmenschlichen, fast teuflischen Maschine und eines schrulligen Verehrers dieser Maschine dargestellt ist. Ganz ähnlich tut Gott im Buche 'Hiob' das, was dem Menschen absurd und ungerecht erscheint. Aber es erscheint eben nur dem Menschen so, und was als letztes Resultat bei Hiob wie bei Kafka sich ergibt, ist die Feststellung, daß das Maß, mit dem der Mensch arbeitet, nicht jenes ist, nach dem in der Welt des Absoluten gemessen wird.
>
> [Since the book of Job in the Bible, God has never been so savagely striven with as in Kafka's *The Trial* and *The Castle*, or in his *In the Penal Colony*, in which justice is presented in the image of a machine thought out with refined cruelty, an inhuman, almost devilish machine, and a crank who worships this machine. Just the same in the Book of Job, God does what seems absurd and unjust to man. But it is *only* to man that this seems so, and the final conclusion arrived at in Job as in Kafka is the confirmation of the fact that the yardstick by which man works is not by that which measurements are taken in the world of the Absolute.][54]
>
> Gilt's Kraft der Starken, so ist der da,
>
> Aber gilt's den Rechtsweg, so heißt es: Wer darf mich vorfordern.
>
> Das ist genau derselbe Richter, zu dem K. im 'Prozeß' nicht vordringen kann; das ist die Schloßherrschaft, die sich nicht sprechen läßt, die immer nur untergeordnete Instanzen ohne Verantwortung vorschreibt, die sehr böse Dinge anstellen.'
>
> ['If I speak of strength, lo, he is strong: and if of judgement, who shall set me a time to plead?'

[53] Moshe Greenberg, 'Job', *The Literary Guide to the Bible*, ed. Robert Alter and Frank Kermode (London: Fontana, 1997), pp. 283–304 (p. 288).

[54] Brod, *Franz Kafka: Eine Biographie*, p. 214; Humphreys Roberts and Winston, trans., *Franz Kafka: A Biography*, pp. 175–6, original emphasis.

That is exactly the same judge to whom K., in *The Trial*, cannot fight his
way: or again, the gentlemen of the Castle, who don't allow themselves to be
spoken to, who always put forward a screen of courts of appeals which have
no responsibility and which do very wicked things.][55]

The Book of Job, *Der Prozeß*, and *Das Schloß* demonstrate that God's
authority is immeasurable, inscrutable, and most of all, infinite. The
readers of the Book of Job know this right from the start, even if Job
does not find out until the end; they 'know—what neither Job nor his
Friends do—that Job's sufferings are designed to test him'.[56] Similarly,
Borges believed that 'when you've read the first page of *The Trial* you know
that he'll never know why he's being judged, why he's being tried'.[57] The
Book of Job relies on 'reversal and subversion', dialogue with 'no predictable
or consistent course of argument', and 'unintelligible sequences'—qualities
that echo the incomprehensible in order to demonstrate God's power.[58]
These traits also feature in Kafka's disjointed works, such as 'Hochzeitsvorbereitungen auf dem Lande' and *Das Schloß*.

Borges admired the Book of Job and Kafka's stories because they both
give the impression of being infinite, which is difficult to do in a finite
piece of writing. Job's suffering seems as if it will have no end and God's
power seems boundless, while Kafka's protagonists find their goals reced-
ing away from them and they discover that the authorities with which
they are confronted are all-powerful. Kafka's novels 'Tienen un número
infinito de capítulos, porque su tema es de un número infinito de postu-
laciones' [Have an infinite number of chapters, because their theme is the
infinite number of possibilities].[59] Yet they lack middle segments, linking
passages, or endings. Borges believed that texts that are infinite yet pared
down were one of Kafka's hallmarks, and that these features are what
allow them to be read as both nightmares and parables. Kafka's texts'
overabundance of and yet lack of detail is reminiscent of nightmares hazily
recalled. And, by virtue of missing key pieces of information, Kafka's
stories give the impression of harbouring secret messages or seeming as
though they might convey universal truths. There is a parallel between the
structure of the stories, which perpetually defer their conclusions, and the
plots about protagonists who search for something unobtainable.

[55] Brod, *Franz Kafka: Eine Biographie*, p. 222; Humphreys Roberts and Winston,
trans., *Franz Kafka: A Biography*, p. 182 (the first part of the quotation is Brod quoting
the Book of Job).

[56] Greenberg, 'Job', p. 286.

[57] Jorge Luis Borges quoted in Richard Burgin, *Conversations with Jorge Luis Borges*
(New York: Holt, 1969), pp. 58–9.

[58] Greenberg, 'Job', p. 283.   [59] Borges, 'Un sueño eterno', p. 238.

In two of Kafka's parables, protagonists seek secret messages but are
prevented from obtaining them by problems akin to Zeno's paradoxes.
In Kafka's 'Vor dem Gesetz' (1914), the countryman's access to the
law is blocked by an infinite number of doors and guards, while in
'Eine kaiserliche Botschaft' [An Imperial Message] (1919), the protagonist waits for a messenger who has to cross an infinitely large
expanse:[60]

Wenn es dich so lockt, versuche es doch, trotz meines Verbotes hineinzu-
gehen. Merke aber: Ich bin mächtig. Und ich bin nur der unterste Türhüter.
Von Saal zu Saal stehn aber Türhüter, einer mächtiger als der andere. Schon
den Anblick des dritten kann nicht einmal ich mehr ertragen.

[If you are so strongly tempted, try and get in without my permission. But
note that I am powerful. And I am only the lowest door-keeper. From hall to
hall, keepers stand at every door, one more powerful than the other. Even the
third of these has an aspect that even I cannot bear to look at.][61]

Der Bote hat sich gleich auf den Weg gemacht; ein kräftiger, ein unermü-
dlicher Mann; einmal diesen, einmal den andern Arm vorstreckend, schafft
er sich Bahn durch die Menge... Aber die Menge ist so groß; ihre Wohn-
stätten nehmen kein Ende.... Aber statt dessen, wie nutzlos müht er sich ab;
immer noch zwängt er sich durch die Gemächer des innersten Palastes;
niemals wird er sie überwinden; und gelänge ihm dies, nichts wäre
gewonnen.... Niemand dringt hier durch und gar mit der Botschaft eines
Toten.—Du aber sitzt an deinem Fenster und erträumst sie dir, wenn der
Abend kommt.

[The messenger immediately sets out on his journey; a powerful, an indefat-
igable man; now pushing with his right arm, now with his left, he cleaves a
way for himself through the throng... But the multitudes are so vast; their
numbers have no end.... But instead how vainly does he wear out his
strength; still he is only making his way through the chambers of the
innermost palace; never will he get to the end of them; and if he succeeded
in that nothing would be gained.... Nobody could fight his way through
here even with a message from a dead man. But you sit at your window when
the evening falls and dream it to yourself.][62]

---

[60] 'Vor dem Gesetz' [Before the Law] is included as a parable in *Der Prozeß* [*The Trial*],
and 'Eine kaiserliche Botschaft' [An Imperial Message] is included as a parable in 'Beim Bau
der chinesischen Mauer' [The Great Wall of China] (1931). Both stories were also
published independently: 'Vor dem Gesetz' appears as a stand-alone text in the Schocken
Gesammelte Schriften, and both stories are included in collection *Ein Landarzt* [The
Country Doctor], which Borges read no later than 1935.
[61] Kafka, 'Vor dem Gesetz', *Erzählungen und kleine Prosa*, p. 144; also Kafka, 'Vor dem
Gesetz', *Drucke zu Lebzeiten* p. 267; Muir and Muir, trans., *The Trial, The Complete
Novels*, p. 120.
[62] Franz Kafka, 'Eine kaiserliche Botschaft', *Erzählungen und kleine Prosa, Gesammelte
Schriften*, Vol. 1 (Berlin: Schocken, 1935), pp. 154–5 (pp. 154–5); also Franz Kafka, 'Eine

Kafka knew of Zeno, having mentioned the paradoxes in his diary: 'Zeno sagte auf eine dringliche Frage hin, ob den nichts ruhe: Ja, der fliegende Pfeil ruht' [Zeno, pressed as to whether anything is at rest, replied: Yes, the flying arrow rests].[63]

Borges first learned about the concept of infinity and Zeno's paradoxes—which he later spotted in Kafka's stories—from his father. In writing about the paradoxes he sometimes recalled both his familial predecessor (Borges *père*) and his literary precursor (Kafka):

> El 'regresus in infinitum' puede ilustrarse, creo que del modo más vívido posible, mediante las paradojas de Zenón de Elea, que dijo que si creíamos en la realidad del tiempo como hecho de instantes y la del espacio como hecho de puntos, el transcurso del tiempo y el movimiento son imposibles, e ilustra esto mediante varias paradojas que fueron refutadas por Aristóteles y comentadas por toda la filosofía después, pero recordaré dos simplemente, ya que en ellas se ve claramente cuál es el modo de Kafka y me permiten recordar a mi padre.

> [*Regresus in infinitum* can be illustrated, perhaps in the most vivid way possible, through the paradoxes of Zeno of Elea, who said that if we believe in the reality of time as being composed of a series of instances and space as a series of consecutive points, the passage of time and movement are impossible. He showed this by way of a variety of paradoxes that were later refuted by Aristotle and commented on by all of philosophy. I will recount two of the simplest versions, which elucidate Kafka's method and give me the chance to remember my father.][64]

Zeno's paradoxes take many forms, but they all produce the same result: motion is an illusion, all goals are unreachable, and infinity is unconquerably large. In one version of the paradoxes, for an arrow to reach a target it first needs to fly half of the distance, but before this it must go one quarter of the distance, and before this an eighth, and so on until it can never leave its starting place at all. In 'La perpetua carrera de Aquiles y la tortuga' [The

---

kaiserliche Botschaft', *Drucke zu Lebzeiten* (Frankfurt: S. Fischer; New York: Schocken, 1994), pp. 280–2 (pp. 281–2); Willa Muir and Edwin Muir, trans., 'The Great Wall of China', *The Complete Stories* (New York: Schocken, 1971), pp. 235–47 (p. 244).

[63] Franz Kafka, *Tagebücher (1910–1923)* (New York: S. Fischer/Schocken, 1948–49), p. 29; also Franz Kafka, *Tagebücher* (New York: Schocken, 1990), p. 29; Joseph Kresh, trans., *The Diaries of Franz Kafka, 1910–1913*, ed. Max Brod (New York: Schocken, 1971), p. 34.

[64] Borges, 'Jorge Luis Borges habla del mundo de Kafka', p. 6. In this essay, Borges discusses his father extensively twice: first with reference to learning about Zeno, and second with reference to learning about idealism. Borges often mentioned his father when he mentioned Kafka, notably in 'An Autobiographical Essay' and 'Un sueño eterno'. With regard to Zeno's paradoxes, Borges *père*, and Kafka, it is curious that Borges *fils* learned about Zeno's paradoxes as a child, and he read Kafka in 1916, but he did not connect the two in writing until 1937, when he wrote his review of *Der Prozeß* for *El Hogar*.

Perpetual Race of Achilles and the Tortoise] (1929) and 'Avatares de la tortuga' [Avatars of the Tortoise] (1939), Borges offered another version:

> Aquiles corre diez veces más ligero que la tortuga y le da una ventaja de diez metros. Aquiles corre esos diez metros, la tortuga corre uno; Aquiles corre ese metro, la tortuga corre un decímetro; Aquiles corre ese decímetro, la tortuga corre un centímetro; Aquiles corre ese centímetro, la tortuga un milímetro; Aquiles Piesligeros el milímetro, la Tortuga un décimo de milímetro y así infinitamente, sin alcanzarla . . .

> [Achilles runs ten times faster than the tortoise and gives the animal a headstart of ten metres. Achilles runs those ten metres, the tortoise one; Achilles runs that metre, the tortoise runs a decimetre; Achilles runs that decimetre, the tortoise runs a centimetre; Achilles runs that centimetre, the tortoise, a millimetre; Fleet-footed Achilles, the millimetre, the tortoise, a tenth of a millimetre, and so on to infinity, without the tortoise ever being overtaken . . .][65]

Borges thought that Kafka's writing was exemplary of Zeno's paradoxes: 'En las novelas, el esquema es siempre el mismo, es algo monótono, se repite el tema del infinito, la paradoja de la tortuga y la flecha' [In the novels, the structure is always the same: somewhat monotonous, it repeats the topic of the infinite, the paradox of the tortoise and the arrow].[66] He identified specific aspects of Zeno's paradoxes in Kafka's 'Vor dem Gesetz', 'Eine alltägliche Verwirrung' [A Common Confusion] (1931), 'Beim Bau der chinesischen Mauer' [The Great Wall of China], and 'Eine kaiserliche Botschaft', all stories that contain endless obstacles or tasks that can never be completed.[67]

Because of the frequency with which Kafka used the structure of Zeno's paradoxes in his stories, Borges saw them as Kafka's modus operandi: 'el "regresus in infinitum" . . . es un proceso intelectual bastante común tratándose de etiología o metafísica, pero raro tratándose de literatura y podríamos decir que fuera de algunos precursores, que de algún modo fueron inventados por él, fue inaugurado por Kafka' [*regresus in infinitum* . . . is an intellectual process which, while fairly common in etiology and metaphysics, is quite rare in literature. We could say that apart from a few precursors, which were in some way invented by him, the process was introduced by Kafka].[68] For Borges, the lack of conclusion in Zeno's

[65] Jorge Luis Borges, 'Avatares de la tortuga', *Discusión*, 1932, *Obras completas*, Vol. 1 (Buenos Aires: Emecé, 1996), pp. 254–8 (p. 254); James Irby, trans., 'Avatars of the Tortoise', *Labyrinths* (London: Penguin, 2000), pp. 237–43 (p. 237).

[66] Jorge Luis Borges, 'Una valoración de Kafka por Jorge Luis Borges', *Clarín: Cultura y nación* 30 Jun. 1983: 1–2 (p. 1).

[67] Jorge Luis Borges, 'Kafka y sus precursores', *Otras inquisiciones*, 1952, *Obras completas*, Vol. 2 (Buenos Aires: Emecé, 1996), pp. 88–90; Borges, 'Franz Kafka: *La metamorfosis*', p. 98; Borges, 'Jorge Luis Borges habla del mundo de Kafka', pp. 6–10.

[68] Borges, 'Jorge Luis Borges habla del mundo de Kafka', p. 5.

paradoxes is built into the very form of Kafka's writing. He saw Kafka's texts as fundamentally Zenoesque, a term used in this study to refer to situations where goals and endings are infinitely far away, and to describe instances where infinity serves as an obstacle that cannot be overcome.

The prospect of Zenoesque obstacles that can never be overcome relates to another element Borges admired in Kafka, that of the labyrinth or maze:

> Uno de los temas predilectos de Kafka fue sin duda, el del laberinto porque él pudo darse cuenta que el mundo donde vivía era un mundo inexplicable, de asombro y perplejidad. Kafka no utiliza la palabra laberinto, porque tiene pudor en usarla porque quizá la sentía demasiado cerca, pero el mundo para él era un laberinto. Kafka llega a la desesperación del laberinto con la idea de la empresa imposible, contrariamente a lo que las literaturas clásicas mostraban que las empresas eran venturosas, de finales felices como '*La Isla de Tesoro*', donde finalmente se llega al tesoro.

> [One of Kafka's favourite themes was, without a doubt, that of the labyrinth, because he realized that the world in which he lived was an inexplicable, amazing and bewildering one. Kafka does not use the word labyrinth—his reservation perhaps stems from the fact that it felt too close—but for him, the world was indeed a labyrinth. Kafka reached the desperation of the labyrinth by way of the idea of an impossible undertaking, which runs contrary to all of those classic books that suggested that adventures were rewarding and had happy endings, as in *Treasure Island*, where they eventually find the treasure.][69]

Although Borges was wrong—Kafka used the word 'labyrinth' nearly a dozen times in 'Der Bau' [The Burrow]—he was right to identify the labyrinth as one of Kafka's predominant motifs. Kafka's characters often find themselves lost in labyrinthine settings, both physically and metaphorically. For example, in 'Eine kaiserliche Botschaft' the emperor's envoy must make his way through a labyrinthine series of palace chambers, staircases, and courts. In *Amerika*, Karl loses himself in 'Treppen, die einander immer wieder folgten' [endless recurring stairs] and 'fortwährend abbiegende Korridore' [corridors with countless turnings] aboard the ship, again in Pollunder's house, and again still in Delamarche's apartment building.[70] Josef K. must navigate the maze-like staircases and chambers of the courts, and also the peculiar, labyrinthine hierarchy of the legal system. K. faces a similar labyrinth, but his is a metaphorical one of hierarchical castle officials

---

[69] Jorge Luis Borges quoted in Dante Escóbar Plata, *Las obsesiones de Borges* (Buenos Aires: Distal, 1989), p. 59.

[70] Franz Kafka, *Amerika: Roman, Gesammelte Schriften*, Vol. 2 (Berlin: Schocken, 1935), p. 11; also Franz Kafka, *Der Verschollene* (New York: Schocken, 1983), p. 8; Willa Muir and Edwin Muir, trans., *America, The Complete Novels* (London: Vintage, 1999), pp. 131–274 (p. 133).

in a physical labyrinth comprised of an endless village crossed by absurd roads that lead K. no closer to the castle yet no further away. These are infinite, Zenoesque labyrinths, where try though the characters may, they cannot reach their goals. As labyrinths, these physical and conceptual structures conceal more than just the way out: they also conceal meanings. Because of the labyrinthine structure of the courts, Josef K. never discovers why he is on trial, and because of the maze of officials governing the castle, K. never learns whether he is to undertake work as a land surveyor. Despite this, Kafka's protagonists continue to search for solutions, maintaining the belief that every maze should have an exit and that even the most absurd situation should have an explanation. Kafka's parables similarly preserve the possibility that meaning exists, even if the parables do not reveal it: the protagonist in 'Eine kaiserliche Botschaft' believes that the messenger is undoubtedly on the way.

3.6 KAFKA AND THE MODEL SHORT STORY

Borges admired Kafka's writing for its brevity as much as for its ability to carry on infinitely. About this preference Borges says,

> Je pense d'abord à ses nouvelles, et moins à ses romans. Il se trouve que je n'ai pas l'habitude des romans. J'ai lu très peu de romans dans ma vie.... Je lis toujours des contes, des nouvelles, parce que dans un roman il y a des bourrages, toujours, tandis qu'un récit de Kipling, de Conrad, un bon récit de Maupassant, peut être essentiel. Un roman ne saurait être essentiel; il y a toujours des digressions, des descriptions. Tandis que dans un conte, chaque mot a une valeur.... Dans le cas de Kafka, si je songe à Kafka je pense tout d'abord à des contes de peu de pages, à *La muraille chinoise*, à *Odradek*, à... *Derrière la porte*, à ses aphorismes aussi. Tandis que les romans sont un peu mécaniques, je trouve.

> [I think a lot about his stories, and less about his novels. I actually am not in the habit of reading novels. I have read very few novels in my lifetime.... I always read tales, stories, because a novel always has padding; but when one reads a story by Kipling, by Conrad, a good story by Maupassant, everything is necessary. A novel does not have to be essential; it is full of digressions, descriptions. By contrast, in a story, every word has weight... In the case of Kafka, if I think of Kafka, I think of his shortest stories, 'The Great Wall of China', 'Odradek', 'Before the Law', and of his aphorisms as well. But I find his novels a bit mechanical.][71]

---

[71] Jorge Luis Borges, 'Kafka, la philosophie, la poésie', *Change International* 3 (1985): 46.

For Borges, Kafka's short stories were part of a storytelling tradition that extended from ancient mythology and biblical parables.

Despite all he said about Kafka, Borges neglected to mention a number of important elements particular to Kafka's short stories, whether intentionally or by accident. These include their portrayals of hope and despair; their inclusion of approximations of the author and of untrustworthy or limited narrators; and their hazy lack of detail. Borges did not mention these features, but an examination of Kafka's stories reveals that these aspects are nonetheless noteworthy for a study of the Kafkian characteristics of Borges's writing.

To start, Kafka's writing treads a line between hope and despair. In stories such as 'Vor dem Gesetz' and in *Der Prozeß* and *Das Schloß*, Kafka's characters persevere when faced with insurmountable problems and unachievable goals. They participate in vast projects that will never be finished, such as building the Great Wall of China. To this end, Kafka often uses a structure in which the story's initial premises are plausible, while the events that follow are not. For example, in *Das Schloß*, it is believable that K. has been called to provide his services as a land surveyor, but the story increases in absurdity as it progresses. These inexplicable circumstances and insurmountable obstacles are reminiscent of Zeno's paradoxes—and of paradoxes more broadly. Paradoxes start with acceptable premises, but they end in situations that are contradictory, illogical, or impossible. In *After Kafka: The Influence of Kafka's Fiction* (1989), Shimon Sandbank proposes two paradoxes that he claims originate in Kafka's writing and later appear in Borges's. He calls the first the paradox of negation as part of affirmation: 'God, to be all-inclusive, must include his negation; to be affirmed he must be negated.'[72] This is a Kafkian, Borgesian version of the barber paradox: if a barber in a small town (where all the men are clean-shaven) shaves only all of the men in the town who do not shave themselves, does the barber shave himself? Bertrand Russell's paradox, a generalization of the barber paradox, asks whether it is possible to have a set of all sets that do not contain themselves.

The second paradox that Sandbank identifies in Kafka is one that he calls the commonplace secret: 'the combination of the singular and the universal, of elimination and accumulation. Since one cannot tell where the secret resides, it may reside anywhere. All things become charged with

---

[72] Shimon Sandbank, *After Kafka: The Influence of Kafka's Fiction* (Athens: U of Georgia P, 1989), p. 91. It is worth noting that Sandbank's paradoxes, like the paradoxes that appear in Borges's and Kafka's writing (and that are discussed here), are literary and not mathematical paradoxes. They are counter-intuitive and absurd, but should not (or cannot) be analysed mathematically.

secrecy, but secrecy itself becomes charged with banality and may prove trivial at any minute.'[73] The commonplace secret suggests that if anything may be the thing that is important, the important may appear to be trivial, a problem Josef K. discovers when he concludes that he must justify his entire life if he is to have the unknown charges against him dismissed.

A third paradox, which Sandbank does not mention, is the sorites paradox. This paradox (with its name derived from the Greek word for heap, *soros*) asks how many grains of sand constitute a heap. If a heap of sand has one grain removed, is it still a heap? Is it still a heap if it has two grains removed? If it has all but one grain of sand removed, it is certainly not a heap, but the boundary between heap and not-heap is unclear. The sorites paradox can also be stated in the opposite direction: one grain of sand does not make a heap, and if one grain does not then two do not either, and if two do then three do not either, and so on. It is impossible to draw the line between what constitutes a heap and what does not. The sorites paradox is based on the vagueness of language—the ambiguity of the term 'heap' makes it impossible to define—and both Borges and Kafka address the shortcomings of language in their stories.

In Kafka's stories, the characters that face these paradoxes often bear some resemblance to the author, in name if not in nature:

> Georg hat so viel Buchstaben wie Franz. In Bendemann ist 'mann' nur eine für alle noch unbekannten Möglichkeiten der Geschichte vorgenommene Verstärkung von 'Bende'. Bende aber hat ebenso viele Buchstaben wie Kafka und der Vokal e wiederholt sich an den gleichen Stellen wie der Vokal a in Kafka.

> [Georg has the same number of letters as Franz. In Bendemann, 'mann' is a strengthening of 'Bende' to provide for all the as yet unforeseen possibilities in the story. But Bende has exactly the same number of letters as Kafka, and the vowel *e* occurs in the same places as does the vowel *a* in Kafka.][74]

The letters in *Samsa* and *Bende*mann (the protagonists of 'Die Verwandlung' and 'Das Urteil' [The Judgement]) follow the same consonant-vowel pattern as *Kafka*. The name Josef K. in *Der Prozeß* suggests Franz K., and K. in *Das Schloß* suggests Kafka. Using characters who seem like they may be ciphers for the author adds a layer of confusion to Kafka's stories. Although it may seem as though Kafka is bolstering the plausibility of his tales by giving his characters names that recall his own, there are as many differences between Kafka and his characters as there are similarities.

---

[73] Ibid., p. 88.
[74] Kafka, *Tagebücher (1910–1923)*, p. 297; also Kafka, *Tagebücher*, p. 492; Joseph Kresh, trans., *The Diaries of Franz Kafka, 1910–1923*, p. 215.

(Notwithstanding this complication, Borges believed that Kafka's stories were based, at least in part, on experiences drawn from his own life.)

The relationship between Kafka and the characters to whom he has given his name is one of the many techniques he used to enhance—yet also undermine—the believability of his tales. For example, his stories are often told from the point of view of untrustworthy narrators. Even when they are written in the third rather than the first person, readers usually know only what the narrator knows. When the readers glimpse disorienting hints of other perspectives, it contributes to the sense of confusion. Neither the characters nor the readers find out why Josef K. is being tried or why Gregor has turned into an insect (or even what sort of insect he is). This ignorance is also a feature of the Book of Job, where Job suffers without knowing why, and it produces the perplexing and nightmarish atmosphere that Borges admired in Kafka.

The nightmarish effect is compounded by narrative techniques such as Kafka's practice of writing fragments and non-sequiturs rather than complete texts—fragments that were often assembled into complete (or semi-complete) works by Brod. For example, in *Amerika*, Karl's story jumps from an apartment where he is living with his acquaintances Robinson, Delamarche, and Brunelda to an interview for the Nature Theatre of Oklahoma:

> In solchen Gedanken schlief Karl ein und nur im ersten Halbschlaf störte ihn noch ein gewaltiges Seufzen Bruneldas, die, scheinbar von schweren Träumen geplagt, sich auf ihrem Lager wälzte.

> Karl sah an einer Straßenecke ein Plakat mit folgender Aufschrift: Auf dem Rennplatz in Clayton wird heute von sechs Uhr früh bis Mitternacht Personal für das Theater in Oklahama aufgenommen!

> [On such thoughts Karl fell asleep, and only in his first light slumber was disturbed by a deep sigh from Brunelda, who was apparently troubled by bad dreams and twisted and turned on her bed.

> At the street corner Karl saw a placard with the following announcement: The Oklahoma Theatre will engage members for its company today at Clayton race-course from six o'clock in the morning until midnight.][75]

While there is a chapter break between these paragraphs, there is no explanation linking one to the other. Karl falls asleep at the end of the penultimate chapter (before the paragraph break). Does this mean that the line that opens the final chapter is meant to introduce a dream? It does not seem so, for the narrative does not intimate that this is the case, and Karl

---

[75] Kafka, *Amerika: Roman*, p. 264, 265; also Kafka, *Der Verschollene*, p. 354, 387; Muir and Muir, trans., *America, The Complete Novels*, p. 260.

shows no sign of waking up at the novel's end. Instead, he boards a train heading for the Nature Theatre, presumably never to return. (It is worth noting that Brod was the one who connected the fragments set in the apartment and at the interview; he may have done so in order to suggest an optimistic conclusion to *Amerika* by way of Karl's escape.)

Compounding the impression that Kafka's stories can be fragmentary or disjointed is the fact that some of his texts have segments that overlap or double back on themselves. This is especially true of longer works, such as 'Hochzeitsvorbereitungen auf dem Lande' and 'Beschreibung eines Kampfes' [Description of a Struggle] (1936). Other works have more than one ending, as in 'Der Jäger Gracchus' [The Hunter Gracchus] (1931) and 'Beim Bau der chinesischen Mauer'. Occasionally they finish without any conclusion at all: 'Blumfeld, ein älterer Junggeselle' [Blumfeld, the Elderly Bachelor] (1936) has two consecutive plots, neither of which reaches a resolution. These unclear, multiple, conflicting, and non-existent endings add to the reader's sense of uncertainty and confusion, and they often leave the characters within the stories perplexed.

Kafka's selective use of detail adds to the fragmentary, ambiguous effect of his narratives. This technique is notable in 'Beim Bau der chinesischen Mauer', where Kafka provides an intermittent excess of detail about the building of the Great Wall among a general lack of information, with the result that what the readers (and the builders) know does not add up to a coherent whole. While it is clear from the title where the story is set, all other identifying geographical and temporal details are obscured. The Great Wall is situated only with respect to internal features: it is 'an ihrer nördlichsten Stelle beendet worden' [finished off at its northernmost corner], converging there 'Von Südosten und Südwesten' [From the southeast and southwest].[76] Without any locations to which these designations can be connected, this information is ultimately meaningless even though it is precise. The story is similarly ambiguous elsewhere: 'In diese Welt drang nun die Nachricht vom Mauerbau. Auch sie verspätet, etwa dreißig Jahre nach ihrer Verkündigung' [The news of the building of the wall now penetrated into this world—late, too, some thirty years after its announcement].[77] Thirty years after the project's announcement is a

---

[76] Franz Kafka, 'Beim Bau der chinesischen Mauer', *Beschreibung eines Kampfes: Novellen, Skizzen, Aphorismen aus dem Nachlass, Gesammelte Schriften*, Vol. 5 (Prague: Heinr. Mercy Sohn, 1936), pp. 67–82 (p. 67); also Franz Kafka, *Nachgelassene Schriften und Fragmente I* (New York: Schocken, 1993), pp. 337–56 (p. 337); Muir and Muir, trans., 'The Great Wall of China', pp. 235–48 (p. 235).

[77] Franz Kafka, 'Fragment zum "Bau der chinesischen Mauer"', *Tagebücher und Briefe, Gesammelte Schriften*, Vol. 6 (Prague: Heinr. Mercy Sohn, 1937), pp. 175–6 (p. 175); also

vague designation that, although it demonstrates how long it takes for news to spread, does not make the actual date of the announcement known. It is also a trivial piece of information in the light of an assertion that the project will take generations to complete. Later, when news arrives about the completion of the wall from a neighbouring province, the language of the message is foreign and archaic-sounding. The news is disregarded as a historical oddity, not an accurate report on current circumstances:

Und nun wurde einmal ein Flugblatt der Aufständischen durch einen Bettler, der jene Provinz durchreist hatte, in das Haus meines Vaters gebracht. Es war gerade ein Feiertag, Gäste füllten unsere Stuben, in der Mitte saß der Priester und studierte das Blatt. Plötzlich fing alles zu lachen an, das Blatt wurde im Gedränge zerissen, der Bettler, der allerdings schon reichlich beschenkt worden war, wurde mit Stößen aus dem Zimmer gejagt, alles zerstreute sich und lief in den schönen Tag. Warum? Der Dialekt der Nachbarprovinz ist von dem unseren wesentlich verschieden, und dies drückt sich auch in gewissen Formen der Schriftsprache aus, die für uns einen altertümlichen Charakter haben. Kaum hatte nun der Priester zwei derartige Seiten gelesen, war man schon entschieden. Alte Dinge, längst gehört, längst verschmerzt. Und obwohl—so scheint es mir in der Erinnerung—aus dem Bettler das grauenhafte Leben unwiderleglich sprach, schüttelte man lachend den Kopf und wollte nichts mehr hören. So bereit ist man bei uns, die Gegenwart auszulöschen.

[Well, one day a leaflet published by the rebels was brought to my father's house by a beggar who had crossed that province. It happened to be a feast day, our rooms were filled with guests, the priest sat in the center and studied the sheet. Suddenly everybody started to laugh, in the confusion the sheet was torn, the beggar, who however had already received abundant alms, was driven out of the room with blows, the guests dispersed to enjoy the beautiful day. Why? The dialect of this neighbouring province differs in some essential respects from ours, and this difference occurs also in certain turns of the written word, which for us have an archaic character. Hardly had the priest read two pages before we had come to our decision. Ancient history told long ago, old sorrows long since healed. And though—so it seems to me in recollection—the gruesomeness of the living present was irrefutably conveyed by the beggar's words, we laughed and shook our heads and refused to listen any longer. So eager are our people to obliterate the present.][78]

Kafka, *Nachgelassene Schriften und Fragmente I*, p. 356; Tania Stern and James Stern, trans., 'The News of the Building of the Wall: A Fragment', *The Complete Stories* (New York: Schocken, 1971), pp. 248–9 (p. 248).

[78] Kafka, 'Beim Bau der chinesischen Mauer', p. 80; also Franz Kafka, *Nachgelassene Schriften und Fragmente II, Apparatband* (Frankfurt: Fischer, 1992), pp. 298–9; Muir and Muir, trans., 'The Great Wall of China', p. 246.

Language conveys meaning only when it is employed as part of an agreed-upon system. In Kafka's story, the use of language varies greatly from one province to the next. The effect conjured by the techniques of ambiguous, flexible language is one of uncertainty and inconclusiveness, and this may partly explain why Kafka's stories have (for Borges) the feeling of being uncertain, agnostic parables.

Borges borrowed the traits he admired in Kafka's writing and many more that he never identified outright, including Kafka's portrayal of hope and despair, his complex use of approximations of the author in his stories, his untrustworthy narrators, and the hazy lack of detail that constitutes so many of his tales. Borges linked Kafka's unreached goals with the ambiguity of language in stories such as 'La biblioteca de Babel' [The Library of Babel] and 'El Congreso' [The Congress]. He also built on Kafka's use of Zeno's paradoxes, his incorporation of biography into fiction, and his predominant themes of subordination, infinity, and the 'patria potestad' throughout his own writing. Eventually, he even tried to resolve some of the literary and philosophical problems that Kafka could not. The next three chapters examine Borges's prose fiction to see how he made use of (and departed from) the things he admired in Kafka.

4

Emulating Kafka in Babylon and Babel

This chapter applies the ideas that Borges admired in Kafka to Borges's own writing. It focuses on the two stories where Borges was open about imitating Kafka's style: 'Quand j'ai écrit *La bibliothèque de Babel* et *La loterie de Babylone*, j'ai tâché d'être Kafka' [When I wrote 'The Library of Babel' and 'The Lottery in Babylon', I tried to be Kafka].[1] Reading these stories in the light of Borges's interpretation of Kafka draws attention to Borges's interest in paradoxes and parables, and to his turn away from Kafka even while emulating him.

4.1 'LA LOTERÍA EN BABILONIA'

Of the two stories Borges openly modelled on Kafka, 'La lotería en Babilonia' [The Lottery in Babylon] was the first one published, appearing in January 1941. It is about a lottery initially held for amusement and financial gain, but which develops over time to include non-pecuniary elements, mandatory participation, and secret draws that control the participants' lives. The story mentions Kafka with 'una letrina sagrada llamada Qaphqa ... que, según opinión general, [*daba*] *a la Compañía*' [a sacred latrine called Qaphqa ... [which] it was generally believed, *gave access to the Company*] that runs the lottery.[2] While this comic misspelling of Kafka with reference to a secret source of power is not enough to prove that the story owes Kafka a debt, it invites the possibility of other connections.

'La lotería en Babilonia' appears to be written as though it is one of Kafka's stories, which are often set in nondescript periods, perhaps in the past, but possibly in the present or even the future. In the opening paragraph, the unnamed first-person narrator identifies himself as branded

---

[1] Jorge Luis Borges, 'Borges sur Kafka', *Change International* 3 (1985): 44–5 (p. 44).

[2] Jorge Luis Borges, 'La lotería en Babilonia', *Ficciones*, 1944, *Obras completas*, Vol. 1 (Buenos Aires: Emecé, 1996), pp. 456–60 (p. 458), original emphasis; Andrew Hurley, trans., 'The Lottery in Babylon', *Fictions*, 1944, *Collected Fictions* (New York: Viking, 1998), pp. 101–6 (p. 104), original emphasis.

with the Hebrew letter bet (ב or B): 'Miren: por este desgarrón de la capa se ve en mi estómago un tatuaje bermejo: es el segundo símbolo, Beth. Esta letra, en las noches de luna llena, me confiere poder sobre los hombres cuya marca es Ghimel, pero me subordina a los de Aleph' [Look here—through this gash in my cape you can see on my stomach a crimson tattoo—it is the second letter, *Beth*. On nights when the moon is full, this symbol gives me power over men with the mark of Gimel, but it subjects me to those with the Aleph].[3] The letter B conjures a link with Borges in the way that the letter K tentatively associates characters with Kafka.

The lottery's draws have denied the narrator his own name and they have also denied him a fixed status, instead providing him with a succession of changing roles: 'Como todos los hombres de Babilonia, he sido procónsul; como todos, esclavo; también he conocido la omnipotencia, el oprobio, las cárceles' [Like all the men of Babylon, I have been proconsul; like all, I have been a slave. I have known omnipotence, ignominy, imprisonment].[4] The lottery has given him all manner of social positions, which he compares to perpetual reincarnation without dying: 'Heráclides Póntico refiere con admiración que Pitágoras recordaba haber sido Pirro y antes Euforbo y antes algún otro mortal; para recordar vicisitudes análogas yo no preciso recurrir a la muerte ni aun a la impostura' [Heraclides Ponticus reports, admiringly, that Pythagoras recalled having been Pyrrhus, and before that, Euphorbus, and before that, some other mortal; in order to recall similar vicissitudes, I have no need of death, nor even of imposture].[5] Although this continual redefinition appears liberating, it actually has the opposite effect. When the narrator says he has known omnipotence, he refers only to a temporary—hence artificial or false—power granted by the lottery, which can be taken from him at any time. Even though the narrator is sometimes empowered by the lottery, he is at the mercy of a system beyond his control or understanding.

At the start, the lottery's power is not pervasive. The participants initially choose whether to buy lots for the prizes, but they lose power as they relinquish the right to regulate the lottery's draws. In this regard, the lottery is similar to any number of orders into which Kafka's characters enter knowingly, discovering later that the system is not within their control: examples of this include the countryman's wait in 'Vor dem

---

[3] Borges, 'La lotería en Babilonia', p. 456; Hurley, trans., 'The Lottery in Babylon', p. 101.
[4] Borges, 'La lotería en Babilonia', p. 456; Hurley, trans., 'The Lottery in Babylon', p. 101.
[5] Borges, 'La lotería en Babilonia', p. 456; Hurley, trans., 'The Lottery in Babylon', p. 101.

Gesetz' [Before the Law], the builders' participation in 'Beim Bau der chinesischen Mauer' [The Great Wall of China], and the performing artist's fast in 'Ein Hungerkünstler' [A Hunger Artist]. For Kafka's characters, the result is that they find themselves subject to a system they cannot comprehend but which they also cannot escape. Just as in Kafka's stories, the lottery in Borges's story comes to control the Babylonians, and their freely instigated changes to the lottery bring about their subjugation to it. For example, when the citizens of Babylon decide to stop paying their fines to undermine the system, they give the Company more control rather than less: 'Todos optaron por la cárcel, para defraudar a la Compañía. De esa bravata de unos pocos nace el todopoder de la Compañía: su valor eclesiástico, metafísico' [In order to thwart the Company, they all chose jail. From that gauntlet thrown down by a few men sprang the Company's omnipotence—its ecclesiastical, metaphysical force].[6] With this change, the Company takes on a meaningful role in the lives of the players, dictating their futures as though it were an arm of God. This transition from the personal to the spiritual recalls the blurring of the levels of the 'patria potestad' in Kafka's stories: in 'Das Urteil' [The Judgement], the father seems to take on some of God's higher power when he hands down a mandate ordering his son Georg to commit suicide.

This view of the lottery as somehow religious (ecclesiastical) and yet also abstract (metaphysical) complements Borges's idea that Kafka's stories are modern, agnostic parables. By describing the lottery in a religious fashion, the narrator draws attention to the lottery's contemporary and eternal echoes: the story mirrors the rise of totalitarianism (of which Borges was critical) and it prefigures the Second World War. It also calls to mind the eternal struggle to understand the role played by fate and chance in life. The result is that 'La lotería en Babilonia' was meaningful to the story's contemporary readers, is meaningful to later readers who identify new layers in the story as a result of their particular historical circumstances, and is meaningful to all readers who see the story as a reflection of the individual's place in the universe. This multi-tiered way of reading one story is similar to the approach Borges took to interpreting Kafka.

Although the lottery can be viewed as metaphysical and ecclesiastical, this does not mean that the citizens of Babylon are excused for the role they play in allowing it to take over their lives. The lottery participants are responsible for the changes in the Company's power, so they are partly to blame when the rules become confused with and even supersede the laws of the city. For example, a thief steals a ticket for which a draw decrees that

---

[6] Borges, 'La lotería en Babilonia', p. 457; Hurley, trans., 'The Lottery in Babylon', p. 102.

the bearer is entitled to have his tongue burnt out; coincidentally this is the same as the punishment for theft of a ticket. Some argue that he should receive the reward, while others are in favour of him receiving the punishment, notwithstanding the fact that the two are the same. In time, the lottery transitions from being optional to mandatory, and entry becomes free of charge. These changes are meant to empower the poorest citizens by including them in the lottery, but they actually strip all Babylonians of any remaining free will. The Company comes to dictate every aspect of the participants' lives. Mapping this onto the 'patria potestad', the Company initially takes on the role of a father who hands out minor rewards and punishments, but it later enforces order in the manner of the state. Eventually, it controls everything, including who will live and who will die, as though it were God. This change in power is highlighted by reading 'La lotería en Babilonia' according to Borges's interpretation of Kafka, since the Kafkian 'patria potestad' is built on the slide from familial authority to divine power.

Borges believed that Kafka's writing was about the relationship between individuals and God, which is precisely what the lottery comes to exemplify once the Company's power over the Babylonians is unending. In Kafka, power is linked with paradox: the paradoxical relationship between individuals and God is the foundation of the parable 'Vor dem Gesetz', where the door to the law exists for the countryman, yet he cannot gain entry through it. A similar paradox that infinitely offers yet denies access to meaning or power is the foundation for the lottery: draws are held to determine everything, yet they determine nothing, because for every decision that is made by a draw, another draw has to be made to determine how it will be carried out, and another to determine who will perform it, and so on to infinity. The narrator explains,

> Imaginemos un primer sorteo, que dicta la muerte de un hombre. Para su cumplimento se procede a un otro sorteo, que propone (digamos) nueve ejecutores posibles. De esos ejecutores, cuatro pueden iniciar un tercer sorteo que dirá el nombre del verdugo, dos pueden reemplazar la orden adversa por una orden feliz (el encuentro de un tesoro, digamos), otro exacerbará la muerte (es decir la hará infame o la enriquecerá de torturas), otros pueden negarse a cumplirla ... Tal es el esquema simbólico. En la realidad *el número de sorteos es infinito.*
>
> [Let us imagine a first drawing, which condemns a man to death. In pursuance of that decree, another drawing is held; out of that second drawing come, say, nine possible executors. Of those nine, four might initiate a third drawing to determine the name of the executioner, two might replace the unlucky draw with a lucky one (the discovery of a treasure, say), another might decide that the death should be exacerbated (death with dishonor, that

is, or with the refinement of torture), others might simply refuse to carry out the sentence.... That is the scheme of the Lottery, put symbolically. *In reality, the number of drawings is infinite.*][7]

This situation emphasizes the lottery's infinite power while also undermining it, slowly eroding the Company's authority to nothing even as it is made stronger. The Company can decree a draw for anything, but nothing can be done without an infinite number of further draws, some of which may subvert the first.

In Babylon, any act may be the result of a secret lottery draw—a situation that recalls Sandbank's commonplace secret. Similarly, something akin to Sandbank's negation as part of affirmation is present even in acts that individuals believe to be the product of their free will, since the set of acts that the Company may decree includes all possible acts, even those performed on another's order or those performed by free will. As a result,

las órdenes que [la Compañía] imparte continuamente (quizá incesantemente) no difieren de las que prodigan los impostores. Además ¿quién podrá jactarse de ser un mero impostor? El ebrio que improvisa un mandato absurdo, el soñador que se despierta de golpe y ahoga con las manos a la mujer que duerme a su lado ¿no ejecutan, acaso, una secreta decisión de la Compañía?

[the orders [the Company] constantly (perhaps continually) imparts are no different from those spread wholesale by impostors. Besides—who will boast of being a mere impostor? The drunken man who blurts out an absurd command, the sleeping man who suddenly awakes and turns and chokes to death the woman sleeping at his side—are they not, perhaps, implementing one of the Company's secret decisions?][8]

This problematic relationship (which orchestrates and yet subverts the power the Company has over the lottery participants) is also intrinsic to Zeno's paradoxes. It should be possible to dictate the lives of the Babylonians through lottery draws, just as it should be possible for Achilles to catch the tortoise, but the goal remains one lottery draw or one step too far away. In both Kafka's and Borges's stories, infinity and Zeno's paradoxes are part of the order (or disorder) governing the laws of their towns, countries, and worlds.

The lottery is subject to more problems and paradoxes than just those described by Zeno and Sandbank. For example, the Company is burdened with impersonal draws that either have no consequences or possibly have terrible ones: 'hay sorteos impersonales, de propósito indefinido: uno

---

[7] Borges, 'La lotería en Babilonia', p. 459, original emphasis; Hurley, trans., 'The Lottery in Babylon', pp. 104–5, original emphasis.
[8] Borges, 'La lotería en Babilonia', p. 460; Hurley, trans., 'The Lottery in Babylon', p. 106.

decreta que... cada siglo se retire (o se añada) un grano de arena de los innumerables que hay en la playa. Las consecuencias son, a veces, terribles' [There are also *impersonal* drawings, whose purpose is unclear. One drawing decrees that... every hundred years a grain of sand be added to (or taken from) the countless grains of sand on a certain beach. Sometimes, the consequences are terrible].⁹ The pieces of sand that the Company moves around recall the sorites paradox, which highlights the insignificance of individual acts such as a single lottery draw or the relocation of a single grain of sand.

While some draws may be meaningless, the lottery and the story that describes it are not similarly devoid of meaning. The story functions as a parable, and it suggests multiple possible interpretations for the lottery's power (or lack thereof):

> Alguna abominablemente insinúa que hace ya siglos que no existe la Compañía y que el sacro desorden de nuestras vidas es puramente hereditario, tradicional; otra la juzga eterna y enseña que perdurará hasta la última noche, cuando el último dios anonade el mundo. Otro declara que la Compañía es omnipotente, pero que sólo influye en cosas minúsculas: en el grito de un pájaro, en los matices de la herrumbre y del polvo, en los entresueños del alba. Otra, por boca de heresiarcas enmascarados, *que no ha existido nunca y no existirá.*
>
> [One scurrilously suggests that the Company ceased to exist hundreds of years ago, and that the sacred disorder of our lives is purely hereditary, traditional; another believes that the Company is eternal, and that it shall endure until the last night, when the last god shall annihilate the earth. Yet another declares that the Company is omnipotent, but affects only small things: the cry of a bird, the shades of rust and dust, the half dreams that come at dawn. Another, whispered by masked heresiarchs, says that *the Company has never existed, and never will.*]¹⁰

Navigating among these possibilities, the narrator concludes with the one with the most ambiguity: 'Otra [conjetura], no menos vil, razona que es indiferente afirmar o negar la realidad de la tenebrosa corporación, porque Babilonia no es otra cosa que un infinito juego de azares' [Another [conjecture], no less despicable, argues that it makes no difference whether one affirms or denies the reality of the shadowy corporation, because Babylon is nothing but an infinite game of chance].¹¹ Although one of the possible

---

⁹ Borges, 'La lotería en Babilonia', p. 459; Hurley, trans., 'The Lottery in Babylon', p. 105, original emphasis.
¹⁰ Borges, 'La lotería en Babilonia', p. 460, original emphasis; Hurley, trans., 'The Lottery in Babylon', p. 106, original emphasis.
¹¹ Borges, 'La lotería en Babilonia', p. 460; Hurley, trans., 'The Lottery in Babylon', p. 106.

meanings of the lottery is that it too is meaningless, the truth remains unclear to the lottery's participants, just as the meaning of the story remains unclear to its readers.

In this regard, 'La lotería en Babilonia' echoes Kafka's 'Zur Frage der Gesetze' [The Problem of Our Laws] (1931), a very short story in which a narrator meditates on the complete impenetrability of the laws that govern his existence:

> Übrigens können auch diese Scheingesetze eigentlich nur vermutet werden. Es ist eine Tradition, daß sie bestehen und dem Adel als Geheimnis anver- traut sind, aber mehr als alte und durch ihr Alter glaubwürdige Tradition ist es nicht und kann es nicht sein, denn der Charakter dieser Gesetze verlangt auch das Geheimhalten ihres Bestandes. Wenn wir im Volk aber seit ältesten Zeiten die Handlungen des Adels aufmerksam verfolgen, Aufschreibungen unserer Voreltern darüber besitzen, sie gewissenhaft fortgesetzt haben und in den zahllosen Tatsachen gewisse Richtlinien zu erkennen glauben, die auf diese oder jene geschichtliche Bestimmung schließen lassen, und wenn wir nach diesen sorgfältigst gesiebten und geordneten Schlußfolgerungen uns für die Gegenwart und Zukunft ein wenig einzurichten suchen—so ist das alles unsicher und vielleicht nur ein Spiel des Verstandes, denn vielleicht bestehen diese Gesetzte, die wir hier zu erraten suchen, überhaupt nicht.

> [The very existence of these laws, however, is at most a matter of presump- tion. There is a tradition that they exist and that they are a mystery confided to the nobility, but it is not and cannot be more than a mere tradition sanctioned by age, for the essence of a secret code is that it should remain a mystery. Some of us among the people have attentively scrutinized the doings of the nobility since the earliest times and possess records made by our forefathers—records which we have conscientiously continued—and claim to recognize amid the countless number of facts certain main tenden- cies which permit of this or that historical formulation; but when in accordance with these scrupulously tested and logically ordered conclusions we seek to adjust ourselves somewhat for the present or the future, every- thing becomes uncertain, and our work seems only an intellectual game, for perhaps these laws that we are trying to unravel do not exist at all.][12]

In Kafka's story, some information about the laws (and about the uni- verse) will always be unknowable—a reality to which the narrator says we must be resigned. Borges implies the same reality with the lottery, an effect that becomes clear when his story is read alongside Kafka's. By employing

[12] Franz Kafka, 'Zur Frage der Gesetze', *Beschreibung eines Kampfes: Novellen, Skizzen, Aphorismen aus dem Nachlass, Gesammelte Schriften*, Vol. 5 (Prague: Heinr. Mercy Sohn, 1936), pp. 90–2 (pp. 90–1); also Franz Kafka, *Nachgelassene Schriften und Fragmente II* (New York: Schocken, 1992), p. 271; Willa Muir and Edwin Muir, trans., 'The Problem of Our Laws', *The Complete Stories* (New York: Schocken, 1971), pp. 437–8 (pp. 437–8).

this Kafkian deferral or inaccessibility of meaning, Borges's narrator emphasizes the importance of the lottery without having to uncover precisely what
it is that makes it important—something he cannot do because he himself
does not know what the lottery means.

Borges merged the uncertainty found in Kafka with a technique to
which he was partial: meta-narratives that draw attention to the nature of
storytelling at the same time as they tell their stories. The inclusion of self-
conscious reflection in the story may represent Borges's turn away from
Kafka, as this sort of meta-narrative (which is not characteristic of Kafka's
works) often appears alongside traits that Borges borrowed from Kafka.
In 'La lotería en Babilonia' Borges played with this technique by echoing
the incomprehensibility of the lottery in the story's frame narrative. The
narrator of 'La lotería en Babilonia' is abroad from Babylon when he tells his
tale. He makes this known with a number of asides, where he reveals his
nostalgia for Babylon, reminiscing about learning the lottery's history from
his father. The narrator refers to the 'queridas costumbres' which he sees
'Ahora, lejos de Babilonia' [belovèd customs... Now, far from Babylon].[13]
He tells his story hastily, because he is about to depart—'Poco tiempo me
queda; nos avisan que la nave está por zarpar' [I have but little time
remaining; we are told that the ship is about to sail]—perhaps to distance
himself from Babylon, or perhaps to return home again.[14] The ambiguity in
his statement makes it hard to tell whether the narrator is fleeing the lottery
or returning to it, which leaves the narrator's intended message unclear.
Through these asides, the narrator highlights his role in telling the story, but
he still leaves the meaning of his tale concealed.

4.2 'LA BIBLIOTECA DE BABEL'

In contrast to 'La lotería en Babilonia', 'La biblioteca de Babel' [The
Library of Babel] is more open about the possibility that it may be a
parable. The story begins with the line 'El universo (que otros llaman la
Biblioteca)' [The universe (which others call the Library)], inviting the
reader to approach the story as an allegory for the universe.[15] Despite this
opening, the tale is not an allegory in the traditional sense, since every

[13] Borges, 'La lotería en Babilonia', p. 456; Hurley, trans., 'The Lottery in Babylon',
p. 101.
[14] Borges, 'La lotería en Babilonia', p. 458; Hurley, trans., 'The Lottery in Babylon',
p. 104.
[15] Jorge Luis Borges, 'La biblioteca de Babel', *Ficciones*, 1944, *Obras completas*, Vol. 1
(Buenos Aires: Emecé, 1996), pp. 465–71 (p. 465); Andrew Hurley, trans., 'The Library of
Babel', *Fictions*, 1944, *Collected Fictions* (New York: Viking, 1998), pp. 112–18 (p. 112).

element does not correlate with an equivalent one on a symbolic level. Rather, in the same vein as 'La lotería en Babilonia', 'La biblioteca de Babel' reads as a problematic Kafkian parable. It is about a library divided into hexagonal cells, each with an identical number of books. The library stretches on as far as the librarian can fathom, a setting similar to the infinite landscapes of 'Eine kaiserliche Botschaft' [An Imperial Message] and 'Beim Bau der chinesischen Mauer'.

As in 'La lotería en Babilonia', 'La biblioteca de Babel' is set in a nondescript location. Its title makes reference to Babel, which gives the tale the feeling of being a biblical or archaic text. This is augmented by the use of odd and old-fashioned language: the peculiar word 'frutas' [spherical fruits] denotes the library's lampshades, 'leguas' [leagues] refers to the distance travelled by the librarian in his lifetime, 'millas' [miles] describes the distances between hexagons where the librarians speak different languages—an allusion to the different languages of the story's namesake, the Tower of Babel—and 'asaz' [quite (antiquated)] describes these languages.[16] As in 'La lotería en Babilonia', the protagonist in 'La biblioteca de Babel' has very few identifying features, not even a name. However, the narrator is a librarian—the job Borges also held at the time of writing the story. Kafka also used this technique, writing about characters that hold the same kind of bureaucratic office jobs as Kafka himself had. All of this gives the story a Kafkian air.

Another Kafkian element is the story's portrayal of paradoxical circumstances. The fact that the narrator cannot read the books presents him with a problem: how is he to act as a librarian if he cannot understand the books? As a way of coping with this problem, the narrator tries to reason his way out of it, but this only leads him to variants on Sandbank's paradoxes. The narrator reasons that each book may contain a hidden meaning. By analogy, so too may the library conceal a secret message. In the commonplace secret, 'that which is unknown can be anywhere, a secret law can be manifested in anything'.[17] In the case of the library of Babel, one book exists that can explain all the others, and the librarian reasons that if he finds this book he will understand the meaning of the library. However, this secret book could be anywhere: it is equally likely to be any of the texts, and since they cannot all be searched, it cannot be found.

Despite this problem, the librarians are determined to uncover the meaning of the library. This leads to further problematic reasoning:

---

[16] Borges, 'La biblioteca de Babel', p. 465, 467; Hurley, trans., 'The Library of Babel', p. 112, 114.

[17] Shimon Sandbank, *After Kafka: The Influence of Kafka's Fiction* (Athens: U of Georgia P, 1989), p. 85.

'Para localizar el libro A, consultar previamente un libro B que indique el sitio de A; para localizar el libro B, consultar previamente un libro C, y así hasta lo infinito' [To locate book A, first consult book B, which tells where book A can be found; to locate book B, first consult book C, and so on, to infinity].[18] The application of Zeno's paradoxes to the search for the book that explains the library demonstrates the futility of the librarians' activity. As in Kafka, it also suggests a dogged determination to try. The same way that the protagonist of 'Eine kaiserliche Botschaft' waits for his message even though it will never come, the librarians in 'La biblioteca de Babel' keep searching for a meaning they will never find.

Paradoxes also play a role in denying the librarians the hope of finding meaning within any one book. The narrator explains that each book is made up of a set number of letters, lines, and pages. For any one book, there are numerous small variants: books exist that differ from each other by one word, one space, or one punctuation mark. It is inevitable that for every book, so too there is a book that contradicts it, which makes it impossible to believe the contents of any single book, even the book that ostensibly explains the library's meaning. This recalls the paradox of negation as part of affirmation. The secret revealed by the one text that confirms the library's purpose is undermined by the existence of some of the other texts. Meaning, while present, can never be known.

This points to yet another problem. Language is variable across the library, so that even if one librarian can find meaning in a text, another librarian (in another hexagon and speaking another language) may not see anything there. Even worse, this other librarian may read something altogether different based on the language he speaks: 'Durante mucho tiempo se creyó que esos libros impenetrables correspondían a lenguas pretéritas o remotas.... [E]s verdad que unas millas a la derecha la lengua es dialectal y que noventa pisos más arriba, es incomprensible' [For many years it was believed that those impenetrable books were in ancient or far-distant languages.... [I]t is true that a few miles to the right, our language devolves into dialect and that ninety floors above, it becomes incomprehensible].[19] Kafka addressed this problem in 'Beim Bau der chinesischen Mauer', where the news of the completion of the wall is disregarded without further consideration by the people of one province because they do not give credence to the archaic language announcing it in the notice brought by a messenger from a neighbouring province. Accurate communication from one province to the next is impossible, just as it is impossible to finish building the infinite wall. Borges used the problems associated with the infinite variability of language to highlight the

---

[18] Borges, 'La biblioteca de Babel', p. 469; Hurley, trans., 'The Library of Babel', p. 117.
[19] Borges, 'La biblioteca de Babel', p. 467; Hurley, trans., 'The Library of Babel', p. 114.

difficulties that language's inadequacies posed for storytellers, thus bringing the focus around to his interest in authorship. Borges's narrator questions whether the story's readers can be assured of understanding what they are reading: 'Tú, que me lees, ¿estás seguro de entender mi lenguaje?' [You who read me—are you certain you understand my language?][20] Depending on how each book is interpreted and what language the readers perceive it to have been written in, the secret explaining the library can be in any or even in all of the books, while the narrator's story can mean anything. The library's message will never be known, because even if it is found, recipients can never be certain they have understood it correctly.

At the end of 'La biblioteca de Babel' the narrator tries to come up with an explanation for the library that circumvents all of the Kafkian problems that stand between him and the library's meaning. Even though he speculates elsewhere that the library has a finite number of books (since he postulates that no two can be identical), he prefers the conclusion that '*La biblioteca es ilimitada y periódica*. Si un eterno viajero la atravesara en cualquier dirección, comprobaría al cabo de los siglos que los mismos volúmenes se repiten en el mismo desorden (que, repetido, sería un orden: el Orden). Mi soledad se alegra con esa elegante esperanza' [*The Library is unlimited but periodic*. If an eternal traveler should journey in any direction, he would find after untold centuries that the same volumes are repeated in the same disorder—which, repeated, becomes order: the Order. My solitude is cheered by that elegant hope].[21] Implicitly, all patterns have order, and order indicates meaning. The narrator hopes that the library conceals its meaning within a code too large for him to grasp. He knows he cannot find it and yet he allows himself to believe in its existence. While Borges's protagonist knows he will never succeed, Kafka's characters often do not. Kafka's countryman continues to wait for access to the law even though he will never gain entry, and another of his characters waits for the emperor's message even though it will never arrive. The librarian's quest echoes Josef K.'s search for an explanation he will never receive for why he is being tried, and it echoes K.'s efforts to gain admission to a castle he will never enter. Kafka's characters wait or search in earnest despite the unachievability of their goals, and Borges's librarian maintains an 'elegante esperanza' [elegant hope] even though he knows the meaning of the library will never be revealed to him.[22] Borges's librarian has faith in some greater order (or, as he calls it, Order), but the source of this order is never named.

---

[20] Borges, 'La biblioteca de Babel', p. 470; Hurley, trans., 'The Library of Babel', p. 118.

[21] Borges, 'La biblioteca de Babel', p. 471, original emphasis; Hurley, trans., 'The Library of Babel', p. 118, original emphasis.

[22] Borges, 'La biblioteca de Babel', p. 471; Hurley, trans., 'The Library of Babel', p. 118.

The librarian's 'elegante esperanza' and his ability to reason through his otherwise incomprehensible situation are foreshadowed by the story's epigraph: 'By this art you may contemplate the variation of the 23 letters...'—which continues in the original—'which may be so infinitely varied, that the words complicated and deduced thence will not be contained within the compass of the firmament; ten words may be varied 40,320 several ways: by this art you may examine how many men may stand one by another in the whole superficies of the earth, some say 148,456,800,000,000.'[23] This quotation from Robert Burton's *The Anatomy of Melancholy* (1621) appears in a section of his book on permutations, Zeno's paradoxes, and libraries—the same ideas that are the subject of 'La biblioteca de Babel'. In *The Anatomy of Melancholy*, Burton proposes the use of intellectual distraction to overcome melancholy, which is precisely what the narrator of Borges's story does: he intellectualizes his circumstance as a way of coping with the melancholy it produces in him. Borges's narrator devises an explanation for the library that places its meaning outside of his reach, thus freeing him from actually having to find it. The narrator's solace is his belief in the library's meaning, even if it is a meaning that he cannot know.

A close reading of 'La biblioteca de Babel' and 'La lotería en Babilonia' alongside Kafka's writing illuminates a feature common in both of Borges's texts but missing from Kafka's: the emphasis on storytelling. Kafka often focused on the action taking place, not the narrator recounting it. Borges, by contrast, employed self-conscious narrators who reflect on the nature of the stories they tell, emphasizing the ability of their tales to provide hope in otherwise intolerable circumstances. The narrators of both 'La lotería en Babilonia' and 'La biblioteca de Babel' use their tales to understand or explain away the problems that permeate their worlds. They acknowledge that their stories are insufficient, yet despite any shortcomings, they persist in telling their tales. For the narrators, telling a story can be a form of the 'elegante esperanza', a last defence against despair in circumstances where all would otherwise be lost. This is not to say that Kafka's writing is devoid of meta-narrative or that it never features a self-conscious awareness on the part of the storyteller, but just to suggest that Borges's writing emphasizes the act of storytelling. This is true not only of Borges's openly Kafkian texts but of many of his other works as well, and the next chapter looks at how Borges combined the elements he admired in Kafka's stories with other techniques and themes to create stories that build upon—rather than just borrow from—Kafka.

[23] Borges, 'La biblioteca de Babel', p. 465; Robert Burton, *The Anatomy of Melancholy*, 1621, Vol. 2 (London: Folio Society, 2005), p. 102.

5

Kafkian Fictions

Kafka's influence on Borges's writing was not limited to 'La lotería en Babilonia' [The Lottery in Babylon] and 'La biblioteca de Babel' [The Library of Babel]. Many of Borges's stories (written both earlier and later) also bear Kafka's mark. Aizenberg suggests that Kafka's influence can be seen in 'El milagro secreto' [The Secret Miracle] from *Ficciones* [*Fictions*], while Sandbank proposes 'Un problema' [A Problem] (1957) from *El hacedor* [*Dreamtigers*] (1960) as a possibly Kafkian text.[1] More than forty years after writing 'La muerte y la brújula' [Death and the Compass] (1942), Borges said, 'I wrote a detective story, in a sense out of Kafka; it was called "Death and the Compass." When it was finished, I felt it was like Kafka, I hope so.'[2] Meanwhile, Borges and Bioy Casares dedicated 'La víctima de Tadeo Limardo' [Tadeo Limardo's Victim] (1942) 'A la memoria de Franz Kafka' [To the memory of Franz Kafka], and a fictional Kafka appears as the creator of a pair of imaginary lovers in Borges's poem 'Ein Traum' [A Dream] (1976).[3] Yet only with respect to one other work (aside from 'La lotería en Babilonia' and 'La biblioteca de Babel') did Borges mention openly trying to emulate Kafka. In 'El Congreso' [The Congress], 'El opaco principio quiere imitar el de las ficciones de Kafka' [The story's murky beginning attempts to imitate the way Kafka's stories begin], but Borges published this story thirty years after he wrote 'La lotería en Babilonia' and 'La biblioteca de Babel' so it is addressed as a special case in Chapter 6.[4]

[1] Edna Aizenberg, 'Kafka, Borges and Contemporary Latin-American Fiction', *Newsletter of the Kafka Society of America* 6.1–2 (1982): 4–13 (p. 6); Shimon Sandbank, *After Kafka: The Influence of Kafka's Fiction* (Athens: U of Georgia P, 1989), p. 96.

[2] Jorge Luis Borges quoted in Alastair Reid, 'Kafka: The Writer's Writer', *Journal of the Kafka Society of America* 2.7 (1983): 20–7 (p. 25).

[3] Jorge Luis Borges, 'La víctima de Tadeo Limardo', *Seis problemas para don Isidro Parodi*, 1942, *Obras completas en colaboración* (Buenos Aires: Emecé, 1979), pp. 85–104 (p. 85); Jorge Luis Borges, 'Ein Traum', *La moneda de hierro*, 1976, *Obras completas*, Vol. 3 (Buenos Aires: Emecé, 1996), p. 154.

[4] Jorge Luis Borges, Epilogue, *El libro de arena*, 1975, *Obras completas*, Vol. 3 (Buenos Aires: Emecé, 1996), pp. 72–3. (p. 72); Andrew Hurley, trans., Afterword, *The Book of Sand*, 1975, *Collected Fictions* (New York: Viking, 1998), pp. 484–5 (p. 484).

Looking at a range of Borges's work from as early as 1936 and as late as 1971 reveals how Kafka's writing had a lasting influence on Borges's. This chapter focuses on Borges's prose fiction chronologically. Starting with 'El acercamiento a Almotásim' [The Approach to Al-Mu'tasim] from 1936 and ending with 'El milagro secreto' from 1943, it divides Borges's writing into three categories: (*i*) stories written before 'La lotería en Babilonia', (*ii*) stories written between 'La lotería en Babilonia' and 'La biblioteca de Babel', and (*iii*) stories written after 'La biblioteca de Babel'. Over the course of these tales, Borges developed the theme of the 'patria potestad' and he refined his use of paradoxes with respect to his ideas about authorship. By reading these stories through the lens of Borges's Kafkian interests, it is possible to see his prose fiction as part of a cohesive body of work, even if the stories are varied enough that there is no single thread connecting them all.

5.1 FROM 'EL ACERCAMIENTO A ALMOTÁSIM' TO 'LAS RUINAS CIRCULARES'

Borges's career as a prose fiction writer began with 'Hombre de la esquina rosada' [Streetcorner Man] in 1933 and the semi-fictional tales in *Historia universal de la infamia* [*A Universal History of Iniquity*] in 1935. In the preface to the second edition of *Historia universal de la infamia* (1954), Borges said that these stories were preparation for his career as a short story writer: 'Son el irresponsable juego de un tímido que no se animó a escribir cuentos y que se distrajo en falsear y tergiversar (sin justificación estética alguna vez) ajenas historias' [They are the irresponsible sport of a shy sort of man who could not bring himself to write short stories, and so amused himself by changing and distorting (sometimes without æsthetic justification) the stories of other men].[5] By contrast, in the preface to the first edition (1935), Borges said he saw his work not as embroidering others' stories but as his own writing, and he credited Robert Louis Stevenson and Chesterton as his literary influences.[6]

---

[5] Jorge Luis Borges, 'Prólogo a la edición de 1954', *Historia universal de la infamia*, 1935, *Obras completas*, Vol. 1 (Buenos Aires: Emecé, 1996), p. 291; Andrew Hurley, trans., 'Preface to the 1954 Edition', *A Universal History of Iniquity*, 1935, *Collected Fictions* (New York: Viking, 1998), pp. 4–5 (p. 4).

[6] Jorge Luis Borges, 'Prólogo a la primera edición', *Historia universal de la infamia*, 1935, *Obras completas*, Vol. 1 (Buenos Aires: Emecé, 1996), p. 289; Andrew Hurley, trans., 'Preface to the First Edition', *A Universal History of Iniquity*, 1935, *Collected Fictions* (New York: Viking, 1998), p. 3.

Borges's hindsight view that he developed as an author by building on the work of others is accurate insofar as his early stories blurred the line between original writing and rewriting. Kristal credits this technique of borrowing from other authors with providing Borges the practice necessary to become a prose fiction writer.[7] Similarly, Bell-Villada suggests that Borges found his voice through reworking and translating:

> What is particularly noteworthy is that the period in which Borges worked on these translations [of Woolf, Faulkner, and Melville], 1937 to 1944, closely coincides with the years when his major fictional works were produced or were in gestation. The time pattern appears too close to be merely casual; Borges was probably well aware that he was dealing with writers whose literary methods were not unlike his, and hence he felt he could learn something from the extensive exposure to them. Borges remarks in a famous essay that Kafka *created* his precursors, that his mode of writing modifies our view of works from the past. In a very real sense, Borges has created his own precursors by recasting them in his native tongue.[8]

Soon after Borges wrote the semi-fictional *Historia universal de la infamia*, he began translating Kafka's stories for the 1938 Losada collection *La metamorfosis*. Through this translation project, Borges further developed the confidence and technique he needed to write stories of his own. This occurred around the same time as Borges *père*'s illness and death, so that when Borges was trying to find his footing as an author and understand his relationship with his father, Kafka offered him the opportunity to do both at once.

The first story Borges wrote following *Historia universal de la infamia* (and which he wrote prior to publishing the Kafka translations in *La metamorfosis*) was 'El acercamiento a Almotásim'. This tale is often regarded as the first of Borges's *ficciones* and therefore the first of his proper, Borgesian (and also Kafkian) short stories. The text employs the fragmented structure that Borges admired in Kafka. It is framed as a review of *El acercamiento a Almotásim*, a novel by the imaginary author Mir Bahadur Alí, and as in Kafka's novels, which skip over the pertinent details of how his characters get from one incident to the next, Borges's review intentionally glosses over middle sections: 'Imposible trazar las peripecias de los diecinueve [capítulos] restantes. Hay una vertiginosa pululación de *dramatis personae*—para no hablar de una biografía que parece agotar los movimientos del espíritu humano (desde la infamia hasta

[7] Efraín Kristal, *Invisible Work: Borges and Translation* (Nashville: Vanderbilt UP, 2002), p. xiv.

[8] Gene Bell-Villada, *Borges and his Fiction: A Guide to his Mind and Art*, 2nd ed. (Austin: U of Texas P, 1999), pp. 36–7, original emphasis.

la especulación matemática) y de una peregrinación que comprende la vasta geografía del Indostán' [It would be impossible to trace the adventures of the remaining nineteen chapters. There is a dizzying pullulation of *dramatis personæ*—not to mention a biography that seems to catalog every motion of the human spirit (from iniquity to mathematical speculation) and a pilgrimage that covers the vast geography of Hindustan].[9] Borges's review does not (or cannot) describe what occurs in the novel's meandering, seemingly infinite middle sections. It emphasizes themes that Bahadur happens to share with Kafka: infinity, stories with deferred or concealed endings, and disjointed narratives that leave out key pieces of information.

El acercamiento a Almotásim shows many of the characteristics Borges admired in Kafka. For example, the opening action is unsettling. The protagonist thinks he may have murdered someone, but he is not sure, nor is he convinced by the religious motives he thinks he may have had to commit the crime. This sense of uncertainty recalls *Der Prozeß* [*The Trial*] and *Das Schloß* [*The Castle*], where Josef K. and K. never find out why they are in their absurd circumstances. As a way out, the protagonist in *El acercamiento a Almotásim* falls in with the lowest of society's low, and he subsequently comes to meet all manner of people as he tries to make sense of his crime. Josef K. and K. similarly interact with all sorts—servants, barmaids, clerks, lawyers, and judges—in pursuit of explanations for and escape (or perhaps even salvation) from their situations.

Kafka's characters and the protagonist of *El acercamiento a Almotásim* try to find a way out of their nightmarish situations by seeking higher truths, be it from a court, a castle official, or God. The protagonist of Bahadur's novel goes on a search for the most exalted man on earth, but in a way reminiscent of Josef K.'s efforts to find out why he is on trial and K.'s efforts to enter the castle, his Zenoesque quest seems impossible: 'El tecnicismo matemático es aplicable: la cargada novela de Bahadur es una progresión ascendente, cuyo término final es el presentido "hombre que se llama Almotásim". El inmediato antecesor de Almotásim es un librero persa de suma cortesía y felicidad; el que precede a ese librero es un santo...' [A technical mathematical formula is applicable here: Bahadur's heavily freighted novel is an ascending progression whose final term is the sensed or foreapprehended 'man called Al-Mu'tasim'. The person immediately preceding Al-Mu'tasim is a Persian bookseller of great courtesy and

---

[9] Jorge Luis Borges, 'El acercamiento a Almotásim', *Historia de la eternidad*, 1936, *Obras completas*, Vol. 1 (Buenos Aires: Emecé, 1996), pp. 414–18 (p. 415); Andrew Hurley, trans., 'The Approach to Al-Mu'tasim', *Fictions*, 1944, *Collected Fictions* (New York: Viking, 1998), pp. 82–7 (p. 84).

felicity; the man preceding the bookseller is a saint . . .].[10] Searching for Almotásim, like searching for the one book in the library of Babel that can explain all of the others, is a regressive process. Where *El acercamiento a Almotásim* differs from 'La biblioteca de Babel', however, is that the protagonist of Bahadur's novel succeeds in his task where the librarian fails.

This marks a point of both convergence with and divergence from Kafka. While Kafka's *Der Prozeß* and *Das Schloß* differ from Bahadur's *El acercamiento a Almotásim* by ending in failure following their comparable, Zenoesque quests, Bahadur's work resembles Kafka's early novel *Amerika* [*America*], in which the protagonist Karl seems to reach his sought-after goal. Bahadur's protagonist finds Almotásim and is said to achieve enlightenment (although the experience and the vision of Almotásim are never described), while Karl arrives at a supposed utopia when he gets to the Nature Theatre of Oklahoma. Like Bahadur, Kafka does not describe this sense of utopia, since Karl only reaches the Nature Theatre after the novel's last page. Almotásim is not depicted, but he is implied to be the source of the protagonist's enlightenment; by contrast, the sinister undertones of Kafka's final chapter suggest that all may not be as it first appears in Karl's utopia. Despite this major difference, the novels share a number of similarities. For example, both are about disgraced protagonists: Karl is seduced by and subsequently impregnates a servant girl, and he is sent off to America as a punishment; Bahadur's protagonist flees fearing punishment for the murder he may have committed. In both, the protagonists are on quests to restore their good names.

In the review that serves as the frame to Borges's story, Borges interprets *El acercamiento a Almotásim* and its quest as a parable about the search for cosmic unity, and he explains the concept of Almotásim by drawing a link with the mythical Simurgh, the King of Birds. According to the legend, a group of birds go on a journey to meet the Simurgh. When they reach his home, 'perciben que ellos son el Simurg y que el Simurg es cada uno de ellos y todos' [they see that they are the Simurgh and that the Simurgh is each, and all, of them].[11] The mystical is individual and also shared; it is unique and all encompassing. By invoking the Simurgh, Borges implies that Almotásim is within Bahadur's protagonist, and he only needs to find him there. It is possible that Borges perceived a link between Kafka and the Simurgh, albeit one that is almost certainly coincidental. In a footnote in 'El acercamiento a Almotásim', Borges writes, 'Saben que el nombre de

---

[10] Borges, 'El acercamiento a Almotásim', p. 416; Hurley, trans., 'The Approach to Al-Mu'tasim', p. 85.

[11] Borges, 'El acercamiento a Almotásim', p. 418; Hurley, trans., 'The Approach to Al-Mu'tasim', p. 87.

su rey quiere decir treinta pájaros; saben que su alcázar está en el *Kaf,* la
montaña circular que rodea la tierra' [They know that the name of their
King means 'thirty birds'; they know that his palace is in the Mountains of
Kaf, the mountains that encircle the earth].[12] The mountain on which the
Simurgh lives is called Kaf, which happens to be the the the first syllable of
Kafka's name, and which can be written as a single letter in Hebrew, kaf or
kaph (כ), pronounced as a letter K. The Czech word *kafka* (or *kavka*)
means 'jackdaw' (a type of crow), which further links Kafka to the birds
that make up the Simurgh. One of the Kafka aphorisms that Borges and
Bioy Casares translated for 'Cuatro reflexiones' was about the crows' belief
that even a single one of their number would be sufficient to destroy
heaven; the existence of this aphorism may have reinforced the link for
Borges between Kafka and the Simurgh (*see* Chapter 3, n. 18).

Borges's next short story after 'El acercamiento a Almotásim' was 'Pierre
Menard, autor del *Quijote*' [Pierre Menard, Author of the *Quixote*], which
(while not overtly Kafkian) is about Zeno's paradoxes. Both the visible and
invisible work of the author Menard, whose obituary constitutes the text,
exhibit a preoccupation with Zeno's paradoxes. Amongst Menard's publications is a catalogue of solutions to them: 'La obra *Les problèmes d'un
problème* (París, 1917) que discute en orden cronológico las soluciones del
ilustre problema de Aquiles y la tortuga' [a work entitled *Les problèmes d'un
problème* (Paris, 1917), which discusses in chronological order the solutions to the famous problem of Achilles and the tortoise].[13] While Menard
used the solutions to the paradoxes for one of his published works, his
unpublished project—writing *Don Quijote* anew—is plagued by Zenoesque problems and is without any solutions to them. Menard concedes
this when he says, 'Mi empresa no es difícil, esencialmente... me bastaría
ser inmortal para llevarla a cabo' [The task I have undertaken is not *in
essence* difficult... If I could just be immortal, I could do it].[14] He believes
that, if he were given infinite time, he would eventually achieve his goal.
With the limited amount of time he has, however, *Don Quijote* remains
beyond Menard's grasp.

Borges associated Zeno's paradoxes with a personal concern, one that is
central to 'Pierre Menard, autor del *Quijote*': the problems an author faces

---

[12] Borges, 'El acercamiento a Almotásim', p. 418, emphasis added; Hurley, trans.,
'The Approach to Al-Mu'tasim', p. 87, emphasis added.

[13] Jorge Luis Borges, 'Pierre Menard, autor del *Quijote*', *Ficciones*, 1944, *Obras com-
pletas*, Vol. 1 (Buenos Aires: Emecé, 1996), pp. 444–50 (p. 445); Andew Hurley, trans.,
'Pierre Menard, Author of the *Quixote*', *Fictions*, 1944, *Collected Fictions* (New York:
Viking, 1998), pp. 88–95 (p. 89).

[14] Borges, 'Pierre Menard, autor del *Quijote*', p. 447; Hurley, trans., 'Pierre Menard,
Author of the *Quixote*', pp. 91–2, original emphasis.

in trying to produce a perfect, unrepeatable text. From as early as the 1926 essay 'Profesión de fe literaria' [A Profession of Literary Faith] Borges showed a preoccupation with the idea of writing something that would act as his unique contribution to the world and that would function as a testament to his individual identity. In 'Profesión de fe literaria', he explained that he hoped one day to produce a text that would represent who he was and that would serve as his justification: 'ya he escrito más de un libro para poder escribir, acaso, una página. La página justificativa, la que sea abreviatura de mi destino, la que sólo escucharán tal vez los ángeles asesores, cuando suene el Juicio Final' [I have already written more than one book in order to write, perhaps, one page. That page that justifies me, that summarizes my destiny, the one that perhaps only the attending angels will hear when Judgment Day arrives].[15] Borges believed that 'toda literatura es autobiográfica, finalmente. Todo es poético en cuanto nos confiesa un destino, en cuanto nos da una vislumbre de él' [all literature, in the end, is autobiographical. Everything is poetic that confesses, that gives us a glimpse of a destiny].[16] He felt he had to translate his own experiences into writing, and that doing so would justify him as a writer.

Over the years, Borges's writing demonstrated a determination to produce the unique, unrepeatable text he described in 'Profesión de fe literaria', and stories such as 'La biblioteca de Babel' and 'Pierre Menard, autor del *Quijote*' show the effect on the author of failing at such a project. In the prologue to *El buitre* [*The Vulture*], 'Jorge Luis Borges habla del mundo de Kafka' [Jorge Luis Borges Talks about the World of Kafka], and 'Un sueño eterno: Palabras grabadas en el centenario de Kafka' [An Eternal Dream: Words Recorded on Kafka's Centenary], Borges dwelt upon what he perceived to be Kafka's sense of failure, as demonstrated by the fact that Kafka supposedly wanted most of his work destroyed when he died.[17] Borges suggested a number of possible reasons for this request, among them Kafka's desire to be absolved of responsibility if his imperfect

[15] Jorge Luis Borges, 'Profesión de fe literaria', *El tamaño de mi esperanza*, 1925 (Buenos Aires: Seix Barral, 1994), pp. 127–33 (pp. 132–3); Suzanne Jill Levine, trans., 'A Profession of Literary Faith', *On Writing* (London: Penguin, 2010), pp. 67–71 (p. 71).

[16] Borges, 'Profesión de fe literaria', p. 128; Levine, trans., 'A Profession of Literary Faith', p. 67.

[17] Jorge Luis Borges, Prologue, *El buitre* (Buenos Aires: La Ciudad, 1979), pp. 7–11 (p. 7); Jorge Luis Borges, 'Jorge Luis Borges habla del mundo de Kafka', *La metamorfosis* (Paraná: Orión, 1982), pp. 5–28 (p. 11); Jorge Luis Borges, 'Un sueño eterno: Palabras grabadas en el centenario de Kafka', *Textos recobrados (1956–1986)* (Buenos Aires: Emecé, 2003), pp. 237–9 (p. 238). It is worth noting that Kafka probably wished for no such thing, and perhaps was even ensuring the reproduction of his work by entrusting it to Brod. In the context of this analysis, however, what matters is that Borges believed Kafka—like Borges *père*—wished for his papers to be destroyed. For more on interpreting Kafka's last wishes, see James Hawes, *Excavating Kafka* (London: Quercus, 2008), pp. 115–19.

works were disseminated, the possibility that Kafka viewed his writing as a private act of faith, and the belief that Kafka would have preferred to have written happier texts had he been able to bring himself to do so (*see* Chapter 3, n. 49 and Chapter 6, n. 23).[18] In 'Un sueño eterno', Borges also pointed out that Borges *père* destroyed his own work (although unlike Kafka, he took matters into his own hands and actually did so).

'Pierre Menard, autor del *Quijote*' uses Zeno's paradoxes to express the artistic frustration of not being able to produce a desired or sought-after text that will vindicate an author's efforts. Menard reasons that an author should be able to write any book if given enough time, and if an author fails it must be due to a lack of time rather than a lack of skill. If this were true, in infinite time Kafka and Borges would have eventually produced the works that they desired. This possibility connects Zeno's paradoxes to the act of writing, therefore linking Borges's affinity for Kafka with his own interest in authorship. Borges's view of Kafka as an author who was dissatisfied with much of his own work may have been what led Borges to make this association.

Borges continued to play with the idea of an impossible project and its relation to authorship, identity, and Zeno's paradoxes in 'Tlön, Uqbar, Orbis Tertius'. This story is usually read as a Borgesian game with idealist philosophy, but reading it in connection with his interest in Kafka produces a different (yet compatible) interpretation. As in many of Kafka's stories, the frame narrative of 'Tlön, Uqbar, Orbis Tertius' is semi-autobiographical. Kafka created protagonists who resembled him; in 'Tlön, Uqbar, Orbis Tertius', Borges took this idea further by casting himself as protagonist, interacting with real people (such as Bioy Casares) and visiting places he knew in real life (including a hotel in Adrogué). Instead of inventing a character who had a vague connection to the author, Borges created a protagonist who appeared to be a version of himself, thus confusing the story's boundaries and the place of the author within it. The result is a text that blurs the line between fact and fiction, which is particularly apt since 'Tlön, Uqbar, Orbis Tertius' is a story about what might happen if fiction were to become reality.

Notable in Borges's blending of the fictional world with the factual one is Herbert Ashe, who features as a friend of the narrator Borges's father in 'Tlön, Uqbar, Orbis Tertius', but who bears a strong resemblance to Borges *père* in real life. Both men are quiet, bookish, and partial to intellectual activities such as games of chess and reading encyclopedias. 'En setiembre de 1937...Herbert Ashe murió de la rotura de un aneurisma' [In

---

[18] Borges, Prologue, *El buitre*, p. 8.

September of 1937 . . . Herbert Ashe died of a ruptured aneurysm]; in real life, Borges *père* died of an aneurysm less than a year after Ashe.[19] Kafka similarly worked his own father into his writing—notably as the domineering Bendemann *père* in 'Das Urteil' [The Judgement]. In Borges's story, the shadowy character of Ashe, although minor, plays an important role in introducing the narrator Borges to 'an unreal world whose apparent coherence undermines confidence in the reality of our own'.[20] This description of the education the narrator Borges receives from Ashe could equally be a description of the lessons in philosophy Borges *fils* received from Borges *père*. For example, Borges once recalled his father teaching him about the unstable nature of memory using a pile of coins: 'Y luego decía: "esta moneda corresponde a una imagen" y luego decía: "yo vuelvo a recordar esa imagen y la represento con otra moneda. Salvo que en la segunda moneda hay una ligera deformación y cuando vuelvo ya no recuerdo la primera moneda sino la primera imagen"' [He would say, 'This coin corresponds to an image', and then, 'When I recall this image, I represent it with another coin. Except that there is a slight distortion in the second coin, and when I return to this memory, I no longer recall the first coin, but rather the first image I have of it'].[21] The coins that later appear in the story as part of a demonstration of the instability of physical objects on Tlön may be an allusion to this childhood lesson.

As well as having a connection with Borges *père*, 'Tlön, Uqbar, Orbis Tertius' has a link with Kafka in the form of the frame narrative. This surrounding story addresses the powers of the text and the limits the author faces in trying to produce or control his writing—limits that Borges saw as related to infinity and Zeno's paradoxes and therefore to Kafka. In the frame narrative, the narrator Borges asserts that it would have been impossible for a single author to create the encyclopedia of Tlön. No one person could have had the time or the skill necessary to write such a work—the encyclopedia is as unfathomable as Menard's *Don Quijote*. If one person wrote it alone, he or she would have had to be 'un infinito Leibniz obrando en la tiniebla y en la modestia', [some infinite Leibniz working in obscurity and self-effacement].[22] The idea that an infinite

[19] Jorge Luis Borges, 'Tlön, Uqbar, Orbis Tertius', *Ficciones*, 1944, *Obras completas*, Vol. 1 (Buenos Aires: Emecé, 1996), pp. 431–43 (p. 433); Andrew Hurley, trans., 'Tlön, Uqbar, Orbis Tertius', *Fictions*, 1944, *Collected Fictions* (New York: Viking, 1998), pp. 68–81 (p. 71).

[20] Donald Shaw, *Borges: Fictions* (London: Grant and Cutler, 1976), p. 15.

[21] Jorge Luis Borges, *Testimonios de mis libros* (Buenos Aires: Revista del Notariado, 1972), p. 7.

[22] Borges, 'Tlön, Uqbar, Orbis Tertius', p. 434; Hurley, trans., 'Tlön, Uqbar, Orbis Tertius', p. 72.

project requires an infinite number of participants invites a comparison with Kafka's 'Beim Bau der chinesischen Mauer' [The Great Wall of China], where a similarly impossible task is undertaken by an unfathomably vast team of individuals:

> Dieses System des Teilbaues wurde auch im Kleinen . . . befolgt. Es geschah dies so, daß Gruppen von etwa zwanzig Arbeitern gebildet wurden, welche eine Teilmauer von etwa fünfhundert Metern Länge aufzuführen hatten, eine Nachbargruppe baute ihnen dann eine Mauer von gleicher Länge entgegen. . . . Natürlich entstanden auf diese Weise viele große Lücken, die erst nach und nach langsam ausgefüllt wurden, manche sogar erst, nachdem der Mauerbau schon als vollendent verkündigt worden war. Ja, es soll Lücken geben, die überhaupt nicht verbaut worden sind, eine Behauptung allerdings, die möglicherweise nur zu den vielen Legenden gehört, die um den Bau entstanden sind, und die, für den einzelnen Menschen wenigstens, mit eigenen Augen und eignem Maßstab infolge der Ausdehnung des Baues unnachprüfbar sind.

> [This principle of piecemeal construction was also applied on a smaller scale. . . . It was done in this way: gangs of some twenty workers were formed who had to accomplish a length, say, of five hundred yards of wall, while a similar gang built another stretch of the same length to meet the first. . . . Naturally in this way many great gaps were left, which were only filled in gradually and bit by bit, some, indeed, not till after the official announcement that the wall was finished. In fact it is said that there are gaps which have never been filled at all, an assertion, however, that is probably merely one of the many legends to which the building of the wall gave rise, and which cannot be verified, at least by any single man with his own eyes and judgment, on account of the extent of the structure.][23]

> Abundan individuos que dominan esas disciplinas diversas, pero no los capaces de invención y menos los capaces de *subordinar* la invención a un riguroso plan sistemático. Ese plan es tan vasto que la contribución de cada escritor es *infinitesimal*. Al principio se creyó que Tlön era un mero *caos*, una irresponsable licencia de la imaginación; ahora se sabe que es un *cosmos* y las íntimas leyes que lo rigen han sido formuladas, siquiera en modo provisional.

> [There are many men adept in those diverse disciplines, but few capable of imagination—fewer still capable of *subordinating* imagination to a rigorous and systematic plan. The plan is so vast that the contribution of each writer is *infinitesimal*. At first it was thought that Tlön was a mere *chaos*, an

---

[23] Franz Kafka, 'Beim Bau der chinesischen Mauer', *Beschreibung eines Kampfes: Novellen, Skizzen, Aphorismen aus dem Nachlass, Gesammelte Schriften*, Vol. 5 (Prague: Heinr. Mercy Sohn, 1936), pp. 67–82 (p. 67); also Franz Kafka, *Nachgelassene Schriften und Fragmente I* (New York: Schocken, 1993), pp. 337–57 (pp. 337–8); Willa Muir and Edwin Muir, trans., 'The Great Wall of China', *The Complete Stories* (New York: Schocken, 1971), pp. 235–47 (p. 235).

irresponsible act of imaginative license; today we know that it is a *cosmos*, and that the innermost laws that govern it have been formulated, however provisionally so.][24]

Both the Great Wall of China and the encyclopedia of Tlön are so large that a massive number of individuals have to be enlisted to carry out the projects. These individuals are controlled by their work, however, rather than being in control of it. The narrator Borges demonstrates this in 'Tlön, Uqbar, Orbius Tertius' by using the words 'subordinar', 'infinitesimal', 'caos', and 'cosmos' [subordinate, infinitesimal, chaos, and cosmos] to describe the relationship between the individual authors of the encyclopedia's segments and the overarching order of Tlön itself. At some point in both stories, the projects are declared complete even though work on them is still continuing. The wall may have gaps and Tlön's laws may only be provisional, but enough has been done to allow the projects to take on lives of their own. Their completion is inevitable yet also inconsequential.

Within the frame narrative, the narrator Borges contrasts the communal act of creating Tlön with his own more modest project, a Quevedian translation of Thomas Browne's *Urn Burial* (1658). In doing so, he places in perspective the idea of an all-encompassing, universal text (such as the encyclopedia of Tlön or the contents of the library of Babel) by juxtaposing it with a smaller, more personal work. His chosen project is a translation of a piece about melancholy (which suggests a link to Burton's *Anatomy of Melancholy*, the text that provides the epigraph for 'La biblioteca de Babel'). About his project, the narrator Borges says, 'yo sigo revisando en los quietos días del hotel de Adrogué una indecisa traducción quevediana (que no pienso dar a la imprenta) del *Urn Burial* de Browne' [through my quiet days in this hotel in Adrogué, I go on revising (though I never intend to publish) an indecisive translation in the style of Quevedo of Sir Thomas Browne's *Urne Buriall*].[25] There are two ways to interpret his actions. First, his translation may be a sign of his resignation. Perhaps he has already accepted that 'El mundo será Tlön' [The world will be Tlön].[26] This act has a parallel in one possible interpretation of Gregor's response to his transformation in Kafka's 'Die Verwandlung' [The Metamorphosis]. After realizing that he has become an insect, Gregor seems to be more focused on getting to work than anything else; similarly, the narrator Borges is focused

---

[24] Borges, 'Tlön, Uqbar, Orbis Tertius', pp. 434–5, emphasis added; Hurley, trans., 'Tlön, Uqbar, Orbis Tertius', p. 72, emphasis added.

[25] Borges, 'Tlön, Uqbar, Orbis Tertius', p. 443; Hurley, trans., 'Tlön, Uqbar, Orbis Tertius', p. 81.

[26] Borges, 'Tlön, Uqbar, Orbis Tertius', p. 443; Hurley, trans., 'Tlön, Uqbar, Orbis Tertius', p. 81.

on completing his own work rather than actively resisting the world's transformation into Tlön.

However, the narrator's translation may also be a response to Tlön in the form of an assertion of his individuality. Although the people around him are losing their identities, the narrator Borges declares his own when he says '*Yo* no hago caso, *yo* sigo revisando' [That makes very little difference to me...I go on revising], with the emphatic employment of the unnecessary 'yo' [I].[27] He focuses on his intellectual activity even when others have given themselves over to the totalitarian world of Tlön.[28] In this regard too, the narrator Borges resembles Gregor from 'Die Verwandlung'. Despite his transformation, Gregor still finds himself moved by his sister's violin playing. If anything, he wonders whether his appreciation of his sister's music has been heightened: 'War er ein Tier, da ihn Musik so ergriff?... Er war entschlossen, bis zur Schwester vorzudringen, sie am Rock zu zupfen und ihr dadurch anzudeuten, sie möge doch mit ihrer Violine in sein Zimmer kommen, denn niemand lohnte hier das Spiel so, wie er es lohnen wollte' [Was he an animal, that music had such an effect upon him?... He was determined to push forward till he reached his sister, to pull at her skirt and so let her know that she was to come into his room with her violin, for no one here appreciated her playing as he would appreciate it].[29] The characters Borges and Gregor find solace— and even some sense of identity—in participating in or observing artistic pursuits at odds with the world around them. The individual's struggle to protect his or her sense of self in a changing world was a concept that Borges associated with Kafka, and Borges highlighted this in his capsule biography of Kafka, where he maintained that Kafka's writing developed in response to the tragedies taking place in the surrounding world. In 'Tlön, Uqbar, Orbis Tertius', this is what the narrator Borges does: he translates Browne as a demonstration of his wariness of Tlön.

The narrator Borges is right to be sceptical of Tlön. The laws that govern the planet make no sense to the narrator Borges (and likely make no sense to Borges's readers), even though they are rigidly structured

---

[27] Borges, 'Tlön, Uqbar, Orbis Tertius', p. 443, original emphasis; Hurley, trans., 'Tlön, Uqbar, Orbis Tertius', p. 81.

[28] See Sarah Roger, 'Translation, Identity, and Jorge Luis Borges', *The Limits of Literary Translation: Expanding Frontiers in Iberian Languages* (Kassel: Reichenberger, 2012), pp. 57–71 for an exploration of the significance of Borges's Quevedian translation of *Urn Burial*.

[29] Franz Kafka, 'Die Verwandlung', *Erzählungen und kleine Prosa, Gesammelte Schriften*, Vol. 1 (Berlin: Schocken, 1935), pp. 69–130 (pp. 119–20); also Franz Kafka, 'Die Verwandlung', *Drucke zu Lebzeiten* (Frankfurt: S. Fischer; New York: Schocken, 1994), pp. 113–200 (pp. 185–6); Willa Muir and Edwin Muir, trans., 'The Metamorphosis', *The Complete Stories* (New York: Schocken, 1971), pp. 89–139 (pp. 130–1).

according to the tenets of idealism. On Tlön, things such as perception and language are relative or problematic. Tlön even owes its existence to a paradox, since Ezra Buckley, the man who funds the encyclopedia, 'descree de Dios, pero quiere demostrar al Dios no existente que los hombres mortales son capaces de concebir un mundo' [did not believe in God, yet he wanted to prove to the nonexistent God that mortals could conceive and shape a world].[30]

If Tlön's origins are based on a paradox, its predecessor country has its roots in ambiguity. Uqbar is set in uncertain geographical boundaries:

> Releyéndolo, descubrimos bajo su rigurosa escritura una fundamental vaguedad. De los catorce nombres que figuraban en la parte geográfica, sólo reconocimos tres—Jorasán, Armenia, Erzerum—, interpolados en el texto de un modo ambiguo. De los nombres históricos, uno solo: el impostor Esmerdis el mago, invocado más bien como una metáfora. La nota parecía precisar las fronteras de Uqbar, pero sus nebulosos puntos de referencia eran ríos y cráteres y cadenas de esa misma región.

> [Rereading it, however, we discovered that the rigorous writing was underlain by a basic vagueness. Of the fourteen names that figured in the section on geography, we recognized only three (Khorosan, Armenia, Erzerum), and they interpolated into the text ambiguously. Of the historical names, we recognized only one: the impostor-wizard Smerdis, and he was invoked, really, as a metaphor. The article seemed to define the borders of Uqbar, but its nebulous points of reference were rivers and craters and mountain chains of the region itself.][31]

This manner of situating Uqbar recalls the barely referential geographical points that mark the limits of Kafka's Great Wall, which are described in vague terms of north, southeast, and southwest (*see* Chapter 3, n. 76). Uqbar is situated with respect to nebulous points: rivers, craters, and mountain chains near Jorosán and Armenia, which are useless indicators because they are mostly internal and partially imaginary. Despite these ambiguous locations, Tlön manages to force its way into the narrator's world. It starts appearing everywhere: a volume of its encyclopedia is found in a hotel bar, an artefact from Tlön shows up in a case of expensive goods shipped from Europe, and it is the cause of a brawl at a pulpería. Although the narrator Borges is sceptical, and although the world of Tlön is not fully described, Tlön manages to establish itself with a physical presence as real as the Great Wall of China.

---

[30] Borges, 'Tlön, Uqbar, Orbis Tertius', p. 441; Hurley, trans., 'Tlön, Uqbar, Orbis Tertius', p. 79.

[31] Borges, 'Tlön, Uqbar, Orbis Tertius', p. 432; Hurley, trans., 'Tlön, Uqbar, Orbis Tertius', p. 69.

'Tlön, Uqbar, Orbis Tertius' resembles Kafka's stories in one other way. Borges admired Kafka's tales because they can function as parables on three different levels: the personal, the contemporary, and the everlasting. The same can be said of 'Tlön, Uqbar, Orbis Tertius'. First, the story is a personal, Borgesian parable for the impossibility of writing a justification-worthy text, because everything will be surpassed in time. Even the narrator's Quevedian *Urn Burial* will be overtaken by the world of Tlön. Second, it is a critique of the rise of Nazism during the period in which the story is written. As Clive Griffin explains,

> In the 1930s, [Borges] saw the rise of seductively simple political philoso-phies. They were, of course, man-made and therefore, like Tlön which is also the product of human intelligence, they were neat and rendered the world comprehensible. That was their fatal attraction. In the face of totalitarian ideologies, like that of Tlön, of Nazism, and of communism which subor-dinate the individual to the masses, the first-person narrator in the story resists by reasserting an identity which had been progressively eclipsed in the story.[32]

Third, if Buckley's reasons for establishing Tlön are to be believed, the story seeks to explain the existence (or non-existence) of God and the limits of God's power (*see* n. 30). Like Kafka's stories, 'Tlön, Uqbar, Orbis Tertius' is a parable as well as a nightmare.

Following 'Tlön, Uqbar, Orbis Tertius', 'Las ruinas circulares' [The Circular Ruins] was published in December 1940, only a month prior to 'La lotería en Babilonia'. 'Las ruinas circulares' is the story of a man who creates a son, a concept that comes from a legend depicted in Gustav Meyrink's *Der Golem* [*The Golem*] (1914), a book Borges admired. The Golem was a sub-human creature created in the attic of the *Altneuschul* in Prague, the synagogue Kafka attended with his father. Borges's story, however, does not take place in Prague. As in many of Borges's and Kafka's stories, the setting is indeterminate, both geographically and temporally: 'su patria era una de las infinitas aldeas que están aguas arriba, en el flanco violento de la montaña, donde el idioma zend no está contaminado de griego y donde es infrecuente la lepra' [his homeland was one of those infinite villages that lie upriver, on the violent flank of the mountain, where the language of the Zend is uncontaminated by Greek and where leprosy is uncommon].[33] The opening of the story situates the

[32] Clive Griffin, 'Philosophy and Fiction', *The Cambridge Companion to Jorge Luis Borges* (Cambridge: Cambridge UP, 2013), pp. 5–15 (p. 12).

[33] Jorge Luis Borges, 'Las ruinas circulares', *Ficciones*, 1944, *Obras completas*, Vol. 1 (Buenos Aires: Emecé, 1996), pp. 451–5 (p. 451); Andrew Hurley, trans., 'The Circular Ruins', *Fictions*, 1944, *Collected Fictions* (New York: Viking, 1998), pp. 96–100 (p. 96).

action within an ambiguous space, using ineffective geographical and temporal markers. At the same time, its references to the 'patria' and the 'infinitas aldeas' associate it with the 'patria potestad' and infinity—two of Borges's key Kafkian themes.

'Las ruinas circulares' breaks down the distinction between dreams and reality. The protagonist's existence is 'consagrado a la única tarea de dormir y soñar' [consecrated to the sole task of sleeping and dreaming], and there is confusion between what happens in his mind while he is asleep and what happens in reality when he is awake.[34] This blurring of sleeping and wakefulness, dreams and reality recalls the Chinese story of a man dreaming of being a butterfly or a butterfly dreaming of being a man, an intellectual game Borges played with elsewhere, such as in 'Nueva refutación del tiempo' [A New Refutation of Time]. Like in the Chinese story, much of the action in 'Las ruinas circulares' takes place in dreams that are so realistic that it is impossible to be certain whether or not they are imagined. Dreams are interpolated into the real world, and the protagonist's real actions are mirrored by the imagined actions of the man he has dreamed.

There is a regressive pattern of creator, creature, and creator in 'Las ruinas circulares' that is reminiscent of Zeno's paradoxes. The creator imagines his creature doing some of the things that he has done, and it transpires at the end of the story that the creator is also a creature who has repeated his creator's actions, and perhaps so on infinitely to an original creator who can never be reached. This possibility is mirrored by the physical placement of the protagonist and his creature. The protagonist is said to have come downriver from 'una de las infinitas aldeas que están aguas arriba' [one of those infinite villages that lie upriver] to undertake his task, while his creature has gone downstream following on from his creator, setting up a Zenoesque spatial pattern in a potentially infinite series.[35]

In a review of Brod's biography of Kafka, published three years earlier, Borges drew attention to an incident from Kafka's life where there was a similar blurring of dreams and reality. Kafka once accidentally woke Brod's father while passing through a room in which Brod's father was taking a nap. On his way past, he commented, 'Le ruego, considéreme un sueño' [Please, consider me a dream].[36] In the context of Brod's biography, this incident is not notable, but Borges singled it out in one of his

---

[34] Borges, 'Las ruinas circulares', p. 451; Hurley, trans., 'The Circular Ruins', p. 97.

[35] Borges, 'Las ruinas circulares', p. 451, 454; Hurley, trans., 'The Circular Ruins', p. 96, 99.

[36] Jorge Luis Borges, 'De la vida literaria: 8 de julio de 1938', *Jorge Luis Borges en 'El Hogar' (1930–1958)* (Buenos Aires: Emecé, 2000), pp. 116–17 (p. 117).

columns, 'De la vida literaria' [On Literary Life], published in *El Hogar*. Kafka's comment suggests the possibility of circumstances where it is impossible to tell for certain when one is awake and when one is dreaming, and it also implies the possibility of a multi-layered dream where one can wake into another dream, rather than into reality—two ideas that fascinated Borges.

In 'Las ruinas circulares' the subject of the protagonist's dreams (and his reality) is the 'patria potestad'. The story is about the disjunction between the authority the protagonist imagines himself possessing and the subordinate position he actually occupies. While the protagonist is dreaming, he has supernatural powers; when he is awake, his existence becomes a nightmare:

> El hombre, un día, emergió del sueño como de un desierto viscoso, miró la vana luz de la tarde que al pronto confundió con la aurora y comprendió que no había soñado. Toda esa noche y todo el día, la intolerable lucidez del insomnio se abatió contra él. Quiso explorar la selva, extenuarse; apenas alcanzó entre la cicuta unas rachas de sueño débil, veteadas fugazmente de visiones de tipo rudimental: inservibles. Quiso consagrar el colegio y apenas hubo articulado unas breves palabras de exhortación, éste se deformó, se borró. En la casi perpetua vigilia, lágrimas de ira le quemaban los viejos ojos.

> [One day the man emerged from sleep as though from a viscous desert, looked up at the hollow light of the evening (which for a moment he confused with the light of dawn), and realized that he had not dreamed. All that night and the next day, the unbearable lucidity of insomnia harried him, like a hawk. He went off to explore the jungle, hoping to tire himself; among the hemlocks he managed no more than a few intervals of feeble sleep, fleetingly veined with the most rudimentary of visions—useless to him. He reconvened his class, but no sooner had he spoken a few brief words of exhortation than the faces blurred, twisted, and faded away. In his almost perpetual state of wakefulness, tears of anger burned the man's old eyes.][37]

The end of the story exposes the limits of the protagonist's power. The dreamer learns that he is also a subordinate: he is a creature as well as a creator. This revelation is similar to the one Georg has at the end of Kafka's 'Das Urteil'. Georg believes he is an independent adult in control of personal and family affairs. However, when he tries to tell his father about plans to inform a friend of his engagement, he discovers that he has been deluded about the extent of his autonomy. Georg's father condemns his son to death by drowning, a command to which Georg remarkably accedes, and the order of the 'patria potestad' is reinstated. Like Georg, just when the protagonist of 'Las ruinas circulares' thinks he has succeeded in creating a

---

[37] Borges, 'Las ruinas circulares', p. 452; Hurley, trans., 'The Circular Ruins', pp. 97–8.

son, he is awakened to the true order of the 'patria potestad': he too is someone else's creature. This discovery recalls Borges's admiration for Kafka's stories as both nightmares and parables. On one hand, 'Las ruinas circulares' is a nightmare: the protagonist's experience is terrifying and the story's actions are far removed from reality. On the other hand, 'Las ruinas circulares' is a parable in the uncertain, Kafkian sense: even though the message is never openly stated, the story serves as a warning about power, reality, success, and delusion.

Although not one of Borges's stories from this period, it is worth mentioning 'Ein Traum' (a poem from Borges's 1976 *La moneda de hierro* [*The Iron Coin*]) in conjunction with 'Las ruinas circulares'. Like 'Las ruinas circulares', Borges's poem is about an individual dreaming another into existence, although in this instance the dreamer is Kafka and his creation is a pair of lovers. The lovers know that Kafka has dreamed them, and they fear that if they try to consummate their relationship, Kafka will wake up and destroy their existence. Meanwhile, Kafka must watch the couple from the sidelines, just as the creator in 'Las ruinas circulares' must watch his creature. Borges's poem takes its title from a Kafka story of the same name about a dreamer and the relationship he has with an individual he has dreamed. In Kafka's story, the dreamer is made to climb into his own grave (and presumably go to his own death) by the character he has dreamed: an artist who is inscribing the name of Kafka's dreamer, Josef K. (the same name as the protagonist of *Der Prozeß*), onto the gravestone. Where Kafka's dreamed man is an artist with power over the man who has dreamed him, the dreamer in Borges's poem is an author who struggles with the limitations of the power he holds over those he has dreamed. Borges's poem is a statement about the author's limited authority in creating and controlling his text.

The stories from 'El acercamiento a Almotásim' through to 'Las ruinas circulares' have settings that range from India to Argentina and styles that range from journalistic to parabolic. However, when they are read with respect to the characteristics that Borges admired in Kafka, they have a cohesiveness about them that may not otherwise be evident. Unlike Kafka's stories, Borges's stories containing Kafkian elements are often also about writing: they challenge the authority of a creator (usually an author) and they question the creator's ability to find or produce something unique and meaningful. A successful act of creation eludes the protagonist in 'Las ruinas ciruclares' and the authors in 'Pierre Menard, autor del *Quijote*' and 'Tlön, Uqbar, Orbis Tertius'. The protagonist of *El acercamiento a Almotásim* ostensibly finds the meaning for which he searches, but the novelist Bahadur is unable to share this with the novel's readers.

In all of these stories, the protagonist questions his identity or struggles to define it. The protagonist of Bahadur's *El acercamiento a Almotásim* is defined by his suspected act of murder, and he subsequently shifts his sense of self onto his quest for Almotásim; the mention of the Simurgh at the end of the story hints at an interpretation where the identity of Almotásim also becomes the protagonist's. Menard is defined by his determination to rewrite *Don Quijote* and his identity is deferred onto his success, which never comes. In 'Tlön, Uqbar, Orbis Tertius', the narrator Borges is defined by his resistance to having the world of Tlön imposed upon him, and he distinguishes himself as an individual through his act of translating—an effort he highlights with his repeated use of 'yo' [I] in the story's final paragraph. Lastly, the protagonist of 'Las ruinas circulares' is defined not as an independent creator, as he initially thinks, but rather as a creature. In most of these cases, this identity-defining or identity-shattering effect is the product of Zeno's paradoxes: there is a Zenoesque search for Almotásim, a need for infinite time to rewrite *Don Quijote*, and a possibly infinite, regressive pattern of creator and creature in 'Las ruinas circulares'.

5.2 BETWEEN THE LOTTERY AND THE LIBRARY: 'EXAMEN DE LA OBRA DE HERBERT QUAIN'

Borges wrote four stories in 1941: 'La lotería en Babilonia', 'Examen de la obra de Herbert Quain' [A Survey of the Works of Herbert Quain], 'La biblioteca de Babel', and 'El jardín de senderos que se bifurcan' [The Garden of Forking Paths]. 'La lotería en Babilonia' and 'Examen de la obra de Herbert Quain' were initially published in *Sur* in January and April respectively, while both 'La biblioteca de Babel' and 'El jardín de senderos que se bifurcan' first appeared in the collection *El jardín de senderos que se bifurcan* in December. Because 'Examen de la obra de Herbert Quain' was published between Borges's two openly Kafkian stories in *El jardín de senderos que se bifurcan* and again between them in *Ficciones*, it may well have been written in the middle; by the same logic, since 'El jardín de senderos que se bifurcan' appeared as the final (and title) story in *El jardín de senderos que se bifurcan*, Borges may have written it last. Although there is no way to confirm this, 'Examen de la obra de Herbert Quain' has many claims to being an intentionally Kafkian story in the vein of 'La lotería en Babilonia' and 'La biblioteca de Babel', and as such it is treated here as a special case.

Even though Borges never mentioned Kafka with respect to 'Examen de la obra de Herbert Quain', the story combines Borges's use of the themes he admired in Kafka with one of his other interests from around this time: his self-conscious writing about authorship. First published in *Sur* in April 1941, 'Examen de la obra de Herbert Quain' appears to have the most in common with 'El acercamiento a Almotásim', 'Pierre Menard, autor del *Quijote*', and 'Tlön, Uqbar, Orbis Tertius'—all pseudo-factual texts about fictional books. However, the texts within 'Examen de la obra de Herbert Quain' each also have aspects of the elements Borges praised in Kafka.

The first of these is Quain's novel, *The God of the Labyrinth*, with a title that invokes two of the topics Borges noted in Kafka's writing: God and labyrinths. Quain's novel is a mystery that is unravelled by the sentence 'Todos creyeron que el encuentro de los dos jugadores de ajedrez había sido casual' [Everyone believed that the chessplayers had met accidentally].[38] This reference to chess recalls the games played by Herbert Ashe in 'Tlön, Uqbar, Orbis Tertius' and also Zeno's paradoxes, which Borges *père* taught to Borges *fils* using a chessboard. Quain's use of a single sentence to reveal the truth underlying *The God of the Labyrinth* also implies that secret workings have been concealed from the characters but shared with the readers, a technique Quain also uses in one of his other works, and which recalls the concealed machinations that take place in Kafka's writings.

Quain's second novel, *April March*, is a fragmentary story made up of one conclusion with nine possible origins. It is a 'novela regresiva, ramificada' [regressively, ramifying fiction], and in this regard, it recalls Borges's description of Kafka's novels:[39]

La crítica deplora que en las tres novelas de Kafka falten muchos capítulos intermedios, pero reconoce que esos capítulos no son imprescindibles. Yo tengo para mí que esa queja indica un desconocimiento esencial del arte de Kafka. El pathos de esas 'inconclusas' novelas nace precisamente del número infinito de obstáculos que detienen y vuelven a detener sus héroes idénticos. Franz Kafka no las terminó, porque lo primordial era que fuesen interminables.

[Critics have complained that Kafka's three novels are missing many intermediate chapters, although they acknowledge that these chapters are not essential. It seems to me that their complaint indicates a fundamental misunderstanding of Kafka's art. The pathos of these 'unfinished' novels stems precisely from the infinite number of obstacles that repeatedly hinder

---

[38] Jorge Luis Borges, 'Examen de la obra de Herbert Quain', *Ficciones*, 1944, *Obras completas*, Vol. 1 (Buenos Aires: Emecé, 1996), pp. 461–4 (p. 462); Andrew Hurley, trans., 'A Survey of the Works of Herbert Quain', *Fictions*, 1944, *Collected Fictions* (New York: Viking, 1998), pp. 107–11 (p. 108).

[39] Borges, 'Examen de la obra de Herbert Quain', p. 462; Hurley, trans., 'A Survey of the Works of Herbert Quain', p. 108.

their identical protagonists. Franz Kafka did not finish his novels because it was essential that they be incomplete.][40]

For Borges, the seemingly infinite number of problems that Kafka's characters come up against in the fragments of his episodic novels make them seem interminable. Quain similarly uses fragmentation to confuse his story's origins, and he contemplates the possibility of using further fragmentation to make *April March* seem interminable: 'No sé si debo recordar que ya publicado *April March*, Quain se arrepintió del orden ternario y predijo que los hombres que lo imitaran optarían por el binario … y los demiurgos y los dioses por el infinito: infinitas historias, infinitamente ramificadas' [I am not certain whether I should remind the reader that after *April March* was published, Quain had second thoughts about the triune order of the book and predicted that the mortals who imitated it would opt instead for a binary scheme … while the gods and demiurges had chosen an infinite one: infinite stories, infinitely branching].[41]

Quain's third work is a play called *The Secret Mirror*, which anticipates the circular play that Borges's protagonist Jaromir Hladík writes in 'El milagro secreto'. *The Secret Mirror* echoes Kafka in the game it plays with the divide between the real and the imagined, between aspiration and reality. The protagonist of Quain's play, John William Quigley, appears to be a semi-biographical version of Quain, just as so many of Kafka's characters were for Kafka: Gregor Samsa, Georg Bendemann, Josef K., and K., among others. Despite his modest existence as a travelling salesman (the same job that Gregor holds), Quigley imagines that he is a gentleman named Wilfred Quarles, who hobnobs with the social elite and is doted on by a wealthy society lady named Ulrica Thrale. The play's two acts reveal the divide between Quigley's inner and outer lives: the first act portrays Quarles's life, with no suggestion that it is Quigley's fantasy; the second act reveals the reality he lives as the downtrodden Quigley.[42] There is a parallel for Quigley's disillusionment in 'Die Verwandlung': although Gregor portrays himself as a well-loved son and brother who has sacrificed himself for his family, over the course of the story, readers realize that Gregor has been manipulated into working on behalf of his self-interested parents and sister. Just as Quigley has imagined his romance with Ulrica, Gregor has imagined his family's need for and appreciation of his sacrifice.

---

[40] Jorge Luis Borges, 'Franz Kafka: *La metamorfosis*', *Prólogos con un prólogo de prólogos*, 1975, *Obras completas*, Vol. 4 (Buenos Aires: Emecé, 1996), pp. 97–9 (p. 98).

[41] Borges, 'Examen de la obra de Herbert Quain', p. 463; Hurley, trans., 'A Survey of the Works of Herbert Quain', p. 110.

[42] In 'La lotería en Babilonia', Borges uses the letter Q in his cypher 'Qaphqa'; the use of Q in Quain, Quigley, and Quarles may hark back to this, and therefore to Kafka.

There are further echoes of 'Die Verwandlung' in Quigley's relationship with Ulrica. While Quigley fantasizes about the upper-class Ulrica Thrale, he 'nunca la ha visto, pero morbosamente colecciona retratos suyos del *Tatler* o del *Sketch*' [has never seen her; he morbidly clips pictures of her out of the *Tatler* or the *Sketch*].[43] Gregor, similarly, frames a picture of 'eine Dame [...] die, mit einem Pelzhut und einer Pelzboa versehen, aufrecht dasaß und einen schweren Pelzmuff, in dem ihr ganzer Unterarm verschwunden war, dem Beschauer entgegenhob' [a lady, with a fur cap on and a fur stole, sitting upright and holding out to the spectator a huge fur muff into which the whole of her forearm had vanished].[44] There is something unsavoury about Quigley's and Gregor's pictures, and Gregor even behaves inappropriately with his photograph: 'da sah er an der im übrigen schon leeren Wand auffallend das Bild der in lauter Pelzwerk gekleideten Dame hängen, kroch eilends hinauf und preßte sich an das Glas, das ihn festhielt und seinem heißen Bauch wohltat. Dieses Bild wenigstens, das Gregor jetzt ganz verdeckte, würde nun gewiß niemand wegnehmen' [he was struck by the picture of the lady muffled in so much fur and quickly crawled up to it and pressed himself to the glass, which was a good surface to hold on to and comforted his hot belly. This picture at least, which was entirely hidden beneath him, was going to be removed by nobody].[45] Gregor clings to the photograph, demonstrating that he is, in some respects, still a man with a man's desires. He acts out his lust in physical contact with the picture: 'er klebte aber fest an dem Glas und mußte sich mit Gewalt losreißen' [he was stuck fast to the glass and had to tear himself loose].[46] Quigley enacts a similar but less lurid desire by writing 'pormenores sórdidos' [sordid details] into his imagined version of Ulrica's life in the first act of *The Secret Mirror*.[47] Through their imaginary relationships, both reveal their (failed) desire to escape their realities.

The Secret Mirror, and indeed all the stories written by the fictional Quain, may have been a testing ground for Borges. For example, Quain undermines the conclusion of *The God of the Labyrinth*, and Borges used the same technique in stories such as 'La forma de la espada' [The Shape of the Sword] (1942) and 'Tema del traidor y del héroe' [Theme of the

---

[43] Borges, 'Examen de la obra de Herbert Quain', p. 464; Hurley, trans., 'A Survey of the Works of Herbert Quain', p. 111.

[44] Kafka, 'Die Verwandlung', p. 69; also Kafka, 'Die Verwandlung', pp. 115–16; Muir and Muir, trans., 'The Metamorphosis', p. 89.

[45] Kafka, 'Die Verwandlung', p. 105; also Kafka, 'Die Verwandlung', p. 165; Muir and Muir, trans., 'The Metamorphosis', p. 118.

[46] Kafka, 'Die Verwandlung', p. 106; also Kafka, 'Die Verwandlung', p. 166; Muir and Muir, trans., 'The Metamorphosis', p. 119.

[47] Borges, 'Examen de la obra de Herbert Quain', p. 464; Hurley, trans., 'A Survey of the Works of Herbert Quain', p. 111.

Traitor and the Hero] (1944)—both of which conclude with twists that encourage the reader to reconsider the narrators' actions, their intentions, and even their identities. As in *April March*, 'El jardín de senderos que se bifurcan' plays with the possibility of forking paths, infinite options, and binary opposites. *The Secret Mirror* and the fictional play *Los enemigos* [*The Enemies*] in 'El milagro secreto' both have plots dreamed by madmen. The stories in 'Examen de la obra de Herbert Quain' allowed Borges to experiment with some of the elements that he admired in Kafka's writing, including secrets, mysteries, infinity, and the confusing nature of time.

Even though 'Examen de la obra de Herbert Quain' is a Kafkian story in its own right, it differs drastically from 'La lotería en Babilonia' and 'La biblioteca de Babel', both of which are highly stylized tales about protagonists isolated within fictional worlds. 'La lotería en Babilonia' and 'La biblioteca de Babel' are first-person accounts, framed as though they are told to provide comfort to their narrators as much as anything else. By contrast, 'Examen de la obra de Herbert Quain' is a detached, humorous commentary on writing. Borges's focus on authorship became, in his later works, one of the points at which he swerved away from Kafka. The conclusion of 'Examen de la obra de Herbert Quain' refers to Quain's self-awareness and his sense of failure as an author. This is a trait shared by Kafka and Borges *père*, and it is an important theme for Borges *fils*'s fictions. At the end of the story, the narrator of 'Examen de la obra de Herbert Quain' mentions Quain's collection of stories called *Statements*, where the reader is left with the impression that he himself has invented the stories' plots, not Quain. The narrator (now identifying himself as Borges) says he borrowed one of Quain's plots for 'Las ruinas circulares'. This makes the story a *mise en abîme*: 'Las ruinas circulares' is the third story of *Ficciones*, and the story Borges claims to have borrowed from Quain is the third in Quain's collection, *Statements*. With this trick, Borges demonstrated his debt to a (fictional) preceding author, and he acknowledged the complex game of attribution, originality, and invention (not to mention an abiding sense of failure) connecting 'Las ruinas circulares' to 'Examen de la obra de Herbert Quain' and to his writing more broadly.

What place does 'Examen de la obra de Herbert Quain' have between 'La lotería en Babilonia' and 'La biblioteca de Babel'? As a story, it brings together Borges's interest in Kafka and his interest in authorship. The Borges stories discussed above (starting with 'El acercamiento a Almotásim' and concluding with 'Las ruinas circulares', all written before 1941) combine the act of creation with fragmentary writing, parables, Zeno's paradoxes, infinity, and the 'patria potestad'—themes that also appear in 'La lotería en Babilonia' and 'La biblioteca de Babel'. Although 'La lotería en Babilonia' and 'La biblioteca de Babel' do not focus on Borges's interest in authorship, 'Examen de la obra de Herbert Quain' demonstrates that at this time Borges was linking aspects from Kafka's work with his own questions about authorship and identity, and that the two interests were not independent from each other.

5.3 FROM 'EL JARDÍN DE SENDEROS QUE SE BIFURCAN' TO 'EL MILAGRO SECRETO'

Looking back on 'La lotería en Babilonia' and 'La biblioteca de Babel', Borges said, 'yo me di cuenta de que no había cumplido mi propósito y que debía buscar otro camino. Kafka fue tranquilo y hasta un poco secreto y yo elegí ser escandaloso' [I realized that I had not fulfilled my purpose and that I had to find another path. Kafka was quiet and even a little secretive, and I had chosen to be outrageous].[48] What is it about Kafkian writing that did not work for Borges? Borges said that Kafka was 'tranquilo' [quiet] while he was 'escandaloso' [outrageous]. This assessment seems accurate: Kafka wrote in an uncomplicated style that gave his stories the air of parables, while Borges created elaborate literary games with carefully constructed frame narratives and the occasional surprise ending. Notwithstanding this difference, Borges's belief that he had not succeeded in emulating Kafka brings to mind his view that Kafka perceived himself to be a failure—an idea that was part of Borges's broader interest in writing about authors, creators, and their sense of inadequacy.

Borges's focus on the author is so prevalent that 'La lotería en Babilonia' and 'La biblioteca de Babel' are the only two Kafkian stories discussed so far that do not openly address either authorship or creation. 'La biblioteca de Babel' is about books, but the books already exist and their creator is distant and unknowable. 'La lotería en Babilonia' has a narrator who is conscious of his role of storyteller, but that does not make the story a meditation on writing. By contrast, 'El acercamiento a Almotásim' is a (fictional) literary critique, 'Examen de la obra de Herbert Quain' and 'Pierre Menard, autor del *Quijote*' are obituaries of fictional authors, 'Pierre Menard, autor del *Quijote*' and 'Tlön, Uqbar, Orbis Tertius' are about writing projects, and even 'Las ruinas circulares' is about an act of creation. Borges's interest in Kafka's literary techniques and his interest in authorship go hand in hand, and many of the stories Borges wrote immediately following 'La lotería en Babilonia' and 'La biblioteca de Babel' also refer

---

[48] Borges, 'Un sueño eterno: Palabras grabadas en el centenario de Kafka', p. 238.

to authorship, particularly 'El jardín de senderos que se bifurcan' and 'El milagro secreto'.

'El jardín de senderos que se bifurcan' is the story of Yu Tsun, a Chinese man from the German colony in Tsingtao, who is spying on behalf of the Germans in the First World War. To alert the Germans to the location of a British artillery park, Yu Tsun murders a man named Stephen Albert. Before he kills Albert, however, Albert tells Yu Tsun about a labyrinthine, bifurcating novel written by one of Yu Tsun's ancestors, Ts'ui Pên. Ts'ui Pên's novel was composed in 'El Pabellón de la Límpida Soledad' [the Pavillion of Limpid Solitude], which may be an allusion to Borges *père*'s lost collection of short stories, *El jardín de la cúpula de oro* [*The Garden of the Golden Dome*] as well as an internal reference to the title of Borges *fils*'s 'El jardín de senderos que se bifurcan'.[49]

There are two stories contained within Borges's text: first, there is the story of Yu Tsun murdering Albert; second, there is the story of Ts'ui Pên's novel. Together, these two stories demonstrate Yu Tsun's obligation to two levels of the 'patria potestad'. On one hand, Yu Tsun is subordinate to the Germans, on whose behalf he is spying. Related to this, he has a responsibility to the Chinese people: 'Lo hice, porque yo sentía que el Jefe tenía en poco a los de mi raza—a los innumerables antepasados que confluyen en mí. Yo quería probarle que un amarillo podía salvar a sus ejércitos' [I did it because I sensed that the Leader looked down on the people of my race—the countless ancestors whose blood flows through my veins. I wanted to prove to him that a yellow man could save his armies].[50] On the other hand, he is indebted to Albert for discovering the meaning of Ts'ui Pên's scorned novel and therefore for restoring the honour of his family. Within the hierarchy of the 'patria potestad', Germany and China represent Yu Tsun's country (patria, fatherland), while Albert and Ts'ui Pên represent the family (pater, father). Problematically, for Yu Tsun to honour one level of the 'patria potestad' he must betray another. The Kafkian nature of this situation is alluded to by reference to Yu Tsun's unnamed, Kafkaesque 'Jefe' [Chief], an authority on a par with those to whom Kafka's characters are often beholden.

Ts'ui Pên's text presents Yu Tsun with an alternative, suggesting that he may not need to choose one level of the 'patria potestad' over another. At any point where a decision has to be made, Ts'ui Pên's novel proposes that

---

[49] Jorge Luis Borges, 'El jardín de senderos que se bifurcan', *Ficciones*, 1944, *Obras completas*, Vol. 1 (Buenos Aires: Emecé, 1996), pp. 472–80 (p. 476); Andrew Hurley, trans., 'The Garden of Forking Paths', *Fictions*, 1944, *Collected Fictions* (New York: Viking, 1998), pp. 119–28 (p. 124).

[50] Borges, 'El jardín de senderos que se bifurcan', p. 473; Hurley, trans., 'The Garden of Forking Paths', p. 121.

all possible options are chosen and the narrative splits into several parts. This means that—at least in Ts'ui Pên's fictional world—there is more than one way for a story to resolve itself. Applying these ideas to Yu Tsun's circumstances, he can honour both elements of the 'patria potestad' in two separate realities. The effect of Ts'ui Pên's bifurcating time is that it creates a Zenoesque, labyrinthine world.

While there may be multiple planes of existence in the story that Ts'ui Pên writes, in Yu Tsun's narrative (presented in Borges's story as a factual report) there is only one way for events to unfold: 'El ejecutor de una empresa atroz debe imaginar que ya la ha cumplido, debe imponerse un porvenir que sea irrevocable como el pasado' [He who is to perform a horrendous act should imagine to himself that it is already done, should impose upon himself a future as irrevocable as the past].[51] Yu Tsun can imagine himself choosing alternatives, but these other possibilities will never occur because he has already decided what he will do. Despite the 'varios porvenires' [several futures] Yu Tsun could have, he sees his obligation to the army as inescapable.[52] He chooses to follow through with his plan, even though it will have negative ramifications for his family under the 'patria potestad'. If he had opted to save Albert, his family's honour could have been restored: Albert could have made Ts'ui Pên's literary accomplishments known.

Yu Tsun's circumstances (in which there is no escape from and no way to satisfy all of his obligations to various levels of authority) are Kafkian, while Ts'ui Pên's novel is a Kafkian nightmare. For Albert, however, the same novel is 'una enorme adivinanza, o *parábola*, cuyo tema es el tiempo; esa causa recóndita le prohíbe la mención de su nombre' [a huge riddle, or *parable*, whose subject is time; that secret purpose forbids Ts'ui Pen the merest mention of its name].[53] From Albert's perspective, Ts'ui Pên's novel can be read as a Kafkian parable for the endless possibilities in infinite time. This dual possibility, where the novel is both a nightmare and a parable, highlights Borges's two ways of reading Kafka's stories: as nightmares detached from reality, and as parables for man's place in the universe.

In 'La muerte y la brújula' Borges moves away from Kafka's ideas even as he emulates them. The story is about two detectives trying to solve the same murder: Erik Lönnrot pursues a logically complex but interesting

---

[51] Borges, 'El jardín de senderos que se bifurcan', p. 474; Hurley, trans., 'The Garden of Forking Paths', p. 121.

[52] Borges, 'El jardín de senderos que se bifurcan', p. 477; Hurley, trans., 'The Garden of Forking Paths', p. 125.

[53] Borges, 'El jardín de senderos que se bifurcan', pp. 478–9, emphasis added; Hurley, trans., 'The Garden of Forking Paths', p. 126, emphasis added.

solution to the crime, while his counterpart Franz Treviranus looks for an empirical solution. Critics have pointed out the significance of the names in the story, particularly the appearances of the colour red in the names of the detective Erik Lönnrot and the murderer Red Scharlach, but no one seems to have seized upon Treviranus's name (Franz), which may be in homage to Kafka. The story, however, is not about Treviranus and his straightforward investigation, but rather about Lönnrot, who searches for the secret name of God, which he thinks has been encoded into a series of murders.

At the end of the story, Lönnrot's complex quest is exposed as foolish when he is lured to a country home where he discovers that he will be Scharlach's final murder victim. The house is a labyrinth with symmetrical rooms and confusing repetitions, recalling the world Kafka describes in his stories: 'Lönnrot avanzó entre los eucaliptos, pisando confundidas generaciones de rotas hojas rígidas. Vista de cerca, la casa de la quinta de Triste-le-Roy abundaba en inútiles simetrías y en repeticiones maniáticas: a una Diana glacial en un nicho lóbrego correspondía en un segundo nicho otra Diana; un balcón se reflejaba en otro balcón; dobles escalinatas se abrían en doble balaustrada' [Lönnrot made his way forward through the eucalyptus trees, treading upon confused generations of stiff red leaves. Seen at closer quarters, the house belonging to the Villa Triste-Le-Roy abounded in pointless symmetries and obsessive repetitions; a glacial Diana in a gloomy niche was echoed by a second Diana in a second niche; one balcony was reflected in another; double stairways opened into a double balustrade].[54] Despite the fact that Borges (wrongly) believed 'Kafka usó jamás la palabra laberinto . . . el mundo fue para él un laberinto' [Kafka never used the word labyrinth . . . for him, the world was indeed a labyrinth].[55] A portrayal of the world in the form of a labyrinth features in Kafka's 'Eine alltägliche Verwirrung' [A Common Confusion] where two men lose track of each other travelling back and forth between two cities. It also appears in the ship and the buildings in which Karl loses himself in *Amerika*, and in *Der Prozeß* and *Das Schloß*, where Josef K. and K. become lost in hallways and stairwells trying to reach the officials who can explain their circumstances. Borges played with the possibility that the world could be a labyrinth in other stories, including 'Los dos reyes y los dos laberintos' [The Two Kings and the Two Labyrinths] (1939) and

---

[54] Jorge Luis Borges, 'La muerte y la brújula', *Ficciones*, 1944, *Obras completas*, Vol. 1 (Buenos Aires: Emecé, 1996), pp. 499–507 (p. 504); Andrew Hurley, trans., 'Death and the Compass', *Fictions*, 1944, *Collected Fictions* (New York: Viking, 1998), pp. 147–56 (p. 153).

[55] Borges, 'Jorge Luis Borges habla del mundo de Kafka', p. 14.

'Abenjacán el Bojarí, muerto en su laberinto' [Ibn-Hakam al-Bokhari, Murdered in His Labyrinth] (1951).

In 'La muerte y la brújula' Scharlach and Lönnrot propose two competing versions of the world as a labyrinth. The first is the labyrinth in which Scharlach traps Lönnrot, and the second is the more elegant alternative that Lönnrot proposes. Lönnrot prefers order to disorder, and just as he pursues a solution to the crime that is spiritual rather than prosaic, he prefers a labyrinth that is divine rather than man-made. In the moment before his death Lönnrot begs Scharlach to create a labyrinth that preserves the elegant principles of the crime he was desperate to uncover:

> En su laberinto sobran tres líneas—dijo por fin—. Yo sé de un laberinto griego que es una línea única, recta. En esa línea se han perdido tantos filósofos que bien puede perderse un mero *detective*. Scharlach, cuando en otro avatar usted me dé caza, finja (o cometa) un crimen en A, luego un segundo crimen en B, a 8 kilómetros de A, luego un tercer crimen en C, a 4 kilómetros de A y de B, a mitad de camino entre los dos. Aguárdeme después en D, a 2 kilómetros de A y de C, de nuevo a mitad de camino. Mátame en D, como ahora va a matarme en Triste-le-Roy.

> ['There are three lines too many in your labyrinth', he said at last. 'I know of a Greek labyrinth that is but one straight line. So many philosophers have been lost upon that line that a mere detective might be pardoned if he became lost as well. When you hunt me down in another avatar of our lives, Scharlach, I suggest that you fake (or commit) one crime at A, a second crime at B, eight kilometers from A, then a third crime at C, four kilometers from A and B and halfway between them. Then wait for me at D, two kilometers from A and C, once again half way between them. Kill me at D, as you are about to kill me at Triste-le-Roy.']56

This ordered labyrinth is a version of Zeno's paradoxes: it is made of an infinite line divided and divided again until it converges on a single (but theoretically unreachable) point. Scharlach tentatively agrees to this alternative, but immediately after, 'Retrocedió unos pasos. Después, muy cuidadosamente, hizo fuego' [He stepped back a few steps. Then, very carefully, he fired], thus dismissing Lönnrot's intellectual labyrinth as an unreality or game.57

By contrasting Scharlach's labyrinth with Lönnrot's, 'La muerte y la brújula' plays with the tensions between two of the aspects of Kafka's writing that Borges admired: the nightmare and the parable. Lönnrot searches for

---

56 Borges, 'La muerte y la brújula', p. 507, original emphasis; Hurley, trans., 'Death and the Compass', p. 156.
57 Borges, 'La muerte y la brújula', p. 507; Hurley, trans., 'Death and the Compass', p. 156.

parabolic crimes with hidden meanings, such as a series of murders rooted in the quest for the tetragammon. His hope is to find order and (ultimately) God, but instead he uncovers a nightmare. The crimes are devoid of meaning aside from pettiness and trickery, and his death in the labyrinthine Triste-le-Roy ends up being meaningless, not meaning-laden. To some extent, the same can be said of Kafka's stories, where characters sometimes die without finding the meaning they have sought. In 'La muerte y la brújula', as in 'El jardín de senderos que se bifurcan', Borges's debt to Kafka is concealed deep within the text. Both stories emphasize nightmares and Zeno's paradoxes, but they do not have the same number of overt allusions to Kafka as some of Borges's earlier tales. In the case of 'La muerte y la brújula', there is no reference to Borges's interest in authorship either. This does not mean, though, that Borges's interest in Kafka had faded.

Borges's final Kafkian work from this period is 'El milagro secreto'. In this story from 1943 (one year after 'La muerte y la brújula'), Borges's debt to Kafka is laid bare from the opening sentence: 'La noche del 14 de marzo de 1939, en un departamento de la Zeltnergasse de Praga, Jaromir Hladík, autor de la inconclusa tragedia *Los enemigos*, de una *Vindicación de la eternidad* y de un examen de las indirectas fuentes judías de Jakob Boehme, soñó con un largo ajedrez' [On the night of March 14, 1939, in an apartment on Prague's Zeltnergasse, Jaromir Hladik, author of the unfinished tragedy *The Enemies*, a book titled *A Vindication of Eternity*, and a study of Jakob Boehme's indirect Jewish sources, dreamed of a long game of chess].[58] The story's protagonist, Hladík, lives on the Zeltnergasse. Kafka lived on the same street at 'Sixt-Haus' (number two) from 1888 to 1889 and at 'Zu den drei Königen' (number three) from 1896 to 1907; his father's shop was located in the second of these houses, and then at Zeltnergasse 12 from 1906 to 1912.[59]

In his dream, Hladík imagines he is meant to be playing a game of chess in a distant tower. His nightmare calls to mind the Tower of Babel, one of the ideas behind the Kafkian 'La biblioteca de Babel', and it also recalls Zeno's paradoxes by way of chessboards, which Borges *fils* remembered Borges *père* using to teach him the paradoxes:

[58] Jorge Luis Borges, 'El milagro secreto', *Ficciones*, 1944, *Obras completas*, Vol. 1 (Buenos Aires: Emecé, 1996), pp. 508–13 (p. 508); Andrew Hurley, trans., 'The Secret Miracle', *Fictions*, 1944, *Collected Fictions* (New York: Viking, 1998), pp. 157–62 (p. 157).

[59] Richard T. Gray, et al., *A Franz Kafka Encyclopedia* (Westport: Greenwood, 2005), p. 263, 305, 303; Daniel Balderston, *Out of Context: Historical Reference and the Representation of Reality in Borges* (Durham: Duke UP, 1993), p. 58; Edna Aizenberg, 'Kafka, Borges and Contemporary Latin-American Fiction', p. 6; František Vrhel, 'Borges y Praga', *El siglo de Borges*, Vol. 1, ed. Alfonso de Toro and Fernando de Toro (Madrid: Iberoamericana; Frankfurt: Vervuert, 1999) I, pp. 439–49 (p. 445).

No lo disputaban dos individuos sino dos familias ilustres; la partida había sido entablada hace muchos siglos; nadie era capaz de nombrar el olvidado premio, pero se murmuraba que era enorme y quizá *infinito*; las piezas y el tablero estaban en una torre secreta; Jaromir (en el sueño) era el *primogénito* de una de las familias hostiles; en los relojes resonaba la hora de la impostergable jugada; el soñador corría por las arenas de un desierto lluvioso y no lograba recordar las figuras ni las *leyes* del ajedrez.

[*The game was played not by two individuals, but by two illustrious families*; it had been started many centuries in the past. No one could say what the forgotten prize was to be, but it was rumored to be vast, perhaps even *infinite*. The chess pieces and the chessboard themselves were in a secret tower. Jaromir (in the dream) was the *firstborn son* of one of the contending families; the clocks chimed the hour of the inescapable game; the dreamer was running across the sand of a desert in the rain, but he could recall neither the figures nor the *rules* [*laws*] of chess.][60]

The chess match is not between two players but between two families, and it is up to Hladík as the firstborn to represent his entire clan (family is the first element in the 'patria potestad', and Kafka, Borges, and Hladík are all firstborn sons). The prize for winning is unknown but possibly infinite, as confirmed by a series of rumours and whispers reminiscent of those that surround Kafka's Great Wall of China. Hladík does not know the rules of the game he is meant to play, a state of ignorance that recalls *Der Prozeß*, where Josef K. does not know the details of his case. Curiously, the rules of Hladík's game are described as 'leyes' [laws], which strengthens the link with *Der Prozeß* and the unknown law to which Josef K. is subject.

When Hladík wakes from his dream, he returns to a world that is equally incomprehensible and equally Kafkian. He is arrested without an explanation, which is what happens to Josef K. The sentence for his execution appears to be handed down 'pour encourager les autres' [to encourage others] and the story's emphasis is on the administration of the execution to the exclusion of the reasons for it: 'Se fijó el día 29 de marzo, a las nueve a.m. Esa demora (cuya importancia apreciará después el lector) se debía al deseo administrativo de obrar impersonal y pausadamente, como los vegetales y los planetas' [The date was set for March 29, at 9:00 a.m. That delay (whose importance the reader will soon discover) was caused by the administrative desire to work impersonally and deliberately, as vegetables do, or planets].[61] Like Josef K. trying to find out

---

[60] Borges, 'El milagro secreto', p. 508, emphasis added; Hurley, 'The Secret Miracle', p. 157, emphasis added.

[61] Borges, 'El milagro secreto', pp. 508–9; Hurley, trans., 'The Secret Miracle', p. 158.

more about his trial, Hladík does everything he can within his limited capabilities to prevent his execution from taking place. The way in which Borges describes Hladík's circumstances is evocative of *Der Prozeß*: Hladík 'Anticipaba *infinitamente el proceso*, desde el insomne amanecer hasta la misteriosa descarga' [He anticipated the *process endlessly*, from the sleepless dawn to the mysterious discharge of the rifles].[62]

While Josef K. seeks an explanation for and help with his circumstances from officials and lawyers, Hladík is forced to find an escape from his situation alone. He tries to imagine all of the possible ways that he can die, reasoning that anticipation never matches reality. In his mind, Hladík 'murió centenares de muertes, en patios cuyas formas y cuyos ángulos fatigaban la geometría, ametrallado por soldados variables, en número cambiante, que a veces lo ultimaban desde lejos; otras, desde muy cerca' [Hladik died hundreds of deaths—standing in courtyards whose shapes and angles ran the entire gamut of geometry, shot down by soldiers of changing faces and varying numbers who sometimes took aim at him from afar, sometimes from quite near].[63] These deaths have a labyrinthine quality about them, featuring endless courtyards similar to those that entrap Lönnrot in Triste-le-Roy.

Hladík's methods of avoiding death are irrational but his fear of dying is not, and it is this fear that connects the story to Borges's interest in authorship. According to the narrator, Hladík has been sentenced to death by the Nazis because he is Jewish and because they believe he is a well-known and successful translator whose execution will arouse public interest. The Nazis wish to make an example out of him. However, Hladík is not a renowned translator but only a mediocre one (rather than an author like Kafka who just felt he was mediocre), and his achievements have been exaggerated in a publisher's catalogue. He is an echo of Borges's version of Kafka: an author whose tragic circumstances were the impetus for his art and who felt his work amounted to nothing. Hladík resolves to correct this prior to his death by making himself the author he wishes he could have been. Notably, 'Hladík había rebasado los cuarenta años' [Hladík was past forty] when he was sentenced to death.[64] Kafka was 40 the year he died and Borges was 40 when he wrote 'El milagro secreto'; Herbert Quain was said to be over 40 before he was acclaimed as a writer. Hladík's vocation is his identity. He is dissatisfied with his writing and

---

[62] Borges, 'El milagro secreto', p. 509, emphasis added; Hurley, trans., 'The Secret Miracle', p. 158, emphasis added. Note that the Spanish word 'infinitamente' (translated here as 'endlessly') is closer in meaning to 'infinitely', while the word for 'process' ('proceso') is used in the title for the Spanish version of Kafka's *Der Prozeß* (*El proceso*).

[63] Borges, 'El milagro secreto', p. 509; Hurley, trans., 'The Secret Miracle', p. 158.

[64] Borges, 'El milagro secreto', p. 509; Hurley, trans., 'The Secret Miracle', p. 158.

therefore is unhappy with person he has been and the image he has presented of himself. Borges similarly felt like a failure, while Borges thought of Kafka as an author who was disappointed with and wanted to destroy the majority of his work.

To become a great author—to vindicate his life in the way that Borges may have been trying to vindicate his father—Hladík needs to finish his play, *Los enemigos*. He beseeches God for the time to do so in a dream that is a model of the 'patria potestad'. In his dream, Hladík meets a librarian who tells him, 'Dios está en una de las letras de una de las páginas de uno de los cuatrocientos mil tomos del Clementinum. Mis padres y los padres de mis padres han buscado esa letra; yo me he quedado ciego buscándola' [God . . . is in one of the letters on one of the pages of one of the four hundred thousand volumes in the Clementine. My parents and my parents' parents searched for that letter; I myself have gone blind searching for it].[65] Concealed within this quotation about fathers, blindness, and unachieved goals (all references to Borges *fils* and Borges *père*) is an allusion to Kafka: Hladík and the librarians are searching in the Clementinum, the Czech national library, which is the second-largest building in Prague (the only one larger is the castle) and the building where Kafka attended university lectures.[66] Although Hladík has roughly the same chance of success as the librarians who search for meaning in 'La biblioteca de Babel', he finds the secret letter and is granted the sought-after time.

Hladík believes that finishing his play will enable him to justify his existence, and in turn it will also allow him to justify God's existence: 'Si de algún modo existo, si no soy una de tus repeticiones y erratas, existo como autor de *Los enemigos*. Para llevar a término ese drama, *que puede justificarme y justificarte*, requiero un año más' [If . . . I do somehow exist, if I am not one of Thy repetitions or errata, then I exist as the author of *The Enemies*. In order to complete the play, *which can justify me and justify Thee as well*, I need one more year].[67] In order for Hladík to affirm God, God needs to affirm Hladík. The dream in which he secures the miracle that will allow him to do so is a counterpoint to his dream from the story's start: the first is a nightmare where Hladík races towards a goal he cannot reach, so that he can participate in a game he cannot play; the second is a parable about achieving a seemingly impossible goal with incredible ease. The first nightmarish dream prefigures reality, anticipating the horrible

[65] Borges, 'El milagro secreto', p. 511; Hurley, trans., 'The Secret Miracle', p. 160.
[66] Vrhel, 'Borges y Praga', p. 447.
[67] Borges, 'El milagro secreto', p. 511, emphasis added; Hurley, trans., 'The Secret Miracle', p. 160, emphasis added.

circumstances in which Hladík finds himself, while the second dream, like the daydreams where Hladík anticipates his death, does not resemble reality at all.

In trying to imagine his death, Hladík finds that his reality is not as rich as his dreams. This concept is echoed in the experiences of the protagonist of Hladík's *Los enemigos*, who has an uneasy (but accurate) feeling that the world he is living in exists in his head: 'Roemerstadt no conoce las personas que lo importunan, pero tiene la incómoda impresión de haberlas visto ya, tal vez en un sueño' [the persons who come to importune Römerstadt are strangers to him, though he has the uneasy sense that he has seen them before, perhaps in a dream].[68] The blurring of the line between dream and reality that Roemerstadt experiences does not affect the audience, who discover that 'Roemerstadt es el miserable Jaroslav Kubin. El drama no ha ocurrido: es el delirio circular que interminablemente vive y revive Kubin' [Römerstadt is the pitiable Jaroslav Kubin. The play has not taken place; it is the circular delirium that Kubin endlessly experiences and reexperiences].[69] Kubin imagines himself to be Roemerstadt, who is engaged to Julia de Weidenau (the object of Kubin's affection), an upper-class woman similar to Ulrica in *The Secret Mirror*. But just as it turns out that Quigley does not actually know Ulrica in Quain's play, in Hladík's play it is revealed that the protagonist is not engaged to Julia, because he is not Roemerstadt. The delusion that Kubin experiences has an implication for the story's frame narrative: Kubin's circumstances reflect Hladík's own, suggesting that Hladík may be dreaming the secret miracle that has allowed him to finish his play.

There are three other possible, minor links between 'El milagro secreto' and Kafka. First, the name Kubin may be a reference to Alfred Kubin, an Austrian illustrator and author who was an acquaintance of Kafka's. Kubin prepared a set of illustrations for Kafka's 'Ein Landarzt' in 1932, although Borges would never have seen them, as they were not published until 1997.[70] Second, *Los enemigos* conceals within it a biographical reference in the guise of Hladík's former lover: 'Vanamente, procuró recordar a la mujer cuyo símbolo era Julia de Weidenau' [Vainly he tried to recall the woman that Julia de Weidenau had symbolized].[71] Kafka similarly encoded the initials of his fiancée Felice Bauer into 'Das Urteil' and Borges may have had Hladík include this (fictional) biographical reference to Julia

[68] Borges, 'El milagro secreto', p. 510; Hurley, trans., 'The Secret Miracle', p. 159.

[69] Borges, 'El milagro secreto', p. 510; Hurley, trans., 'The Secret Miracle', p. 160.

[70] Sela Bozal, 'Franz Kafka/Alfred Kubin: *Ein Landarzt*. La parabola sin clave', *Cuadernos de Filología Alemana* 1 (2009): 73–88, Web. 10 Nov. 2014 (p. 74).

[71] Borges, 'El milagro secreto', p. 511; Hurley, trans., 'The Secret Miracle', p. 161.

in *Los enemigos* in homage to Kafka.[72] Third, Borges may have incorporated Kafka's struggle as a writer into Hladík's sense of failure, so that 'El milagro secreto' can be read as a commentary on authorship, the dissatisfaction Borges thought Kafka felt with his writing, and Borges's aspiration to justify his existence through his work. In this Kafkian vein, 'El milagro secreto' reads as both a nightmare about the hopelessness of the author's struggle to write a text that justifies the author's existence and an inconclusive parable about the possibility of accomplishing this elusive task.

From 'El acercamiento a Almotásim' in 1936 through to 'El milagro secreto' in 1943, Borges's stories show Kafka's influence. They make use of the themes and techniques that Borges admired in Kafka's works, and they also employ elements that Borges never mentioned but which resonate with Kafka's writing. Reading Borges's writing from the 1930s and 1940s with a focus on Kafka's influence, the concepts of subordination and infinity emerge as common threads in much (though not all) of his work. From Kafka, Borges borrowed the 'patria potestad' and the problems and paradoxes that illustrate it; by incorporating these ideas into his own work alongside his interests in authorship, frame narratives, and self-conscious stories about writing, he produced texts that were influenced by yet also expanded on Kafka's writing. After openly emulating Kafka in 'La lotería en Babilonia' and 'La biblioteca de Babel', Borges said, 'I was aping Kafka. But Kafka was a genius, and I am only a man of letters. I couldn't go on being Kafka.'[73] However, in 'La lotería en Babilonia', 'La biblioteca de Babel', and many of the stories that followed, Borges was not merely aping Kafka. He was building on Kafka to produce works that were distinctly his own. In later years, Borges deviated from Kafka to draw on other influences and to address other concerns. It would not be until the 1970s that he would return to openly emulating Kafka. When he did so, it was in a newly nuanced fashion that contrasted aspects he admired in Kafka's writing with those he wished to emulate from the works of Chesterton.

[72] Franz Kafka, *Tagebücher (1910–1923)* (New York: S. Fischer/Schocken, 1948–49), p. 297; also Franz Kafka, *Tagebücher* (New York: Schocken, 1990), p. 492; Joseph Kresh, trans., *The Diaries of Franz Kafka, 1910–1923* (London: Minerva, 1992), p. 215.
[73] Jorge Luis Borges quoted in Margaret Byrd Boegman, 'Paradox Gained: Kafka's Reception in English from 1930 to 1949 and his Influence on the Early Fiction of Borges, Beckett, and Nabokov' (unpublished doctoral dissertation, U of California, Los Angeles, 1977), p. 213.

6

The Congress of the World

Borges returned to acknowledging Kafka's influence on his writing with 'El Congreso' [The Congress], a story that was published as a stand-alone text in 1971 and subsequently included in *El libro de arena* [*The Book of Sand*] in 1975. At 5800 words, 'El Congreso' is Borges's longest story; only 'Tlön, Uqbar, Orbis Tertius' and 'El inmortal' [The Immortal] rival it in length, at 5700 words and 5100 words respectively. 'El Congreso' may have originally been much longer, perhaps even a novella, as suggested by the story's wandering plot, its subplots, and its substantial character development, all of which are uncommon in Borges's shorter works.

Not only is 'El Congreso' Borges's longest story, it may have also been his longest in the making. The text had a substantial gestation period, with Borges first referring to it in 1945:

> *¿Qué prepara usted?*
>
> Para el remoto y problemático porvenir, una larga narración o novela breve, que se titulará *El Congreso* y que conciliará (hoy no puedo ser más explícito) los hábitos de Whitman y los de Kafka.
>
> [*What are you working on?*
>
> For the distant and problematic future, a long story or short novel, which will be called *El Congreso*, and which will reconcile (I cannot currently be more precise) the tendencies of Whitman and Kafka.][1]

Around the time of the story's publication in 1971, Borges said, '"El Congreso" is a story that has been haunting me for the last thirty or forty years', which would date it to the early 1930s.[2] Although it is impossible to determine when Borges actually conceived of or began writing 'El Congreso', it is probably from after he started writing prose fiction with 'Hombre de la esquina rosada' [Streetcorner Man] in 1933 but from

[1] Jorge Luis Borges, 'De la alta ambición en el arte', *Textos recobrados (1931–1955)* (Buenos Aires: Emecé, 2001), pp. 352–4 (p. 353).

[2] Jorge Luis Borges quoted in Ronald Christ, Alexander Coleman, and Norman Thomas di Giovanni, 'Borges at NYU: 8 April 1971', *Prose for Borges*, eds. Charles Newman and Mary Kinzie (Evanston: Northwestern UP, 1974), pp. 396–411 (p. 411).

before he published *El Aleph* [*The Aleph*] in 1949. This period overlapped with Borges's most prolific phase as a fiction writer, including the time during which he translated and tried to emulate Kafka. It also coincided with the years of Borges *père*'s illness and death.

'El Congreso' tells the story of a journalist named Alejandro Ferri, a member of a mysterious association of people (or congressmen) trying to assemble 'un Congreso del Mundo que representaría a todos los hombres de todas las naciones' [a Congress of the World, which would represent all people of all nations].[3] As part of the Congress, Ferri is sent to London to search for a universal language, which he fails to find. While there, Ferri falls in love with a girl named Beatriz Frost, and during sexual relations, he experiences a sense of union similar to the one sought by the congressmen. When Ferri discovers that Beatriz is not in love with him, he returns to Buenos Aires to fulfil his obligations to the Congress and its chairman, Alejandro Glencoe. Ferri arrives home to learn that—even without his research—Glencoe has discovered that the Congress has always existed and every congressman (indeed, everyone in the world) is already a member. The congressmen celebrate the completion of their project with an all-night carriage ride around Buenos Aires where they share in a sense of pantheistic unity. They disband the next day, never to meet again.

6.1 KAFKA: PROBLEMS AND PARADOXES

Borges was open about Kafka's influence on 'El Congreso', mentioning him in conjunction with the story in 'An Autobiographical Essay', in interviews, and in the epilogue to *El libro de arena*, where he said: 'El opaco principio quiere imitar el de las ficciones de Kafka; el fin quiere elevarse, sin duda en vano, a los éxtasis de Chesterton o de John Bunyan' [The story's murky beginning attempts to imitate the way Kafka's stories begin; its ending attempts, no doubt unsuccessfully, to ascend to the ecstasy of Chesterton or John Bunyan].[4] Based on this comment, it seems as though Borges was using 'El Congreso' to return to Kafka, while also distancing himself from Kafka's influence by turning to that of other authors—particularly Chesterton and Bunyan. This possibility is reinforced by a close reading of 'El Congreso', which reveals not only the

[3] Jorge Luis Borges, 'El Congreso', *El libro de arena*, 1975, *Obras completas*, Vol. 3 (Buenos Aires: Emecé, 1996), pp. 20–32 (p. 23); Andrew Hurley, trans., 'The Congress', *The Book of Sand*, 1975, *Collected Fictions* (New York: Viking, 1998), pp. 422–36 (p. 426).

[4] Jorge Luis Borges, Epilogue, *El libro de arena*, 1975, *Obras completas*, Vol. 3 (Buenos Aires: Emecé, 1996), pp. 72–3 (p. 72); Andrew Hurley, trans., Afterword, *The Book of Sand*, 1975, *Collected Fictions* (New York: Viking, 1998), pp. 484–5 (p. 484).

lasting impact of the Kafkian concepts of subordination, infinity, and the 'patria potestad', but also the extent to which Borges embraced the influence of Chesterton as an alternative to Kafka.

When Borges said that the beginnings of 'El Congreso' were Kafkian, he was referring not only to its initial premises but also to its title:

> ¿El título tiene algún significado especial; alguna connotación política—me refiero a la 'institución Congreso'—, algo más allá de lo que representa del cuento?
>
> No. Ninguna connotación especial. Salvo que quiere entenderse como ello el sentido de homenaje que tiene a Kafka. *El congreso* a mí me hace recordar títulos de Kafka, por ejemplo *El castillo*, *El proceso* ...
>
> [*Does the title have some special significance; some political connotation—I am referring to the 'Congressional institution'—something beyond what is portrayed in the story?*
>
> No. No special significance, unless you want to interpret it in the sense that it is in homage to Kafka. For me, *El Congreso* brings to mind Kafka's titles, such as *The Castle*, *The Trial*...][5]

Like *Das Schloß* and *Der Prozeß*, 'El Congreso' leaves many details unexplained, and its conclusion leaves the sought-after (and once-glimpsed) Congress out of reach. The two obsessions that Borges identified in Kafka—subordination and infinity—both appear in the story's major plot points: in Glencoe's efforts to establish the Congress, in Ferri's trip to London in search of a universal language, and in the attempts of Twirl (one of the congressmen) to assemble a congressional library. These aspects of the story mark a return to the paradoxes and problems that featured in many of Borges's earlier Kafkian works, and they also set the stage for Borges's turn away from Kafka in the story's somewhat uncharacteristic conclusion.

The text's central thread is Glencoe's plan for a Congress with representatives for all of the world's citizens, a project that is beset by problems related to infinity. Foremost among these problems are those that the congressmen face when they try to define the criteria for their members:

> Sugirió que, sin ir más lejos, don Alejandro Glencoe podía representar a los hacendados, pero también a los orientales y también a los grandes precursores y también a los hombres de barba roja y a los que están sentados en un sillón. Nora Erfjord era noruega. ¿Representaría a las secretarias, a las noruegas o simplemente a todas las mujeres hermosas? ¿Bastaba un ingeniero para representar a todos los ingenieros, incluso los de Nueva Zelandia?

[5] Vicente Zito Lema, 'Jorge Luis Borges y su ultimo libro: "El Congreso" que yo soñé (1973)', *El otro Borges: Entrevistas (1960–1986)*, ed. Fernando Mateo (Buenos Aires: Equis, 1997), pp. 38–48 (p. 45).

[He suggested, therefore, that (to take but one example) don Alejandro Glencoe might represent ranchers, but also Uruguayans, as well as founding fathers and red-bearded men and men sitting in armchairs. Nora Erfjord was Norwegian. Would she represent secretaries, Norwegians, or simply all beautiful women? Was one engineer sufficient to represent all engineers, even engineers from New Zealand?][6]

There are two obstacles inherent in the congressmen's approach to defining their membership. The first lies in determining whether there can be fewer categories than there are people in the world. The second lies in trying to decide which categories any individual member of the Congress will represent. This second problem is contained in the amusingly absurd suggestion that Glencoe stand for all men sitting in armchairs. Since all men will eventually sit down and no man can stay seated forever, it is unlikely that the individuals who fill the categories (if the categories can ever be established) can be chosen with any degree of certainty. As Twirl points out, 'Planear una asamblea que representara a todos los hombres era como fijar el número exacto de los arquetipos platónicos, enigma que ha atareado durante siglos la perplejidad de los pensadores' [Designing a body of men and women which would represent all humanity was akin to fixing the exact number of Platonic archetypes, an enigma that has engaged the perplexity of philosophers for centuries].[7] Borges was no stranger to this problem, having written many works about the impossibility of capturing in writing even a single Platonic archetype.

No matter how many categories the congressmen define, the number they require to ensure that their membership is exhaustive perpetually slips away from them in a manner reminiscent of Zeno's paradoxes. The categories the congressmen propose for the Congress's members are either too broad or too narrow to be useful. This problem seems to be resolved when Glencoe realizes at the story's end that everyone in the world is a member of the Congress. However, this discovery reveals another Kafkian problem. By uncovering the fact that the Congress has been everywhere all along, Glencoe shows it to be a version of the commonplace secret: 'the divine scheme of the universe is unknowable, and therefore classification and representation are impossible, and therefore an account of things must include them all.'[8]

Similar Kafkian problems are present in the story's subplots. Twirl's efforts to establish a congressional library start out as a modest project

---

[6] Borges, 'El Congreso', p. 24; Hurley, trans., 'The Congress', p. 427.

[7] Borges, 'El Congreso', p. 24; Hurley, trans., 'The Congress', pp. 427–8.

[8] Shimon Sandbank, *After Kafka: The Influence of Kafka's Fiction* (Athens: U of Georgia P, 1989), pp. 90–1.

supposedly meant to help the congressmen with their research, but (like the Congress itself, which grows to include the world's citizens) the library expands to contain every possible book. The process of doing so evokes Zeno's paradoxes:

> Twirl... había invocado a Plinio el Joven, según el cual no hay libro tan malo que no encierre algo bueno, y había propuesto la compra indiscriminada de colecciones de *La Prensa*, de tres mil cuatrocientos ejemplares de *Don Quijote*, en diversos formatos, del epistolario de Balmes, de tesis universitarias, de cuentas, de boletines y de programas de teatro.... Los desmesurados paquetes iban apilándose ahora, sin catálogo ni fichero, en las habitaciones del fondo y en la bodega del caserón de don Alejandro.

> [Twirl had invoked Pliny the Younger—who had affirmed that there was no book so bad that it didn't contain some good—to suggest that the Congress indiscriminately purchase collections of *La Prensa*, thirty-four hundred copies (in various formats) of *Don Quijote*, Balmes' *Letters*, and random collections of university dissertations, short stories, bulletins, and theater programs.... The enormous packages now began piling up, uncatalogued and without card files, in the back rooms and wine cellar of don Alejandro's mansion.][9]

The library becomes an indiscriminate collection of useless, disordered texts that are no help to the congressmen. Ferri describes it as like being 'en el centro de un círculo creciente, que se agranda sin fin, alejándose' [at the center of an ever-widening, endlessly expanding circle that seemed to be moving farther and farther beyond one's reach].[10] If the Zenoesque library were to continue growing, it might one day contain all possible books, just like the library in 'La biblioteca de Babel' [The Library of Babel]. As Borges has shown, the repercussions of such a library are terrible: the existence of every possible book undermines the meaning contained within any one book, while the possibility that there is meaning somewhere in the library is compromised by the fact that it cannot necessarily be found.

Ultimately, however, the congressional library produces a positive outcome. Twirl may have established the library in order to hinder (and not affirm) the Congress, but his creation—in mirroring Glencoe's project— leads Glencoe to the realization that the Congress has existed all along. Twirl concedes this when he says, 'He querido hacer el mal y hago el bien' [I have tried to do evil yet I have done good].[11] Motivated by the discovery that Twirl's actions have engendered, Glencoe burns the library books and sells the ranch where the congressmen were to meet, erasing the Congress's

---

[9] Borges, 'El Congreso', p. 29; Hurley, trans., 'The Congress', p. 433.
[10] Borges, 'El Congreso', p. 25; Hurley, trans., 'The Congress', p. 428.
[11] Borges, 'El Congreso', p. 32; Hurley, trans., 'The Congress', p. 435.

physical presence. In doing so, he extends the Congress to include the entire world.

One of the points at which the congressional project echoes Kafka is in the quest to find an ideal language. In 'Beim Bau der chinesischen Mauer' [The Great Wall of China], ambiguous and archaic language renders communication between neighbours impossible and the limits of the Great Wall difficult to define. In 'El Congreso', a similar lack of a shared language prevents the potential congressmen from conversing with each other. Ferri cannot speak with the gauchos on Glencoe's ranch, while those who attend the congressional meetings offer each other language lessons to facilitate communication among themselves. Ferri travels to London to search for an ideal language, but he fails to find a solution to the Congress's problems. Perhaps as a nod to this, Ferri is credited with writing *Breve examen del idioma analítico de John Wilkins* [*A Brief Examination of the Analytic Language of John Wilkins*] based on his research. His book is an echo of Borges's 'El idioma analítico de John Wilkins' [John Wilkins's Analytical Language], which explores the 'ambigüedades, redundancias y deficiencias' [ambiguities, redundancies, and deficiencies] of ideal and artificial languages, ultimately dismissing them as impractical.[12] The shortcomings that plague Wilkins's analytic language as arbitrary and baseless are reminiscent of the shortcomings that the congressmen face when trying to choose their members and build their library. They are also reminiscent of the shortcomings that prevent Kafka's villagers from sharing news of the Great Wall. Language is insufficient because of its infinite variability, and because of the slide in meaning that this variability brings. Trying to pin down a more exact language, like trying to define the Platonic archetypes, is a problem for which Ferri (and Borges) can find no solution.

6.2 BORGES *PÈRE*: FATHER AND SON

The problems and paradoxes of 'El Congreso' are rooted in one of what Borges referred to as the two obsessions in Kafka's writing: infinity. Kafka's other obsession, subordination, also features in the story, where it serves as the bridge between Borges's interest in Kafka and his obligation to Borges *père*, and where it subsequently connects the story to Borges's desire for 'El Congreso' to echo Chesterton. As Borges explained in his

---

[12] Borges, 'El Congreso', p. 20; Hurley, trans., 'The Congress', p. 422; Jorge Luis Borges, 'El idioma analítico de John Wilkins', *Otras inquisiciones*, 1952, *Obras completas*, Vol. 2 (Buenos Aires: Emecé, 1996), pp. 84–7 (p. 85); Eliot Weinberger, trans., 'John Wilkins' Analytical Language', *Selected Non-Fictions* (New York: Viking, 1999), pp. 229–32 (p. 231).

writing on Kafka, subordination is implicit in the 'patria potestad'—the structure that pulls together the authority of the father, the fatherland, and the patriarchy. In 'El Congreso', the 'patria potestad' features twice: in the surrogate father–son relationship that Ferri develops with Irala and Glencoe, and in the subtly intimated God–Man relationship that appears during the celebratory carriage ride. The first of these versions of the 'patria potestad' reinforces Borges's assertion that the story's initial premises are Kafkian, while the second version marks Borges's turn towards Chesterton in the conclusion.

The lowest level of the 'patria potestad' is that of the son's subordination to his father. Borges believed that Kafka's writing grew (in part) out of his relationship with his father, and the same may be true of Borges's writing. In support of this, it is possible to connect Borges *fils*'s composition of 'El Congreso' with Borges *père*'s *El caudillo* [*The Chieftain*], especially in light of Borges mentioning the two in proximity to each other in 'An Autobiographical Essay':

> At present, I am finishing a long tale called 'The Congress'. Despite its Kafkian title, I hope it will turn out more in the line of Chesterton. The setting is Argentine and Uruguayan. For twenty years, I have been boring my friends with the raw plot. Finally, as I was telling it to my wife, she made me see that no further elaboration was needed. I have another project that has been pending for an even longer period of time—that of revising and perhaps rewriting my father's novel *The Caudillo*, as he asked me to years ago. We had gone as far as discussing many of the problems; I like to think of the undertaking as a continued dialogue and a very real collaboration.[13]

Earlier in 'An Autobiographical Essay', Borges says he wanted to rewrite *El caudillo* 'in a straightforward way, with all the fine writing and purple patches left out', because he felt partly to blame for its failings.[14] The mention of *El caudillo* alongside 'El Congreso' suggests that the two texts may have been related in Borges's mind. This possibility is reinforced by reading Borges's use of the 'patria potestad' in 'El Congreso' through the lenses of *El caudillo* and Borges *fils*'s obligations to Borges *père*.

Borges suggested that writing was a vocation that could be passed down by a father to his son. This inheritance features in Ferri's belief that he is obliged to write the story of the Congress on Irala's behalf: 'La pluma de José Fernández Irala, el inmerecidamente olvidado poeta de *Los mármoles*, era la predestinada a esta empresa, pero ya es tarde' [It was the pen of José

---

[13] Jorge Luis Borges, 'An Autobiographical Essay', *The Aleph and Other Stories: 1933–1969*, trans. and ed. Norman Thomas di Giovanni (London: Jonathan Cape, 1968), pp. 203–60 (p. 259).

[14] Borges, 'An Autobiographical Essay', pp. 219–20.

Fernández Irala, the undeservedly forgotten poet of *Los mármoles* [*The Marbles*], that fate had destined for this enterprise, but now it is too late].[15] For Irala, 'el periodista escribe para el olvido y que su anhelo era escribir para la memoria y el tiempo' [the journalist writes to be forgotten, while he himself wanted to write to be remembered, and to last]; Ferri takes up his charge by becoming a writer to perpetuate Irala's memory.[16] In doing so, Ferri hopes to accomplish what Irala could not. Just as Ferri is obliged to Irala, he seems to have a similar responsibility to Glencoe, whose accomplishments in creating the Congress will not be known unless Ferri publicizes them with his tale. These filial bonds echo Borges's own, since it fell to Borges *fils* to succeed where Borges *père* could not.

The idea that Irala and Glencoe can be viewed as father figures is borne out by a close reading of the text. Irala takes Ferri under his wing when Ferri first moves to Buenos Aires, and he arranges Ferri's invitation to the Congress. A familial connection between the two is hinted at by similarities in their names: Ferri's surname combines the first portions of Fernández and Irala; Fernández links to *Martín Fierro* by way of José Hernández and therefore back to Ferri again, since Ferri and Fierro are similar; the first syllables in Ferri and Irala both refer to iron.[17] Their relationship is also implied by Ferri's description of Irala in a way that recalls Borges *père*. Irala is the author of a collection of poetry whose classical title, *Los mármoles*, evokes the modernista style Borges *père* favoured. As with Borges *père*'s writing, only those with a personal connection to the author remember Irala's work. There is a similar link between Ferri and Glencoe, also courtesy of their shared name: 'En el tranvía [Irala] me dijo que las reuniones preliminares tenían lugar los sábados y que don Alejandro Glencoe, tal vez movido por mi nombre, ya había dado su firma' [On the trolley, Irala told me that the preliminary meetings took place on Saturday and that don Alejandro Glencoe, perhaps inspired by my name, had already given leave for me to attend].[18] Glencoe gives Ferri access to libraries and books, and he funds Ferri's research trip abroad. In exchange, Ferri works to foster (and subsequently preserve) Glencoe's accomplishment. All of this calls to mind Borges *fils*'s relationship with Borges *père*: their shared name, the son's sense of owing a debt to his father for facilitating and encouraging his development as a writer, and the son's need to compensate for the father's shortcomings as an author.

---

[15] Borges, 'El Congreso', p. 21; Hurley, trans., 'The Congress', p. 423.
[16] Borges, 'El Congreso', p. 21; Hurley, trans., 'The Congress', p. 424.
[17] Peter Standish, '"El Congreso" in the Works of J. L. Borges', *Hispanic Review* 55.3 (1987): 347–59, *JSTOR*, Web, 7 Nov. 2009 (p. 350).
[18] Borges, 'El Congreso', p. 22; Hurley, trans., 'The Congress', p. 424.

While Ferri is largely positive about his relationships with Glencoe and Irala, Borges believed that Kafka's writing revealed tensions with his father. Kafka's stories are sometimes about a son's sense of being beholden to and controlled by a father figure; this is particularly true of 'Das Urteil' [The Judgement]. Just as Borges saw Kafka's writing as growing out of his negative relationship with Kafka *père*, Borges *fils* may have identified Borges *père*'s sense of inferiority compared to his deceased war-hero father (Borges *grand-père*) in *El caudillo*. Alicia Jurado has hesitantly pointed to *El caudillo*'s biographical resonances: 'El joven personaje de *El Caudillo*, Carlos Dubois, tímido, introspectivo, amigo de los libros y soñador, pudo reflejar al autor de la novela' [The young character in *El caudillo*, Carlos Dubois, is shy, introspective, a book-lover and a dreamer, and could be a reflection of the novel's author].[19] Similarly, Antonio Pagés Larraya has written, 'No sugiero un ingenuo paralelo Tavares-Dubois, Borges padre e hijo. Pero no hay sin duda un éxtasis de la conciencia en todo lo que este texto desenmascara' [I am not suggesting an ingenuous parallel between Tavares and Dubois, between Borges father and son. But there is obviously a delightful sense of awareness brought about by all that this text reveals].[20] With an eye to a specific connection between Dubois and Borges *père*, Williamson has suggested that *El caudillo* portrays Borges *père*'s sense of inadequacy compared to his father, a sentiment that is translated into the relationship between the strong, successful Tavares and the weak, intellectual Dubois.[21]

The significance of the father–son relationship in Borges *père*'s novel makes it possible to read *El caudillo* alongside Kafka. For example, Kafka's Georg Bendemann and Borges *père*'s Dubois both attempt to gain their fathers' respect by demonstrating their independence through romances and by taking control of family affairs. In response, Bendemann *père* (as a father) and Tavares (as a surrogate) deny their sons' passage into adulthood by sentencing them to death: Georg Bendemann complies with his father's order to commit suicide, and Tavares has Dubois murdered. Like Kafka, Borges *père* made use of philosophies such as Zeno's paradoxes and eternal return; a sense of failure pervades both their works. While it would have been improbable for Kafka to have read Borges *père*'s writing or for Borges *père* to have read Kafka's, Borges may have perceived these similarities. In the manner of 'Kafka y sus precursores' [Kafka and His

---

[19] Alicia Jurado, Prologue, *El caudillo* (Buenos Aires: Academia Argentina de Letras, 1989), pp. 11–23 (p. 14).

[20] Antonio Pagés Larraya, '*El caudillo*: Una novela del padre de Borges', *Repertorio Latinoamericano* 2nd ser. 5.36 (1979): 3–6 (p. 6).

[21] Edwin Williamson, *Borges, A Life* (London: Viking, 2004), p. 30.

Precursors], a reading of Kafka can help make sense of Borges *père* and a reading of *El caudillo* can help make sense of 'El Congreso'.

If Borges *fils* saw echoes of his father's novel in Kafka's writing, he may have incorporated aspects of Kafka into 'El Congreso' as a way of mediating or responding to Borges *père*'s influence. Williamson has suggested that 'Borges composed *The Congress* on the pattern of his father's novel, and . . . that he was seeking in part to fulfil his dying father's request that he rewrite *El Caudillo*'.[22] Williamson's assertion that Borges *fils* was rewriting Borges *père*'s novel with 'El Congreso' is supported by similarities between the two works. Both involve powerful patriarchs (Tavares, Glencoe), sinister advisers (El Gringo, Twirl), and romances cut short (Dubois and Marisabel, Ferri and Beatriz). In both, the son succumbs to the expectations of the father (or surrogate father).

The possibility that Borges was rewriting *El caudillo* in 'El Congreso' is augmented by the fact that his story shows *modernista* echoes. By drawing on Kafka and Chesterton, among others, and by loosely redrafting *El caudillo*, Borges was borrowing from pre-existing texts—a *modernista* trait that features heavily in Borges's works, and not just in 'El Congreso'. More uncharacteristically, 'El Congreso' made use of the *modernista* trope of rejecting the material world in favour of erotic fulfilment and cosmic harmony, of which there are three instances in his story: (*i*) Ferri's tryst with Beatriz, (*ii*) the burning of the congressional library, and (*iii*) the celebratory carriage ride. These moments mark rejections of the physical world in favour of the spiritual one, and they provide a sense of fulfilment that is unusual for Borges's stories.

6.3 CHESTERTON: GOD AND MAN

The (tentatively) happy conclusion to 'El Congreso' marks a departure from Kafka, whose presence in the story—as Borges himself noted—was limited to its beginning. While it is not the purpose of this study to analyse all of Borges's precursors (or even all three of Chesterton, Bunyan, and Whitman—the other influences Borges named with reference to 'El Congreso'), it is productive to look at one to understand why Borges may have turned away from Kafka in 'El Congreso' even as he returned to openly emulating him him after a nearly thirty-year break.

Of the authors who Borges mentions with respect to 'El Congreso', the one who provides the strongest contrast with Kafka is Chesterton. In his

[22] Ibid., p. 250.

critical writing, Borges is clear about the fundamental difference in authorial intent that separates Kafka from Chesterton. He says that Kafka 'Hubiera preferido la redacción de páginas felices y su honradez no condescendió a fabricarlas' [would have preferred to write a few happy pages, but his honor would not let him fabricate them]; by contrast, he says that Chesterton 'Hubiera podido ser un Edgar Allan Poe o un Kafka; prefirió—debemos agradecérselo—ser Chesterton' [could have been an Edgar Allan Poe or a Kafka, but he chose—and for this we should be thankful—to be Chesterton].[23] In choosing to emulate Chesterton for the conclusion to 'El Congreso', Borges may have been making a similar, conscious decision to swerve away from Kafka and towards a happier, Chestertonian sort of writing.

Although critics tend to compare Borges's writing to Chesterton's Father Brown stories, 'El Congreso' most resembles *The Man Who Was Thursday: A Nightmare* (1908). The novel is about Gabriel Syme, who is hired by the chief of the secret police to join a seven-member anarchists' council on which he adopts the persona of Thursday and is expected to participate in a bombing. During one of the council meetings, the anarchist chief Sunday reveals that Tuesday is really an undercover police-man, and Syme begins to worry for his safety. Syme is pursued by Friday, who confronts him and reveals that he is also a policeman. A series of chases occur, and eventually all of the anarchists are exposed as policemen. The story concludes when they are invited to a party thrown by Sunday, who admits to being the chief anarchist, the police chief, and also 'Pan, or Nature, or God'.[24] The policemen celebrate this discovery with a dance orchestrated by Sunday to mark their union with the pantheistic.

Like 'El Congreso', *The Man Who Was Thursday* is about a secret council with members who reveal their identities to each other gradually. It involves betrayals and plots to undermine collective projects, and it concludes with a celebration that also marks a failure. In Chesterton, this is the failure to defeat the anarchists, while in Borges this is the failure to establish the Congress. Most strikingly, both *The Man Who Was Thursday* and 'El Congreso' reach fully realized, mystical moments of transcendence. When Sunday shows himself to be an embodiment of the pantheistic,

[23] Jorge Luis Borges, Prologue, *El buitre* (Buenos Aires: La Ciudad, 1979), pp. 7–11 (p. 8); Eliot Weinberger, trans., 'Franz Kafka, The Vulture', *Selected Non-Fictions* (New York: Viking, 1999), pp. 501–3 (p. 501); Jorge Luis Borges and María Ester Vázquez, 'Nuestro siglo', *Introducción a la literatura inglesa*, 1965, *Obras completas en colaboración* (Buenos Aires: Emecé, 1979), pp. 850–7 (p. 851).
[24] Kingsley Amis, 'The Poet and the Lunatics', 1971, *G. K. Chesterton: A Half Century of Views*, ed. D.J. Conlon (Oxford: Oxford UP, 1987), pp. 269–73 (p. 271).

Syme experiences 'an unnatural buoyancy in his body and a crystal simplicity in his mind' as though he were 'in possession of some impossible good news'.[25] This is likely to have been the feeling to which Borges was referring when he said that he was hoping to emulate a Chestertonian conclusion to 'El Congreso'. There are two parts of Borges's story that approximate this Chestertonian sense of ecstasy: one reworks a similar scene from *El caudillo*, while the other echoes *The Man Who Was Thursday*.

The first moment of ecstasy in 'El Congreso' is Ferri's tryst with Beatriz. Alluded to in the story's title (a pun on sexual congress), Ferri's union with Beatriz may be the Congress the others have been seeking.[26] During their affair, Ferri experiences what seems to be a sense of oneness where he feels himself joined to Beatriz:

> Oh noches, oh compartida y tibia tiniebla, oh el amor que fluye en la sombra como un río secreto, oh aquel momento de la dicha en que cada uno es los dos, oh la inocencia y el candor de la dicha, oh la unión en la que nos perdíamos para perdernos luego en el sueño, oh las primeras claridades del día y yo contemplándola.

> [Oh nights, oh shared warm darkness, oh the love that flows in shadow like a secret river, oh that moment of joy in which two are one, oh innocence and openness of delight, oh the union into which we entered, only to lose ourselves afterward in sleep, oh the first soft lights of day, and myself contemplating her.][27]

This experience has a precedent in *El caudillo*, when Dubois is joined with Marisabel to experience a sense of being outside of time and the self:

> Todo su ser sacudido por el salmo de su deseo y la ternura de Marisabel que parecía decir: Soy tuya. En mi rostro la primavera de las rosas es eternal, el sol de mis ojos no se abate nunca. He escuchado de los labios del mundo el cantar de amores y lo he amasado en besos para que tú lo comprendas mejor. Las manzanas de mis pechos maduraron el huerto de Paraíso, soy la seda de los nidos, la sombra adormecida bajo el bochorno solar. . . . Una sola curva de mi cuerpo, vaso sagrado, arca de los destinos de la raza.

> [His entire being was shaken by the psalm of his desire and the tenderness of Marisabel, who seemed to say: I am yours. In my face, the roses spring eternal, the sun of my eyes will never set. I have heard the song of lovers from the lips of the world and I have gathered it together in kisses so that you will better understand it. The apples of my breast ripen in the orchard of

---

[25] Gilbert Keith Chesterton, *The Man Who Was Thursday: A Nightmare* (New York: Random House, 2001), p. 182.

[26] Standish, '"El Congreso" in the works of J. L. Borges', p. 351.

[27] Borges, 'El Congreso', pp. 28–9; Hurley, trans., 'The Congress', p. 432.

Paradise, I am the silk of the nests...A single bend of my body, sacred vessel, ark of the destinies of the human race.][28]

Both Borges *père* and Borges *fils* describe sexual congress in a lyrical fashion, employing nature imagery and hyperbolic language reminiscent of the Song of Songs. In light of this, Williamson has suggested that the language of Borges's text links 'El Congreso' with Borges *père*'s 'El cantar de los cantares', contributing further to the possibility that Borges *fils* was trying to improve upon his father's writing with his story.[29]

Where 'El Congreso' and *El caudillo* differ from each other is in Ferri's and Dubois's responses to their romances. Dubois's sense of oneness fades the morning after his congress with Marisabel. He is overcome by the feeling that he has disappointed Tavares, which he tries to rectify by asking for Marisabel's hand in marriage, but Tavares has Dubois killed. By contrast, when Ferri cannot persuade Beatriz to marry him, he realizes that their connection was limited and fleeting, and if he is to help with Glencoe's project, he needs to find a lasting union that can be shared among all those who seek the Congress. Tavares forcibly brings Dubois back to his obligations, while Ferri voluntarily returns to the 'patria potestad'. Unlike Dubois, who is killed on the orders of his surrogate father, Ferri is rewarded by his surrogate father with an experience of oneness that surpasses his union with Beatriz.

Chesterton provided Borges with the alternative to Ferri's short-lived, limited experience of oneness. *The Man Who Was Thursday* offers a positive portrayal of the 'patria potestad' by celebrating the relationship between God and Man. It concludes with an all-encompassing glimpse of the divine—an experience that Borges borrows for the climax of 'El Congreso'. Like Syme's pantheistic dance, Ferri's celebratory carriage ride takes in the entire world. Both scenes are affirmations of the existence of a cosmic unity:

> Algo de lo que entrevimos perdura—el rojizo paredón de la Recoleta, el amarillo paredón de la cárcel, una pareja de hombres bailando en una esquina sin ochava, un atrio ajedrezado con una verja, las barreras del tren, mi casa, un mercado, la insondable y húmeda noche—pero ninguna de esas cosas fugaces, que acaso fueron otras, importa. Importa haber sentido que nuestro plan, del cual más de una vez nos burlamos, existía realmente y secretamente y era el universo y nosotros.

> [Something of what we glimpsed that night remains—the reddish wall of the Recoleta, the yellow wall of the prison, two men on a street corner dancing the tango the way the tango was danced in the old days, a checkerboard

---

[28] Jorge Guillermo Borges, *El caudillo*, 1921 (Buenos Aires: Academia Argentina de Letras, 1989), p. 147.

[29] Williamson, *Borges, A Life*, p. 401.

entryway and a wrought-iron fence, the railings of the railroad station, my house, a market, the damp and unfathomable night—but none of these fleeting things (which may well have been others) matters. What matters is having felt that the institution of ours, which more than once we had made jests about, truly and secretly existed, and that it was the universe and ourselves.]

Syme seemed to see every shape in Nature imitated in some crazy costume. There was a man dressed as a windmill with enormous sails, a man dressed as an elephant, a man dressed as a balloon; the two last, together, seemed to keep the thread of their farcical adventures.... There were a thousand other such objects, however. There was a dancing lamp-post, a dancing apple-tree, a dancing ship. One would have thought that the untamable tune of some mad musician had set all the common objects of field and street dancing an eternal jig.[30]

Ferri and Syme both experience visions of the universe where everyday things are joined together in an ecstatic whole. Through the pantheistic dance that Sunday orchestrates, Chesterton's policemen realize that they collectively represent God's creation. The congressmen similarly discover that they are 'un pájaro que es todos los pájaros, un sol que es todas las estrellas y el sol' [a bird that is all birds, a sun that is the sun and yet all stars].[31] Borges's congressmen are the mystical Simurgh: they are the divine both individually and collectively, and they are connected in a oneness that is antithetical to the hierarchy of the 'patria potestad'.

The clarity, knowledge, and wholeness the congressmen experience as the fulfilment of their project is hinted at but unachieved (or at least undescribed) in many of Borges's Kafkian stories: it is the sought-after union with Almotásim in 'El acercamiento a Almotásim' [The Approach to Al-Mu'tasim], it is the discovery of the secret letter in the Clementinum in 'El milagro secreto' [The Secret Miracle], and it is the 'elegante esperanza' [elegant hope] that motivates the narrator in 'La biblioteca de Babel'. By contrast, the conclusion to *The Man Who Was Thursday* offered Borges a resolution to the Kafkian problems of subordination, infinity, and the 'patria potestad'. It provided him with a model for consciously choosing an earnest, happy ending of the sort that Kafka was unable to write.

'*And yet, and yet...*' in typical Borgesian fashion, the celebratory feeling that marks the successful completion of the congressmen's project cannot be sustained.[32] Perhaps because it was so out of character, Borges

---

[30] Borges, 'El Congreso', p. 32; Hurley, trans., 'The Congress', pp. 435–6; Chesterton, *The Man Who Was Thursday: A Nightmare*, p. 175.

[31] Borges, 'El Congreso', p. 31; Hurley, trans., 'The Congress', p. 435.

[32] Borges, 'Nueva refutación del tiempo', *Otras inquisiciones*, 1952, *Obras completas*, Vol. 2 (Buenos Aires: Emecé, 1996), pp. 135–49 (p. 149), original emphasis.

abandoned his attempt at Chestertonian happiness even before he finished 'El Congreso'. In the frame narrative, Ferri concedes that although pantheistic oneness might exist, writing is not the route to finding or holding onto it. The shortcomings of language, the impossibility of writing certain texts, and the inevitable passage of time all stand between the author and the experience he wishes to convey. Ferri finds that these obstacles prevent him from repeating his experience of ecstasy: 'Sin mayor esperanza, he buscado a lo largo de los años el sabor de esa noche; alguna vez creí recuperarla en la música, en el amor, en la incierta memoria, pero no ha vuelto, salvo una sola madrugada, en un sueño' [With no great hope, through all these years I have sought the savor of that night; once in a great while I have thought I caught a snatch of it in a song, in lovemaking, in uncertain memory, but it has never fully come back to me save once, one early morning, in a dream].[33] This frustration contrasts starkly with the experience of Chesterton's Syme, who 'could never see one of those particular objects' from the pantheistic dance 'without thinking that it was a strayed reveller from that revel of masquerade'.[34] Syme repeatedly relives his moment of pantheistic oneness, but Ferri cannot even fully remember his. When he tries to address this loss by writing his story, he finds that language is just as insufficient for describing the Congress as it was for creating it in the first place. Ferri's sense of ecstasy during the congressional carriage ride is as limited and temporary as his sense of union with Beatriz. He has glimpsed Chestertonian happiness, but nothing more.

Borges's story differs from Chesterton's novel insofar as the happiness that Ferri experiences is fleeting. By contrast, it differs from Kafka's stories insofar as Ferri is able to experience happiness at all. As such, 'El Congreso' ends in a manner unique to Borges. A sought-after goal is grasped, only to be snatched away again in the frame narrative—a technique Borges used in many other stories, including 'El jardín de senderos que se birfurcan' [The Garden of Forking Paths] and 'El milagro secreto'. While 'El Congreso' may not achieve the enduring ecstasy that Borges identified in Chesterton, the happiness that is attained is not completely undone by the Kafkian problems and paradoxes that Borges admired and emulated. 'El Congreso' combines Kafkian subordination, infinity, and the 'patria potestad' with a Chestertonian sense of ecstasy and pantheistic oneness to produce a story that, while not Borges's most successful, is evocative of his aims, interests, and obligations as a writer and a son.

---

[33] Borges, 'El Congreso', p. 32; Hurley, trans., 'The Congress', p. 436.
[34] Chesterton, *The Man Who Was Thursday*, pp. 181–2, 175.

7

Writing about Kafka, Writing about Writing

In 1957, Borges published 'Borges y yo' [Borges and I], a short piece about the boundary between biography and fiction. Barely more than a paragraph long, it explores the tension between Borges's private and public selves. In the text, the narrator Borges explains how things that used to belong to his private identity are incorporated into his public identity once he includes them in his writing. This means that the interests that Borges once thought of as central to who he was—his fascination with the suburbs, and later with time and infinity—have become public property. Through his writing, Borges engendered a fictional son, an avatar of himself made up of all the things about which he wrote. His writing preserved a public persona who continued to exist in the minds of his readers even when he (the private Borges) developed new interests and therefore ceased to be the person his readers believed him to be.

The idea that there are two versions of the author—one who exists for the author and another who exists for the readers—is related to Borges's views on literary precursors. In 'Tlön, Uqbar, Orbis Tertius', Borges imagined a world where readers drew connections between two unrelated literary works by attributing both to the same imaginary writer. He offered an applied version of this approach to reading in 'Kafka y sus precursores' [Kafka and His Precursors], where he suggested that readers could assign meaning to an author's works based on their own past reading, regardless of whether the author in question had (or even could have) read those texts.

For an author who played so often with the concepts of identity and attribution, 'Borges y yo' has a surprisingly melancholy tone. In the text's final line, the narrator wonders, 'No se cual de los dos escribe esta pagina' [I am not sure which of us it is that's writing this page], a statement that seems to highlight Borges's resignation to—or his fear of—losing himself through his writing.[1] Elsewhere, Borges expressed an inverse fear, which

---

[1] Jorge Luis Borges, 'Borges y yo', *El hacedor*, 1960, *Obras completas*, Vol. 2 (Buenos Aires: Emecé, 1996), p. 186; Andrew Hurley, trans. 'Borges and I', *The Maker*, 1960, *Collected Fictions* (New York: Viking, 1998), p. 324.

was that without writing he would leave nothing behind for posterity, and therefore he would have done nothing to justify his existence. Thus Borges is caught in a double bind: he cannot leave a legacy if he does not write, but he will lose his private sense of self to his public persona if he does write. With this in mind, the narrator of 'Borges y yo' defends his decision to relinquish himself to his public persona, who he hopes will be able to use the material he (the private Borges) has provided to write a text that will serve as a justification for them both. The hope that such a work is possible is at the core of many of Borges's pieces on writing and identity: it appears in his early theoretical essay, 'Profesión de fe literaria' [A Profession of Literary Faith], and it features in some of his stories that resonate most strongly with Kafka, including 'Pierre Menard, autor del *Quijote*' [Pierre Menard, Author of the *Quixote*] (the text that Borges claimed precipitated his career as a short story writer), 'Las ruinas circulares' [The Circular Ruins], 'El milagro secreto' [The Secret Miracle], and even 'El Congreso' [The Congress].

Among the reasons that Borges admired Kafka, one that he often mentioned was the fact that Kafka's writing grew out of personal experiences such as his dull job and his difficult relationship with his father. Borges felt that Kafka used these biographical details in a way that responded to and yet also surpassed them. For example, Borges said that Kafka's relationship with his father was the basis for his writing about subordination and the 'patria potestad', but that Kafka extended his stories' scope so that they could also be read as a depiction of the individual's relationship with the state and subsequently with God. A single short story such as 'Vor dem Gesetz' [Before the Law] could be about Kafka's relationship with his father, the circumstances of a twentieth-century citizen navigating an incomprehensible bureaucracy, and the timeless relationship between God and Man, all at the same time.

Borges viewed Kafka as one of the greatest writers of the modern age because his stories turned personal experiences into explorations of the incomprehensibility of the individual's place in the universe. Kafka's texts were simultaneously personal and general, timely and timeless, nightmares and allegories. By balancing these dualities, Kafka's stories overcame the problem that Borges worried about in 'Borges y yo'. In writing stories that portrayed deeply personal concepts in a way that could also be read as universal, Kafka was able to insert himself into his texts while also maintaining some distance from them.

Kafka's ability to write texts that could be both biographical and allegorical is perhaps a reason why Borges was so drawn to him. Although Borges's initial impressions of Kafka from reading him in his youth were not favourable, he came to admire Kafka's writing for its ability to blend the personal with the timeless. Borges subsequently borrowed themes and traits from Kafka, both overtly and covertly, for his own short stories. Kafka's influence on Borges is strongest in Borges's works from the 1930s and 1940s, particularly the stories from *Ficciones* [*Fictions*] that made use of the Kafkian themes of subordination, infinity, and the 'patria potestad'. Although Borges only attributed two stories to Kafka outright—'La lotería en Babilonia' [The Lottery in Babylon] and 'La biblioteca de Babel' [The Library of Babel]—Kafka's influence pervaded many of his texts from this time. Borges combined the things he admired in Kafka with his own interest in writers and writing to produce stories such as 'Examen de la obra de Herbert Quain' [A Survey of the Works of Herbert Quain]—works about the problems and paradoxes faced by the writer.

As Borges came into his own as a short story writer, he moved away from Kafka's influence. Just as Borges described in 'Borges y yo', he left behind Kafkian themes of subordination and infinity for other interests, such as betrayal, duels, and gauchos. However, Borges never fully abandoned Kafka. This was because he was still using him as a model for negotiating the father–son relationship, which Borges saw as one of Kafka's central themes, and which struck a personal chord with Borges. The father–son relationship returned to the fore in Borges's final attempt at Kafkian writing in the late story 'El Congreso'. In this uncharacteristically long work, Borges revisited unreachable goals and the son's obligation to his father. Perhaps in an effort to resolve these concerns, he also drew on Chesterton for a happy conclusion that would be out of place in Kafka. By emulating Chesterton, Borges permitted his protagonist two experiences of ecstasy—moments in which he glimpsed resolutions to the problems and paradoxes that plagued him. However, these moments of happiness were short lived. Borges may have been unconvinced by them, and his scepticism may not have allowed him to write them in earnest. In the final paragraphs of 'El Congreso', Borges suggested that while it might be possible to reach a seemingly impossible, Kafkian goal, such a resolution could never be captured in writing.

Borges showed that Kafkian objectives are worthy of pursuit, even if he never fully documented the moment in which these long-sought goals were secured. Instead, his focus was on the 'elegante esperanza'— the elegant hope—that motivates his characters as they struggle to understand the library of Babel, to find Almotásim, to reach the Congress, to write the justification-worthy text. In Borges' stories, these goals may be glimpsed or sometimes even briefly grasped, but they are never fully experienced or never described in their entirety. For Borges, depicting the struggle to achieve them was enough.

Annotated Bibliography

WORKS BY BORGES THAT MENTION KAFKA

Borges's writings on Kafka are presented here in chronological order based on their initial publication dates. The dates and sources provided in bold at the head of the entries refer to the texts' first publication, and not to the dates on which they were written; the citations below are for the sources from which the texts have been obtained. For texts where Kafka is mentioned in passing, the notes only refer to the context in which Kafka appears without providing a summary of the rest of the piece. The entries here are only for texts written by Borges; interviews where Borges mentioned Kafka are not included.

2 June 1935 (*La Prensa*)
Borges, Jorge Luis. 'Las pesadillas y Franz Kafka'. *Textos recobrados (1931–1955)*. Buenos Aires: Emecé, 2001. 110–14.

In this essay, Borges recounts the history of dreams and nightmares in literature. He focuses on real dreams (not prophetic ones or ones used purely as literary devices), and he suggests that the first real dream in literature is William Wordsworth's 'The Prelude' (1805). Wordsworth's dream refigures things seen by the dreamer when he is awake.

Kafka's dreams are different because they are not continuous or rooted in reality. Each has the air of nightmare about it. Borges explains that some psychologists think nightmares are the product of feeling physically unwell. Instead, he proposes a reciprocal arrangement, where feeling unwell causes the nightmare but the nightmare also results in feeling unwell. The horror of the nightmare is that the dreamer is temporarily under the influence of something strong but also illusory.

In Kafka's 'Eine kaiserliche Botschaft' [An Imperial Message], an individual waits for a message that has been sent to him by an emperor. No matter how long he waits, the message will never reach him, and he will spend his entire life anticipating its arrival. For Borges, while it is possible to interpret this story as symbolic, its strength is in its lack of symbolism. Borges thinks that as an allegorist, Kafka is in good company as old as the history of writing, but as a writer of disinterested stories, Kafka is unique.

March 1936 (*Obra n°4*)
Borges, Jorge Luis. 'Alfredo Cahn: Cuentistas de la alemania libre'. *Textos recobrados (1931–1955)*. Buenos Aires: Emecé, 2001. 163–4.

Borges says that the symbol is the device most common in German literature, and he cites Kafka as an example of an author who favoured symbols.

1936 (*Historia de la eternidad*, Viau y Zona)
Borges, Jorge Luis. 'Los traductores de *Las 1001 Noches*'. *Historia de la eternidad.*
1936. *Obras completas.* Vol. 1. Buenos Aires: Emecé, 1996. 397–413.

Borges compares translations of *The Thousand and One Nights*. At the end of the
article he wonders how Kafka would have translated *The Thousand and One Nights*
if he had tried.

6 August 1937 (*El Hogar*)
Borges, Jorge Luis. '*The Trial*, de Franz Kafka'. *Textos cautivos.* 1986. *Obras
completas.* Vol. 4. Buenos Aires: Emecé, 1996. 306.

Borges reviews an English translation of Kafka's *Der Prozeß* [*The Trial*].
He summarizes its plot and points out the similarities between it, *Das Schloß* [*The
Castle*], 'Eine kaiserliche Botschaft' [An Imperial Message], and 'Eine alltägliche
Verwirrung' [A Common Confusion]. Kafka's stories are nightmares, and even
though it is possible to give them a religious interpretation, it is not necessary to do
so. They are stories about unreachable goals, infinity, and Zeno's paradoxes.

29 October 1937 (*El Hogar*)
Borges, Jorge Luis. 'Franz Kafka: Biografía sintética'. *Textos cautivos.* 1986. *Obras
completas.* Vol. 4. Buenos Aires: Emecé, 1996. 326.

For Borges, 'Los hechos de la vida de [Kafka] no proponen otro misterio que el de
su no indagada relación con la obra extraordinaria' [The events of [Kafka's] life
propose no other mystery than their unexplored connection with his extraordinary
work].[1] In this capsule biography, Borges lists the major events in Kafka's life: he
was born to middle-class parents in a Jewish neighbourhood in Prague, he studied
law, and he died from tuberculosis. Borges offers a short review of each of Kafka's
three novels. *Amerika* [*America*] ends with the protagonist finding utopia, while
Der Prozeß [*The Trial*] and *Das Schloß* [*The Castle*] remind Borges of Zeno's
paradoxes because their protagonists never reach their goals. Borges also lists his
favourites amongst Kafka's short stories, including 'Vor dem Gesetz' [Before the
Law], 'Eine kaiserliche Botschaft' [An Imperial Message], and 'Beim Bau der
chinesischen Mauer' [The Great Wall of China].

13 May 1938 (*El Hogar*)
Borges, Jorge Luis. 'De la vida literaria: 13 de mayo de 1938'. *Jorge Luis Borges en
'El Hogar' (1930–1958).* Buenos Aires: Emecé, 2000. 106–7.

In his literary news column, Borges mentions that *La Nouvelle Revue Française* has
published a translation of Kafka's 'Die Verwandlung' [The Metamorphosis].

---

[1] Jorge Luis Borges, 'Franz Kafka: Biografía sintética', *Textos cautivos*, 1986, *Obras
completas*, Vol. 4 (Buenos Aires: Emecé, 1996), p. 326.

8 July 1938 (*El Hogar*)
Borges, Jorge Luis. 'De la vida literaria: 8 de julio de 1938'. *Jorge Luis Borges en 'El Hogar' (1930–1958)*. Buenos Aires: Emecé, 2000. 116–17.

Borges recounts an anecdote from Brod's biography of Kafka. One afternoon, when Kafka was visiting Brod's house, he accidentally disturbed Brod's father who was taking a nap. Passing quietly through the room, Kafka whispered, 'Le ruego, considéreme un sueño' [Please, consider me a dream].[2]

October 1938 (*Sur* n° 49)
Borges, Jorge Luis. 'Una exposición afligente'. *Jorge Luis Borges en 'Sur' (1931–1980)*. Barcelona: Emecé, 1999. 155–7.

Borges comments on a revised version of *Geschichte der deutschen National-Literatur* [*A History of German Literature*] that omits authors because they are Jewish or because their works do not bolster the National Socialist agenda. Among the omitted authors are Heinrich Heine, Bertolt Brecht, and Kafka. Of those who have been excluded, Borges says that three—Kafka, Johannes Becher, and Alfred Döblin—belong to a class of extraordinary writers. Borges is horrified that they (and indeed all Jewish writers) have been excluded.

1938 (*La metamorfosis*, Losada)
Borges, Jorge Luis. 'Franz Kafka: *La metamorfosis*'. *Prólogos con un prólogo de prólogos*. 1975. *Obras completas*. Vol. 4. Buenos Aires: Emecé, 1996. 97–9.

Borges starts this prologue to a collection of short stories by emphasizing Kafka's Jewishness and also his relationship with his father: 'Era enfermizo y hosco: íntimamente no dejó nunca de menospreciarlo su padre y hasta 1922 lo tiranizó. (De ese conflicto y de sus tenaces meditaciones sobre las misteriosas misericordias y las ilimitadas exigencias de la patria potestad, ha declarado él mismo que procede todo su obra)' [He was sickly and sullen; his father never stopped secretly despising him and tyrannized him up until 1922. (Kafka himself has said that all of his work, including his persistent meditations on the mysterious compassions and endless demands of the 'patria potestad', derived from this conflict)].[3] He highlights other biographical details, including Kafka's failed relationships, his job with the insurance board, the influence of the First World War on his writing, and his death from tuberculosis.

With respect to Kafka's writing, Borges comments 'Dos ideas . . . rigen la obra de Franz Kafka. La subordinación es la primera de las dos; el infinito, la segunda' [Two ideas . . . pervade the work of Franz Kafka. The first is subordination, and

[2] Jorge Luis Borges, 'De la vida literaria: 8 de julio de 1938', *Jorge Luis Borges en 'El Hogar' (1930–1958)* (Buenos Aires: Emecé, 2000), pp. 116–17 (p. 117).

[3] Jorge Luis Borges, 'Franz Kafka: *La metamorfosis*', *Prólogos con un prólogo de prólogos*, 1975, *Obras completas*, Vol. 4 (Buenos Aires: Emecé, 1996), pp. 97–9 (p. 97).

the second infinity].[4] He gives examples of these traits in Kafka's novels and short stories. Kafka's stories seem interminable, which Borges sees as a manifestation of Zeno's paradoxes and of infinity. His stories conjure intolerable situations, particularly the incomprehensibility of the individual's place in the universe. For Borges, this makes Kafka one of the greatest writers of the modern age.

December 1939 (*Sur* n° 63)
Borges, Jorge Luis. 'Avatares de la tortuga'. *Discusión*. 1957. *Obras completas*. Vol. 1. Buenos Aires: Emecé, 1996. 254–8.

Borges discusses infinity and the ways in which it functions as a literary device in the works of authors such as Kafka. Borges traces infinity back to Zeno's paradoxes and explains a number of different versions of the paradoxes.

1940 (*La invención de Morel*, Losada)
Borges, Jorge Luis. 'Adolfo Bioy Casares: *La invención de Morel*'. *Prólogos con un prólogo de prólogos*. 1975. Buenos Aires: Emecé, 1996. 25–7.

With reference to Bioy Casares's *La invención de Morel* [*The Invention of Morel*] (1940), Borges discusses the history of the adventure story. He mentions the pursuit of the infinite in the fables of Thomas De Quincey, which remind him of Kafka's stories.

January 1941 (*Sur* n° 76)
Borges, Jorge Luis. 'La lotería en Babilonia'. *Ficciones*. 1944. *Obras completas*. Vol. 1. Buenos Aires: Emecé, 1996. 456–60.

This story about a Kafkaesque lottery mentions a secret latrine named Qaphqa where patrons believe they can deposit messages for the company that controls the lottery.

August 1941 (*Sur* n° 83)
Borges, Jorge Luis. 'Un film abrumador'. *Jorge Luis Borges en 'Sur' (1931–1980)*. Barcelona: Emecé, 1999. 199–200.

Reviewing *Citizen Kane* (1941), Borges recalls the nihilism of Kafka and the labyrinths of Chesterton.

August 1942 (*Sur* n° 95)
Borges, Jorge Luis. 'Michael Sadleir: *Fanny by Gaslight*'. *Jorge Luis Borges en 'Sur' (1931–1980)*. Barcelona: Emecé, 1999. 254–5.

In this book review, Borges discusses the difference between characters he finds believable but who are situated in implausible plots, and plots he finds believable

---

[4] Ibid., pp. 97–8.

with unmemorable characters. About Kafka, he writes, 'Creo en los tribunales infinitos y en el Castillo impenetrable de Kafka, pero no en sus borrosos protagonistas' [I believe in Kafka's infinite trials and the impenetrable Castle, but not in his vague protagonists].[5]

1942 (H. Bustos Domecq, *Seis problemas para don Isidro Parodi*, Sur)

Borges, Jorge Luis, and Adolfo Bioy Casares. 'La víctima de Tadeo Limardo'. *Seis problemas para don Isidro Parodi*. 1942. *Obras completas en colaboración*. Buenos Aires: Emecé, 1979. 85–104.

This detective story is dedicated 'A la memoria de Franz Kafka' [To the memory of Franz Kafka].[6]

January 1943 (*La Nación*)

Borges, Jorge Luis. 'La última invención de Hugh Walpole'. *Textos recobrados (1931–1955)*. Buenos Aires: Emecé, 2001. 207–10.

With reference to Walpole's stories, which portray a chaotic version of reality and confuse good with bad, Borges says that Walpole is 'uno de los primeros panegiristas ingleses de Kafka' [one of the first English eulogists of Kafka].[7]

December 1944 (*Sur* n° 122)

Borges, Jorge Luis. 'Francisco Ayala: *El hechizado*'. *Jorge Luis Borges en 'Sur' (1931–1980)*. Barcelona: Emecé, 1999. 280–1.

Borges discusses instances of Zeno's paradoxes in literature. Among them are Ayala's *El hechizado* [*The Bewitched*] (1944) and 'los seis volúmenes de Franz Kafka' [Franz Kafka's six volumes].[8] He refers to the distressing nature of Zeno's paradoxes in Kafka's writing.

1944 (*Latitud* n° 1)

Borges, Jorge Luis. 'De la alta ambición en el arte'. *Textos recobrados (1931–1955)*. Buenos Aires: Emecé, 2001. 352–4.

In response to a short questionnaire about his writing, Borges says that he is working on 'una larga narración o novela breve, que se titulará *El Congreso* y que conciliará (hoy no puedo ser más explícito) los hábitos de Whitman y los de Kafka'

[5] Jorge Luis Borges, 'Michael Sadleir: *Fanny by Gaslight*', *Jorge Luis Borges en 'Sur' (1931–1980)* (Barcelona: Emecé, 1999), pp. 254–5 (p. 254).

[6] Jorge Luis Borges and Adolfo Bioy Casares, 'La víctima de Tadeo Limardo', *Seis problemas para don Isidro Parodi*, 1942, *Obras completas en colaboración* (Buenos Aires: Emecé, 1979), pp. 85–104 (p. 85).

[7] Jorge Luis Borges, 'La última invención de Hugh Walpole', *Textos recobrados (1931–1955)* (Buenos Aires: Emecé, 2001), pp. 207–10 (p. 208).

[8] Jorge Luis Borges, 'Francisco Ayala: *El hechizado*', *Jorge Luis Borges en 'Sur' (1931–1980)* (Barcelona: Emecé, 1999), pp. 280–1 (p. 280).

[a long story or short novel, which will be called *The Congress*, and which will reconcile (I cannot currently be more precise) the tendencies of Whitman and Kafka].[9]

1944 (*Bartleby*, Emecé)
Borges, Jorge Luis. Prologue. *Bartleby*. By Herman Melville. Trans. Jorge Luis Borges. Buenos Aires: Edicom, 1969. 9–13.

In a prologue to *Bartleby, the Scrivener* (1853), Borges suggests that Melville's novel foreshadowed Kafka's stories about human behaviour.

1945 (*La humillación de los Nortmore*, Emecé)
Borges, Jorge Luis. 'Henry James: *La humillación de los Northmore*'. *Prólogos con un prólogo de prólogos*. 1975. *Obras completas*. Vol. 4. Buenos Aires: Emecé, 1996. 94–6.

With reference to Henry James, Borges mentions his own translations of Kafka.

July 1946 (*Sur* n° 141)
Borges, Jorge Luis. 'Nuestro pobre individualismo'. *Otras inquisiciones*. 1952. *Obras completas*. Vol. 2. Buenos Aires: Emecé, 1996. 36–7.

Borges discusses the problems with determining what constitutes Argentine national identity. He says that Europeans believe the universe is an ordered cosmos, while Argentines believe it is chaotic. European literature reflects this ordered view: in Kafka's stories, the individual seeks his or her place within the order of the cosmos, no matter how low this place may be.

September–October 1947 (*Realidad* vol. 2 n° 5)
Borges, Jorge Luis. 'Nota sobre el *Quijote*'. *Páginas de Jorge Luis Borges*. Ed. Alicia Jurado. Buenos Aires: Celtia, 1982. 175–7.

In a footnote to a discussion of *Don Quijote*, Borges recalls Kafka's speculation that Cervantes's novel was really a product of Sancho's imagination and the result of Sancho reading too many adventure books.

October 1947 (*Los Anales de Buenos Aires* n° 20–2)
Borges, Jorge Luis. 'Sobre Chesterton'. *Otras inquisiciones*. 1952. *Obras completas*. Vol. 2. Buenos Aires: Emecé, 1996. 72–4.

In a discussion of Chesterton's writing, Borges suggests that Chesterton 'se defendió de ser Edgar Allan Poe o Franz Kafka, pero que algo en el barro de su yo

---

[9] Jorge Luis Borges, 'De la alta ambición en el arte', *Textos recobrados (1931–1955)* (Buenos Aires: Emecé, 2001), pp. 352–4 (p. 353).

propendía a la pesadilla, algo secreto, y ciego y central' [restrained himself from being Edgar Allan Poe or Franz Kafka, but something in the makeup of his personality leaned toward the nightmarish, something secret, and blind, and central].[10] He compares two parables: the first is Kafka's 'Vor dem Gesetz' [Before the Law] from *Der Prozeß [The Trial]* and the second is from John Bunyan's *The Pilgrim's Progress* (1678). In the former a man waits but never is admitted to the law, while in the latter a man forces his way into a castle to earn eternal glory. Borges speculates that Chesterton—a religious man—'dedicó su vida a escribir la segunda de las parábolas, pero algo en él propendió siempre a escribir la primera' [devoted his life to the writing of the second parable, but something within him always tended to write the first].[11]

March 1948 (*Escritura* n° 3)
Borges, Jorge Luis. 'El enigma de Ulises'. *Textos recobrados (1931–1955)*. Buenos Aires: Emecé, 2001. 254–7.

Borges wonders about Dante's portrayal of Ulysses in the eighth pit of the eighth circle of hell. He compares the incomprehensible God of Dante with the incomprehensible and absurd God of Kafka.

1948 (Emecé)
Borges, Jorge Luis. 'Quevedo'. *Otras inquisiciones*. 1952. *Obras completas*. Vol. 2. Buenos Aires: Emecé, 1996. 38–44.

In a discussion of the work of Francisco de Quevedo, Borges points out that many authors have something about their writing that makes their work unique. For Kafka, it is his unending labyrinths.

July 1949 (*Cursos y conferencias*, vol. 35)
Borges, Jorge Luis. 'Nathaniel Hawthorne'. *Otras inquisiciones*. 1952. *Obras completas*. Vol. 2. Buenos Aires: Emecé, 1996. 48–63.

In this long essay on Hawthorne, Borges compares Hawthorne's story 'Wakefield' (1837) to Melville's writing and to Kafka's. He says that Kafka's work can be situated within the context of Judaism, and Hawthorne's work can be situated within the context of the Old Testament. He speculates that had Kafka written 'Wakefield', the story would have ended differently.

October 1949 (*La Nación*)
Borges, Jorge Luis. 'Edgar Allan Poe'. *Textos recobrados (1931–1955)*. Buenos Aires: Emecé, 2001. 263–5.

---

[10] Jorge Luis Borges, 'Sobre Chesterton', *Otras inquisiciones*, 1952, *Obras completas*, Vol. 2 (Buenos Aires: Emecé, 1996), pp. 72–4 (p. 73); Ruth L. C. Simms, trans., 'On Chesterton', *Other Inquisitions: 1937–1952* (Austin: U of Texas P, 2000), pp. 82–5 (p. 84).
[11] Borges, 'Sobre Chesterton', p. 74; Simms, trans., 'On Chesterton', p. 85.

Borges labels literature of the twentieth century 'desventurado' [unhappy] because of the 'infiernos elaborados' [intricate hells] of Kafka, Henry James, and Poe.[12]

11 February 1951 (or 20 August 1975, according to the date following the author's signature) (*Los orilleros*, Losada)
Borges, Jorge Luis, and Adolfo Bioy Casares. Prologue. *Los orilleros*. 1955. *Obras completas en colaboración*. Buenos Aires: Emecé, 1979. 199–200.

In this prologue to screenplays written by Borges and Bioy Casares, Borges compares the quests in the two films to the infinite quests in Kafka (to gain admission to the castle) and in Melville (to find Moby Dick).

19 August 1951 (*La Nación*)
Borges, Jorge Luis. 'Kafka y sus precursores'. *Otras inquisiciones*. 1952. *Obras completas*. Vol. 2. Buenos Aires: Emecé, 1996. 88–90.

Notwithstanding the fact that Borges thinks Kafka is a unique author, he sees shades of Kafka's writing in the works of others. In particular, Borges says that Kafka's writing is the literary embodiment of Zeno's paradoxes, with *Der Prozeß* [*The Trial*] being a perfect example. After reading Kafka, Borges noticed Zeno's paradoxes in a ninth-century Chinese story, in Kierkegaard, in Browning, in Bloy, and Lord Dunsany. Borges points out that texts by all of these authors resemble Kafka but this does not mean that they resemble each other. Kafka's writing pulls them together. Although it is possible that the texts written before Kafka anticipated his writing, what is more likely (according to Borges) is that our reading of Kafka modifies our reading of earlier authors.

1953 (*El Martín Fierro*, Columba)
Borges, Jorge Luis, and Margarita Guerrero. 'Martín Fierro y los críticos'. *El Martín Fierro*. 1953. *Obras completas en colaboración*. Buenos Aires: Emecé, 1979. 557–61.

In the conclusion to this piece on the critical reception of *Martín Fierro* (1872 and 1879), Borges mentions Ezequiel Martínez Estrada's *Muerte y transfiguración de Martín Fierro* [*Death and Transfiguration of Martín Fierro*] (1948), which he says is a dreamlike recreation of *Martín Fierro* by an author in the same class as Melville and Kafka.

14 November 1954 (*La Nación*)
Borges, Jorge Luis. 'Vindicación de *Bouvard et Pécuchet*'. *Discusión*. 1957. *Obras completas*. Vol. 1. Buenos Aires: Emecé, 1996. 259–62.

---

[12] Jorge Luis Borges, 'Edgar Allan Poe', *Textos recobrados (1931–1955)* (Buenos Aires: Emecé, 2001), pp. 263–5 (p. 263).

Borges considers the infinite task of Bouvard and Pécuchet, and he speculates that Gustave Flaubert's book implies eternity, as do Kafka's stories.

July 1955 (Noticias gráficas)
Borges, Jorge Luis. 'Jorge Luis Borges, encrucijada de admiraciones y negaciones, nos habla de su labor futura'. *Textos recobrados (1931–1955)*. Buenos Aires: Emecé, 2001. 367–71.

In an interview about his upcoming work, Borges refers to an introduction he is writing for the complete works of Kafka. (Note: no such text seems to exist.)

1955 (*Leopoldo Lugones*, Troquel)
Borges, Jorge Luis, and Betina Edelberg. 'El modernismo'. *Leopold Lugones*. 1955. *Obras completas en colaboración*. Buenos Aires: Emecé, 1979. 463–9.

In a chapter on modernismo, Borges mentions the frequency with which mythology is used or alluded to in modern literature. He lists Kafka's writing as an example of mythology employed to represent an individual's circumstances.

10 February 1956 (*El Hogar*)
Borges, Jorge Luis. '¿Qué sabe usted de teatro?' *Jorge Luis Borges en 'El Hogar' (1930–1958)*. Buenos Aires: Emecé, 2000. 175–7.

In a literary quiz, one of Borges's questions is: Which is the only Kafka work written for the theatre? (*i*) 'Die Verwandlung' [The Metamorphosis], (*ii*) 'Der Gruftwächter' [The Warden of the Tomb] (1936), or (*iii*) 'Ein Hungerkünstler' [A Hunger Artist]? The answer is given on the following page as 'Der Gruftwächter'.

1963 (*Cuentos breves y maravillosos*, Ministerio de educación)
Borges, Jorge Luis. 'Álvaro Menen Desleal: Cuentos breves y maravillosos'. *El círculo secreto: Prólogos y notas*. Buenos Aires: Emecé, 2003. 34–6.

Borges mentions Kafka's 'Beim Bau der chinesischen Mauer' [The Great Wall of China] with reference to a collection of fantastic short stories.

1965 (*Introducción a la literatura inglesa*, Columba)
Borges, Jorge Luis, and María Esther Vázquez. 'Nuestro siglo'. *Introducción a la literatura inglesa*. 1965. *Obras completas en colaboración*. Buenos Aires: Emecé, 1979. 850–7.

In a section on Chesterton in the history of English literature, Borges remarks that Chesterton wanted to write in the manner of Poe or Kafka, but happily he wrote in the manner of Chesterton.

1967 (*Introducción a la literatura norteamericana*, Columba)
Borges, Jorge Luis, and Esther Zemborain de Torres. *Introducción a la literatura norteamericana*. Buenos Aires: Columba, 1967.

This book provides an overview of North American literature, and on several occasions Borges invokes Kafka as a point of comparison. He refers to the setting of Melville's *Bartleby, the Scrivener* as Kafkian, and he also says that the mysterious world of Henry James has much in common with Kafka.[13]

1968 (*The Aleph and Other Stories: 1933–1969*, Jonathan Cape)
Borges, Jorge Luis. 'An Autobiographical Essay'. *The Aleph and Other Stories: 1933–1969*. Trans. and ed. Norman Thomas di Giovanni. London: Jonathan Cape, 1968. 203–60.

In his autobiographical essay, Borges recalls his relationship with his father, and he reminisces about his father teaching him about infinity and Zeno's paradoxes. He says that 'La biblioteca de Babel' [The Library of Babel] is written in the manner of Kafka. About 'El Congreso', he says, 'Despite its Kafkian title, I hope it will turn out more in the line of Chesterton.'[14]

1968 (*This Craft of Verse*, Harvard UP)
Borges, Jorge Luis. 'The Telling of the Tale'. *This Craft of Verse*. Ed. Calin-Andrei Mihailescu. Cambridge: Harvard UP, 2000. 43–55.

Borges says that modern adventures in literature end in failure: 'When we read Franz Kafka's *The Castle*, we know that the man will never get inside the castle. That is to say, we cannot really believe in happiness and in success.'[15] Borges suggests that Kafka wanted his books destroyed because he could not write happy ones.

19 April 1970 (*El informe de Brodie*, Emecé)
Borges, Jorge Luis. Prologue. *El informe de Brodie*. 1970. *Obras completas*. Vol. 2. Buenos Aires: Emecé, 1996. 399–400.

Borges opens this prologue by referring to Rudyard Kipling's late stories, which he says are as labyrinthine and as tormented as Kafka's and Henry James's. Borges does so to give context to his own late writing.

---

[13] Jorge Luis Borges and Esther Zemborain de Torres, *Introducción a la literatura norteamericana* (Buenos Aires: Columba, 1967), p. 26, 40.

[14] Jorge Luis Borges, 'An Autobiographical Essay', *The Aleph and Other Stories: 1933–1969*, trans. and ed. Norman Thomas di Giovanni (London: Jonathan Cape, 1968), pp. 203–60 (p. 259).

[15] Jorge Luis Borges, 'The Telling of the Tale', *This Craft of Verse*, ed. Calin-Andrei Mihailescu (Cambridge: Harvard UP, 2000), pp. 43–55 (p. 49).

1972 (*El oro de los tigres*, Emecé)
Borges, Jorge Luis. 'Los cuatro ciclos'. *El oro de los tigres*. 1972. *Obras completas*. Vol. 2. Buenos Aires: Emecé, 1996. 504.

Borges identifies four main plots in literature: a valiant fight, a journey, a quest, and a sacrifice. Borges says Kafka's stories are exemplary of the third type of story—the quest—and he says that Kafka's quests never end happily.

26 November 1974 (*Prólogos con un prólogo de prólogos*, Torres Agüero)
Borges, Jorge Luis. Prologue. *Prólogos con un prólogo de prólogos*. 1975. *Obras completas*. Vol. 4. Buenos Aires: Emecé, 1996. 13–14.

In this prologue, Borges offers a résumé of the texts for which he has written prologues. With reference to Kafka, he mentions 'las eleáticas postergaciones' [the Eleatic deferrals] of Zeno.[16] He goes on to contemplate the history and theory of the prologue, and he reflects on how his views of the books he has prefaced have changed over time.

3 February 1975 (*El libro de arena*, Emecé)
Borges, Jorge Luis. Epilogue. *El libro de arena*. 1975. *Obras completas*. Vol. 3. Buenos Aires: Emecé, 1996. 72–3.

In the epilogue to *El libro de arena* [*The Book of Sand*], Borges mentions that with 'El Congreso' [The Congress], 'El opaco principio quiere imitar el de las ficciones de Kafka; el fin quiere elevarse, sin duda en vano, a los éxtasis de Chesterton o de John Bunyan' [The story's murky beginning attempts to imitate the way Kafka's stories begin; its ending attempts, no doubt unsuccessfully, to ascend to the ecstasy of Chesterton or John Bunyan].[17]

27 October 1975 (*Libro de sueños*, Torres Agüero)
Borges, Jorge Luis. Prologue. *Libro de sueños*. Buenos Aires: Torres Agüero, 1976. 2–4.

In the prologue to this anthology of dreamlike stories, Borges mentions Kafka's 'puros juegos' [pure games] in conjunction with Lewis Carroll's.[18] He says there are a number of different ways for stories to convey both daydreams and nightmares.

---

[16] Jorge Luis Borges, Prologue, *Prólogos con un prólogo de prólogos*, 1975, *Obras completas*, Vol. 4 (Buenos Aires: Emecé, 1996), pp. 13–14 (p. 13).

[17] Jorge Luis Borges, Epilogue, *El libro de arena*, 1975, *Obras completas*, Vol. 3 (Buenos Aires: Emecé, 1996), pp. 72–3 (p. 72); Andrew Hurley, trans., Afterword, *The Book of Sand*, 1975, *Collected Fictions* (New York: Viking, 1998), pp. 484–5 (p. 484).

[18] Jorge Luis Borges, Prologue, *Libro de sueños* (Buenos Aires: Torres Agüero, 1976), pp. 2–4 (p. 2).

1976 (*Sur* n° 338–9)
Borges, Jorge Luis. 'Problemas de la traducción: El oficio de traducir'. *Jorge Luis Borges en 'Sur' (1931–1980)*. Barcelona: Emecé, 1999. 321–5.

Borges shares his views on translation. He says he prefers translating poetry to translating the prose of authors such as Kafka or Faulkner. Translating prose just means changing words from one language to another, which Borges says he does not find satisfying.

1976 (*La moneda de hierro*, Emecé)
Borges, Jorge Luis. 'Ein Traum'. *La moneda de hierro*. 1976. *Obras completas*. Vol. 3. Buenos Aires: Emecé, 1996. 154.

In this poem, Borges imagines a dialogue between Kafka and two characters Kafka has dreamed. In a note on the collection, Borges describes the poem as 'una mera curiosidad psicológica o, si el lector es muy generoso, de una inofensiva parábola del solipsismo' [a mere psychological curiosity or, if the reader is very generous, an inoffensive solipsistic parable].[19]

1978 (*El congreso del mundo*, Franco Maria Ricci)
Borges, Jorge Luis. 'El congreso del mundo'. 1978. *Textos recobrados (1956–1986)*. Buenos Aires: Emecé, 2003. 210–11.

In a prologue to a special tetralingual edition of 'El Congreso' [The Congress], Borges discusses epic stories and happy endings, two things that are uncharacteristic in modern writing. Modern writing has more in common with Henry James, Kafka, and Zeno's paradoxes. Borges says this is because 'Somos menos valientes que nuestras padres' [We are not as courageous as our fathers].[20]
    Borges says 'El Congreso' [The Congress] is about a project that results in a mystical experience and an intimate, secret victory. He says, 'Confieso que la compartida experiencia mística que es la justificación de este cuento—quizá el más largo de cuantos ha ejercitado mi pluma—es del todo ajena a mi vida' [I confess that the shared mystical experience that is the justification for this story—perhaps the longest of the stories that I have ever penned—is completely foreign to me].[21]

1978 (*Libro de las ruinas*, Franco Maria Ricci)
Borges, Jorge Luis. 'Libro de las ruinas'. *El círculo secreto: Prólogos y notas*. Buenos Aires: Emecé, 2003. 156–65.

---

[19] Jorge Luis Borges, 'Ein Traum', *La moneda de hierro*, 1976, *Obras completas*, Vol. 3 (Buenos Aires: Emecé, 1996), p. 154.
[20] Jorge Luis Borges, 'El congreso del mundo', 1978, *Textos recobrados (1956–1986)* (Buenos Aires: Emecé, 2003), pp. 210–11 (p. 210).
[21] Ibid., p. 211.

Borges refers to Kafka's characters as professionals at defeat who appear in stories that end unhappily.

1979 (*El buitre*, La Ciudad)
Borges, Jorge Luis. Prologue. *El buitre*. By Franz Kafka. Buenos Aires: La Ciudad, 1979. 7–11.

In the prologue to a collection of Kafka stories, Borges recalls Virgil's and Kafka's dying wishes to have their writing destroyed. He speculates that Virgil and Kafka did this to liberate themselves from the burden of feeling responsible for spreading their work. Despite Kafka's request, Brod, his executor, did not honour Kafka's wishes. Borges remembers first reading Kafka in 1917. He was unimpressed by what he read, but later recognized his error. He has changed his view about Kafka and now sees him as one of the greatest writers of his time.

Borges identifies a connection between Kafka's writing, the Book of Job, and Judaism. He believes that for Kafka, writing is an act of faith. Borges notes a parallel in Kafka's writing between his sense of guilt towards his father and the Jews' sense of guilt towards God. Two themes form the basis of his writing— subordination and infinity—and Borges gives examples of both from all three of Kafka's novels and from a selection of his short stories. For Borges, Kafka's principal merit is his ability to conjure intolerable situations, which always feature a German– Jewish man at the bottom of an incomprehensible cosmic hierarchy.

1982 (*La metamorfosis*, Orión)
Borges, Jorge Luis. 'Jorge Luis Borges habla del mundo de Kafka'. *La metamorfosis*. Paraná: Orión, 1982. 5–28.

Borges discusses *regresus in infinitum*, which he sees as Kafka's modus operandi. He links this with Zeno's paradoxes, which he recalls learning about from his father. Borges describes a few ways of portraying Zeno's paradoxes (such as with a chessboard and with the story of Achilles and the tortoise). Kafka makes use of Zeno's paradoxes in his novels and short stories. Borges says he prefers Kafka's short stories, because he thinks that humans have a natural attraction to short stories, while novels are unnatural.

Borges recalls how Kafka wanted his works destroyed on his deathbed (as did Virgil), but his executor disobeyed his wishes. Borges wonders why Kafka would have wanted this, and he suggests that perhaps it was because Kafka wished he could have written happier prose. *Amerika [America]*, Kafka's first novel, is an allegory for the heavens, and it reminds Borges of Dante's *Paradiso*.

The labyrinth is one of Kafka's main themes. Borges says that Kafka never used the word labyrinth, but that this does not matter. Borges distinguishes between chaos and a labyrinth: in chaos, there is no order; in a labyrinth there is an order that is meant to be confusing. The universe, says Borges, has an order but this order is labyrinthine and created by God. The whole of philosophy is an effort to understand this order. Borges relates this quest for understanding to idealism, which he learned about from his father. According to idealism, we can only know things that we perceive with our senses; according to Kafka we cannot know anything at all. Borges thinks the idea of an unknowable order is at the heart of *Amerika* [*America*], *Der Prozeß* [*The Trial*], *Das Schloß* [*The Castle*], 'Die Verwandlung' [The Metamorphosis], and many of Kafka's other stories.

The impossible task is Kafka's other main theme. This distinguishes Kafka's writing from much of the literature that preceded it, which focused on tasks that could be completed. The happy ending is no longer fashionable in fiction; the most recent book Borges can recall with a happy ending is Stevenson's *Treasure Island* (1883). By contrast, *Don Quijote* is one of the first books to end with a failed quest. Kafka's stories also end in this way.

Kafka's stories lack detail, which makes them accessible to all people at all times. Again, this is a feature that makes Kafka's writing unique. Kafka's protagonists are examples of modern individuals: they are slaves who are happy to be enslaved. Kafka lived in a time when individuals were enslaved to the state, and as an example of this, Borges points to the passport, which is part of a bureaucratic system to track and control people. Borges suggests that this sort of reality is documented in and predicted by Kafka.

This does not mean that Kafka's writing is only relevant to people enslaved to the state. Even when things have changed and bureaucracy and Kafkaesque governments no longer exist, humans will still have a relationship with an incomprehensible God. This relationship is also exemplified by Kafka's writing. For Borges, the merit of Kafka's writing is its ability to represent an individual's relationship with God, not Kafka's particular historical circumstances.

1982 (*Autobiografía de Irene*, Gaglianone)
Borges, Jorge Luis. 'Silvina Ocampo: *Autobiografía de Irene*'. El círculo secreto: *Prólogos y notas*. Buenos Aires: Emecé, 2003. 210–11.

In this prologue, Borges refers to Kafka as the 'creador de un orbe eleático de infinitas postergaciones' [creator of an Eleatic world of infinite deferrals].[22]

30 June 1983 (*Clarín*)
Borges, Jorge Luis. 'Una valoración de Kafka por Jorge Luis Borges'. *Clarín: Cultura y nación* 30 June 1983: 1–2.

Borges recalls the first books he read in German, and his reaction to the beauty of the language. He remembers reading a Kafka story in 1917, and later reading Kafka's three novels and his short stories. He says the novels are repetitive and connected to Zeno's paradoxes: 'el esquema es siempre el mismo, es algo monótono, se repite el tema del infinito, la paradoja de la tortuga y la flecha' [the structure is always the same, it is somewhat monotonous, it repeats the topic of the

---

[22] Jorge Luis Borges, 'Silvina Ocampo: *Autobiografía de Irene*', El círculo secreto: *Prólogos y notas* (Buenos Aires: Emecé, 2003), pp. 210–11 (p. 210).

infinite, the paradox of the tortoise and the arrow].[23] Alongside the infinite, solitude is another important theme in Kafka's writing.

Borges discusses his translations of Kafka and the stories included in *La metamorfosis* [*The Metamorphosis*]. He prefers Kafka's shortest stories, and his favourite is 'Beim Bau der chinesischen Mauer' [The Great Wall of China]. He admires Kafka's stories because they could have been written during any age; they are not reflections of their time. For Borges, 'Esa atemporalidad . . . es una forma de eternidad' [This atemporality . . . is a form of eternity] that reminds him of the fables in *The Thousand and One Nights* and of fairy tales.[24] Kafka's writing is about the relationship between individuals and the universe, although not in a particularly religious way.

Borges says he tried to write 'dos cuentos que trataban de ser cuentos de Kafka' [two stories that were trying to be Kafka stories], 'La lotería en Babilonia' [The Lottery in Babylon] and 'La biblioteca de Babel' [The Library of Babel], but he did not succeed, since only Kafka can write like Kafka.[25] Borges says he is the only writer in Argentina who has tried to emulate Kafka.

3 July 1983 (*El País*)
Borges, Jorge Luis. 'Un sueño eterno: Palabras grabadas en el centenario de Kafka'. *Textos recobrados (1956–1986)*. Buenos Aires: Emecé, 2003. 237–9.

Borges recalls first reading Kafka in 1916, when he was learning German. He points out that what separates Kafka from contemporaries such as George Bernard Shaw and Chesterton is that Kafka's stories are timeless fables. According to Borges, Kafka's preferred theme is 'el hombre contra el Estado' [man against the State].[26]

Borges is partial to Kafka's short stories over his novels, since the novels never conclude. Borges says his favourite Kafka story is 'Beim Bau der chinesischen Mauer' [The Great Wall of China] and he mentions his attempts to emulate Kafka: 'Yo he escrito también algunos cuentos en los cuales traté ambiciosa e inútilmente de ser Kafka. Hay uno, titulado "La biblioteca de Babel" y algún otro, que fueron ejercicios en donde traté de ser Kafka' [I have also written some stories in which I ambitiously but unsuccessfully tried to be Kafka. There is one, called 'La biblioteca de Babel' and another one, which were exercises where I tried to be Kafka].[27]

Borges recalls that Kafka wanted all of his works to be destroyed upon his death, as did Virgil, and as did Borges's father. We are lucky that Kafka's literary executor disobeyed. Kafka is 'uno de los grandes autores de toda la literatura'

---

[23] Jorge Luis Borges, 'Una valoración de Kafka por Jorge Luis Borges', *Clarín: Cultura y nación* 30 June 1983: 1–2 (p. 1).
[24] Ibid.
[25] Ibid., p. 2.
[26] Jorge Luis Borges, 'Un sueño eterno: Palabras grabadas en el centenario de Kafka', *Textos recobrados (1956–1986)* (Buenos Aires: Emecé, 2003), pp. 237–9 (p. 238).
[27] Ibid.

[one of the great authors of all of literature], and Borges says, 'Para mí es el primero de ese siglo' [In my view, he is the best of this century]—even better than Joyce.[28] Kafka is a dreamer whose dreams have become part of the universe's shared memory. One day his biography may be forgotten but his stories will never be.

28 December 1983 (*Newsletter of the Kafka Society of America*)
Borges, Jorge Luis. 'Franz Kafka'. *Franz Kafka: A Centennial Celebration. Newsletter of the Kafka Society of America*. Philadelphia: The Kafka Society of America, 1983. 3.

Borges meditates on the responsibility of the author to turn the things he has been given—the sun, the moon, betrayals, loneliness, and history—into writing. He highlights Kafka's Jewishness and his knack for writing 'quiet, uncanny nightmares in a crystal clear style'.[29] He concludes by referring to Kafka as the 'major classic writer of our bewildered and bewildering century'.[30]

8 March 1984 (*Clarín*)
Borges, Jorge Luis. 'La hipocresía argentina'. *Textos recobrados (1956–1986)*. Buenos Aires: Emecé, 2004. 309–11.

Borges recalls giving a talk about Kafka in New York, after which one of the audience members thanks him for the talk, saying that by discussing Kafka, Borges 'había mejorado . . . la imagen argentina' [Had improved Argentina's image].[31]

November 1984 (*Minotauro* n° 8)
Borges, Jorge Luis. 'Los caminos de la imaginación'. *Textos recobrados (1956–1986)*. Buenos Aires: Emecé, 2004. 243.

Borges says that fantastic literature can be divided into two categories: the first is oneiric, as in the stories of Henry James and Kafka; the second is scientific, as in the stories of H.G. Wells and Ray Bradbury.

May 1985 (Change International)
Borges, Jorge Luis. 'Borges sur Kafka'. *Change International* 3 (1985): 44–5.

According to Borges, 'Quand j'ái écrit *La bibliothèque de Babel* et *La loterie de Babylone*, j'ai tâche d'être Kafka' [When I wrote 'The Library of Babel' and 'The Lottery in Babylon', I tried to be Kafka].[32] Borges discusses his attempts to write

---

[28] Ibid.

[29] Jorge Luis Borges, 'Franz Kafka', *Franz Kafka: A Centennial Celebration, Newsletter of the Kafka Society of America* (Philadelphia: The Kafka Society of America, 1983), p. 3.

[30] Ibid.

[31] Jorge Luis Borges, 'La hipocresía argentina', *Textos recobrados (1956–1986)* (Buenos Aires: Emecé, 2004), pp. 309–11 (p. 309).

[32] Jorge Luis Borges, 'Borges sur Kafka', *Change International* 3 (1985): 44–5 (p. 44).

in a Kafkian fashion, and he compares Kafka's writing to Coleridge's, Shakespeare's, and Dante's.

Borges mentions first reading Kafka in 1917, in either the journal *Die Aktion* or the journal *Sturm*, and he locates this reading with respect to the First World War and German Expressionism. Borges's first reading of Kafka did not impress him, but he later changed his opinion, realizing that he saw something great and did not recognize it at the time.

Borges situates Kafka's writing within his life, noting that his Jewishness and the First World War leave their impressions on his texts. Despite this context, Borges still sees Kafka's writing as outside the history of literature; it is in a class of its own with its portrayal of the fantastic. He suggests that Kafka's writing captures the cosmos in miniature, and that it can be compared to the Book of Job—a text Borges cites as Kafka's favourite. Centuries from now, when the historical circumstances of Kafka's writing have been forgotten, Kafka's works will still be remembered and admired.

1988 (no original source or date available)

Borges, Jorge Luis. 'David Garnett: *De dama a zorro, Un hombre en el zoológico, La vuelta del marinero*'. *Biblioteca personal: Prólogos*. 1988. *Obras completas*. Vol. 4. Buenos Aires: Emecé, 1996. 511.

Borges compares David Garnett's *Lady into Fox* (1922) with Kafka's stories. He says the two resemble each other, although Kafka's writing is desperate and overwhelming, while Garnett's is ironic.

1988 (no original source or date available)

Borges, Jorge Luis. 'Dino Buzzati: *El desierto de los tártaros*'. *Biblioteca personal: Prólogos*. 1988. *Obras completas*. Vol. 4. Buenos Aires: Emecé, 1996. 457.

Borges refers to Kafka's use of Zeno's paradoxes, which he sees as a reflection of tedious bureaucracy. He says that Buzzati's writing is different, because it is hopeful and reminiscent of epics.

1988 (no original source or date available)

Borges, Jorge Luis. 'Franz Kafka: *América*'. *Biblioteca personal: Prólogos*. 1988. *Obras completas*. Vol. 4. Buenos Aires: Emecé, 1996. 454.

Borges contextualizes Kafka's life with respect to the First World War, German Expressionism, Joyce, and Kafka's biography. He mentions 'la desavenencia con el padre' [Kafka's tension with his father], his office job, his isolation, and his death from tuberculosis. For Borges 'El destino de Kafka fue transmutar las circunstancias y las agonías en fábulas' [Kafka's destiny was to transform circumstances and agonies into fables] which Kafka did by writing nightmares.[33] Judaism is central to

---

[33] Jorge Luis Borges, 'Franz Kafka: *América*', *Biblioteca personal: Prólogos*, 1988, *Obras completas*, Vol. 4 (Buenos Aires: Emecé, 1996), p. 454.

Kafka's writing even if he never mentioned it by name. Borges acknowledges Kafka as 'el gran escritor clásico de nuestro atormentado y extraño siglo' [the great classic writer of our tormented and strange century].[34]

1988 (no original source or date available)
Borges, Jorge Luis. 'Gilbert Keith Chesterton: *La cruz azul y otros cuentos*'. *Biblioteca personal: Prólogos*. 1988. *Obras completas*. Vol. 4. Buenos Aires: Emecé, 1996. 455.

Borges opens this piece by saying, 'Es lícito afirmar que Gilbert Keith Chesterton (1874–1936) hubiera podido ser Kafka' [it is fair to say that Gilbert Keith Chesterton (1894–1936) could have been Kafka] before comparing Chesterton's nightmarish writing to *Der Prozeß* [*The Trial*] and *Das Schloß* [*The Castle*].

1988 (no original source or date available)
Borges, Jorge Luis. 'Herman Melville: *Benito Cereno, Billy Budd, Bartleby, el escribiente*'. *Biblioteca personal: Prólogos*. 1988. *Obras completas*. Vol. 4. Buenos Aires: Emecé, 1996. 470–1.

Borges suggests that Melville's *Bartelby, The Scrivener* prefigured Kafka's writing. Melville's protagonist 'es un hombre oscuro que se niega tenazmente a la acción' [an enigmatic man who stubbornly refuses to act].[35]

1988 (no original source or date available)
Borges, Jorge Luis. 'Juan José Arreola: *Cuentos fantásticos*'. *Biblioteca personal: Prólogos*. 1988. *Obras completas*. Vol. 4. Buenos Aires: Emecé, 1996. 510.

Borges suggests that Kafka's writing influenced Juan José Arreola's *El guardagujas* [*The Switchman*] (1952), although Arreola's writing is not as good as Kafka's.

1995 (no original source or date available)
Borges, Jorge Luis. 'Gilbert Keith Chesterton: *El ojo de Apolo*'. *Prólogos de La Biblioteca de Babel*. Madrid: Alianza, 1995. 65–8.

About Chesterton, Borges says, 'Puedo haber sido Kafka o Poe pero valerosamente optó por la felicidad o fingió haberla hallado' [He could have been a Kafka or Poe, but he valiantly opted for happiness or feigned to have found it].[36]

---

[34] Ibid.
[35] Jorge Luis Borges, 'Herman Melville: *Benito Cereno, Billy Budd, Bartleby, el escribiente*', *Biblioteca personal: Prólogos*, 1988, *Obras completas*, Vol. 4 (Buenos Aires: Emecé, 1996), pp. 470–1 (p. 470).
[36] Jorge Luis Borges, 'Gilbert Keith Chesterton: *El ojo de Apolo*', *Prólogos de La Biblioteca de Babel* (Madrid: Alianza, 1995), pp. 65–8 (pp. 65–6).

APPENDIX I

Works by Kafka that Borges Read

A NOTE ON THE APPENDIX

This appendix provides a list of all of the stories by Kafka that Borges mentioned by name, reviewed, or translated. The list does not take into account stories for which there exists no original text by Kafka, such as those Borges mentioned reading in the German journals *Die Aktion* or *Sturm* in 1916 or 1917. It also does not include works that appear in volumes that Borges owned if he made no particular mention of them in his writing or in interviews. Borges's Kafka collection included the first and fifth volumes of the *Gesammelte Schriften* (the Schocken Complete Works), which he may have read as early as 1936; only the works from these volumes that Borges specifically mentioned are listed below. He also owned Kafka's *Hochzeitsvorbereitungen auf dem Lande* [*Wedding Preparations in the Country*], which he received as a birthday gift from Bioy Casares in 1953.[1]

There is some confusion over what books Borges actually read. In 'Un sueño eterno: Palabras grabadas en el centenario de Kafka' [An Eternal Dream: Words Recorded on Kafka's Centenary], Borges said that he read a collection of Kafka's stories called *Once cuentos* [*Eleven Stories*] in 1916.[2] There is no evidence in German or Spanish of a collection called *Once cuentos* (or any name resembling it), nor is there any Kafka collection containing eleven stories. There is a single story called 'Elf Söhne' [Eleven Sons], which was first published in the 1919 collection, *Ein Landarzt* [*A Country Doctor*]. When Borges claimed to have read *Once cuentos*, he was probably referring to one of two collections. The first possibility is the 1913 collection *Betrachtung* [*Meditation*], which contains eighteen stories. *Betrachtung* was Kafka's first published book of short stories, and Borges said that he read Kafka's first book. The second possibility is the 1919 collection *Ein Landarzt*, containing fourteen stories, which Borges also read. It is also conceivable that Borges only read 'Elf Söhne', which appears in *Ein Landarzt*. However, this story first appeared in print in 1919, and Borges said he initially read Kafka in 1916 or 1917. Out of eighty-nine short stories by Kafka published in Borges's lifetime, Borges read at least forty-one stories and many more as fragments. Borges also read all three of Kafka's novels: *Amerika* [*America*], *Der Prozeß* [*The Trial*], and *Das Schloß* [*The Castle*].

[1] Adolfo Bioy Casares, *Borges* (Buenos Aires: Destino, 2006), p. 85.
[2] Jorge Luis Borges, 'Un sueño eterno: Palabras grabadas en el centenario de Kafka', *Textos recobrados (1956–1986)* (Buenos Aires: Emecé, 2003), pp. 237–9 (p. 237).

WORKS BY KAFKA THAT BORGES
MENTIONED IN WRITING

1916

Once cuentos [*Eleven Stories*], probably the German-language collection *Betrachtung* [*Meditation*], which includes:

'Kinder auf der Landstraße' [Children on a Country Road]
'Entlarvung eines Bauernfängers' [Unmasking a Confidence Trickster]
'Der plötzliche Spaziergang' [The Sudden Walk]
'Entschlüsse' [Resolutions]
'Der Ausflug ins Gebirge' [Excursion into the Mountains]
'Das Unglück des Junggesellen' [Bachelor's Ill Luck]
'Der Kaufmann' [The Tradesman]
'Zerstreutes Hinausschaun' [Absent-minded Window-gazing]
'Der Nachhauseweg' [The Way Home]
'Die Vorüberlaufenden' [Passers-by]
'Der Fahrgast' [On the Tram]
'Kleider' [Clothes]
'Die Abweisung' [Rejection]
'Zum Nachdenken für Herrenreiter' [Reflections for Gentlemen-jockeys]
'Das Gassenfenster' [The Street Window]
'Wunsch, Indianer zu werden' [The Wish to Be a Red Indian]
'Die Bäume' [The Trees]
'Unglücklichsein' [Unhappiness]

1935

'Beim Bau der Chinesischen Mauer' [The Great Wall of China]
Der Prozeß [*The Trial*]
Ein Landarzt [*The Country Doctor*], which includes:

'Der neue Advokat' [The New Advocate]
'Ein Landarzt' [A Country Doctor]
'Auf der Galerie' [Up in the Gallery]
'Ein altes Blatt' [An Old Manuscript]
'Vor dem Gesetz' [Before the Law]
'Schakale und Araber' [Jackals and Arabs]
'Ein Besuch im Bergwerk' [A Visit to a Mine]
'Das nächste Dorf' [The Next Village]
'Eine kaiserliche Botschaft' [An Imperial Message]
'Die Sorge des Hausvaters' [The Cares of a Family Man]
'Elf Söhne' [Eleven Sons]
'Der Mord/Ein Brudermord' [A Fratricide]
'Ein Traum' [A Dream]
'Ein Bericht für eine Akademie' [A Report to an Academy]

1937

'Der Bau' [The Burrow]
'Ein Hungerkünstler' [A Hunger Artist]
'Forschungen eines Hundes' [Investigations of a Dog]
'Zur Frage der Gesetze' [The Problems of Our Laws]
'Der Kreisel' [The Top]
'Der Geier' [The Vulture]
Das Schloß [*The Castle*]

1938

'Eine alltägliche Verwirrung' [A Common Confusion]
'Die Verwandlung' [The Metamorphosis]
Amerika/Der Verschollene [*America/The Man Who Disappeared*]

1955

'Das Schweigen der Sirenen' [The Silence of the Sirens]
'Die Wahrheit über Sancho Pansa' [The Truth about Sancho Panza]
Die Zürauer Aphorismen [*The Zürau Aphorisms*] (also known as 'Betrachtungen über Sünde, Hoffnung, Leid und den wahren Weg' [Reflections on Sin, Suffering, Hope, and the True Way])

1956

Der Gruftwächter [*The Warden of the Tomb*]

1967

'Das Stadtwappen' [The City Coat of Arms]
'Eine Kreuzung' [A Crossbreed]
'Erstes Leid' [First Sorrow]
'Josefine, die Sängerin oder Das Volk der Mäuse' [Josephine the Singer, or the Mouse Folk]
'Prometheus' [Prometheus]
Hochzeitsvorbereitungen auf dem Lande [*Wedding Preparations in the Country*]

APPENDIX II

Jorge Guillermo Borges's Poetry

Note: Original spelling and punctuation have been preserved.

Borges, Jorge Guillermo. 'Momentos'. *Nosotros* 7.18 (1913): 147–8.

MOMENTOS

I

Enmudeciste . . . y luego,
con el hosco silencio fué el olvido
nevando sobre el ruego
del Amor en tu pecho entumecido.
5   Yo, no puedo olvidar, ni callar puedo
porque el Dolor es lengua que no calla
nunca, nunca. Por eso sobre el ledo
ritmo del verso mi dolor restalla;
manando de una fuente que no cesa
10   de glosar monocorde la tristeza
del humano vivir; ¡falaz quimera!
Y mi vida espejada en la corriente,
se contempla a sí misma en el doliente
espejo del pasado . . . y nada espera!

II

15   Y nada espero. Toda Vida es trunca.
Las horas dan, lo que las horas quitan.
Nunca vuelve el pasado, ¿sabes? ¡nunca!
ni las dichas pasadas resucitan.
En el recuerdo inmoble ¡ay! apenas
20   dibujan sus siluetas ilusorias,
las dichas y las penas,
dichas y penas que no tienen glorias.
La noche azul, aquel jardín callado,
los jazmines más blancos que la luna.
25   ¿Dime, no vierten claridad alguna?
¿Son de horas muertas que no tienen dueño?
Nunca torna el pasado.
Dime ¿te quise?, ¿fué verdad o sueño?

III

Sueño o verdad, al fin, es vana empresa
30   penetrar en el Alma de las Cosas.

El fatigante aliento de las rosas
perfuma, lo demás no me interesa!
Y si todo es mudanza y no es posible
las Horas modelar en bronce eterno,
35 y al empuje del Tiempo irresistible
la Primavera pasa y el Invierno,
protéico yo también a otros lugares,
es fuerza que me aleje sin agravios.
—Así la vida entiendo—
40 y por la noche que no tuvo azahares
y por el beso que no halló tus labios,
he aquí mi mano. ¿Ves? yo te la tiendo!

Borges, Jorge Guillermo. 'El cantar de los cantares'. *Gran guignol* 1.2 (1920):
5–7.

EL CANTAR DE LOS CANTARES

I
Este es el cantar de los cantares
que fué del Rey de Reyes Salomón,
amor es cuna de diez mil pesares.
Acuerde Dios al Rey gloria y favor.

5 Este es el cantar de los cantares,
y todo hombre nacido de mujer,
cuando gusta la fruta en los Pomares
Bendice la memoria del Gran Rey.

II
Este es el pesar de los pesares.

III
10 Agua que baña la caldeada roca;
vino de olvido, voluptuosa Paz.
Bésame con el beso de tu boca.
¡Arda en tu aliento la canción nupcial!

IV
Tus ojos son cisternas donde el cielo
15 de la noche estival copia sus astros,
¡tus ojos que en la hora de los besos
se ocultan en sus celdas de alabastro!

Tu cabello es la noche que distiende
sobre tus hombros perfumado manto,
20 sobre tus hombros y desnudos senos
¡timbales que el amor bate en sus cantos!

Tu boca es una cinta de escarlata,
ascua de un fuego que encendió el amor,
¡para aclamar el triunfo de las horas
25   en las siestas henchidas de pasion!

V

Canta, poeta, canta,
la túnica levanta
que cubre de tu amor la desnudez.

Vierte los pomos llenos
30   de myrra entre sus senos
¡y en su abrazo perfúmate después!

VI

El jardín y los patios señoriales
donde la guardia bate el atambor,
el huerto florecido y los trigales
35   que el oro rinden de la espiga al sol.

El lecho de la alcoba perfumada
donde el amor su lámpara cuidó,
recuerdan las ternuras de la amada,
sus tesoros, la alondra de su voz.
40   Las mantas de mi lecho la recuerdan
¡de su cuerpo conservan el calor!

VII

Morena es mi adorada cual la noche
que sus morenas carnes amasó,
la negra noche se enredó en sus trenzas
45   y en sus ojos profundos se durmió.

La negra noche de desnudos brazos,
la loca noche de desnudos pies,
que cual la amada llega silenciosa
y silenciosa aléjase después.

50   Morena es mi adorada cual la sombra
que amor escoje para amarse bien,
como el oculto nido en que sus besos
¡el canto cantan del perdido Edén!

VIII

Tu nombre es el zumbido de las alas
55   en torno a la colmena rica en miel,
es el claro llamar de las campanas
en torres de la astral Jerusalén!

Es el áureo contento de la huerta
dormida al sol en otoñal quietud,

60   el gajo roto al peso de la fruta,
        ¡tu nombre es el perfume y es la luz!

                        IX
        O Sulamita, lirio de los lirios,
        jardín de las doncellas de Sulém,
        ¿qué estrella en ascuas te indicó el camino
65   a este mi reino de Jerusalén,
        donde la gloria de tus ojos tienen
        enfermo y triste el corazón del rey?

        ¿Qué verde falda, qué región dorada
        de trigo y pleno sol te vió nacer,
70   en qué cielo enjoyado te miraste,
        dónde hallaron tus labios leche y miel?
        ¡Que por la dicha de tu rostro late
        enfermo y triste el corazón del rey!

                        X
        ¡Deja que el sol te bese en la esplendente
75   copa del amplio día; bebe luz!
        te cele el viejo bosque y la silente
        noche tiemble de amor y de inquietud.

        Tu eres el ala que sostiene el canto
        en las heridas cuerdas del laúd,
80   del vagabundo viento eres el llanto,
        del amplio cielo la mirada azul.

                        XI
        ¡Oh torre de marfil! ¡Oh llama de oro
        que en esplendor de luz anuncia el día!
        ¡Oh lámpara de plata de mi noche!

Borges, Jorge Guillermo. 'Del Poema de Omar Jaiyám'. *Gran Guignol* 1.1 (1920): 8.

DEL POEMA DE OMAR JAIYÁM

Omar Jaiyám nació a fines del undécimo siglo, en la ciudad de Naishapur. Dedicóse a las matemáticas, especializándose en la astronomía. Fué también un alegre camarada. Al morir, sus amigos reunieron sus coplas, a la manera persa, no según su carácter, sino según la letra inicial de cada una. Setecientos años después Fitzgerald cinceló esa admirable versión inglesa de las coplas que consagrara en Occidente la perenne fama de Omar. Este y Fitzgerald se complementan y armonizan. El persa dió tal vez la visión enjoyada del Oriente, la obsesión fatalista, el fondo de amargura y el otro su exquisito genio poético, un instrumento ya perfecto cuando Shakespear escribiera sus dramas, la arquitectura del poema, la pulsación sonora de la línea excelsa.

La actitud filosófica de Omar es muy sencilla. El presente enciérralo todo, es la sombra del pasado y va en fuga hacia la nada. Hay que abrazar en el presente el breve placer de las horas.

Este hedonismo es indudablemente antiguo como la civilización. Desde los griegos de la escuela cirenáica hasta Stirner, mil pensadores lo profesan y es diariamente practicado por todos nosotros a pesar de los frenos de ascetismo religioso y moral. Como se vé, la filosofía de Omar es lisa y plana y por eso mismo nos atrae; por eso mismo que no se eleva a inmensidades azules, que no promete felicidades lejanas sino que siempre es egoísta y fácil, inmediata y sincera.

I   El Mundo es sólo el cuadro iluminado
que arroja la Linterna del Juglar
cuya vela es el Sol, y nuestras Vidas,
Sombras que vienen, Sombras que se van.

II   Y si el Vino que bebes y la loca
Caricia de la Amada morirán,
como todo en la vida pasa y muere,
que más ni menos te pondrán quitar?

III   Bebe conmigo el fruta de la viña
mientras arda la Rosa en el Rosal
y cuando el Angel de la Muerte tienda
A tí su Copa, riente beberás.

IV   El Mundo es un tablero cuyos cuadros
son Noches y son Días, y el Azar
a su antojo nos mueve como a Piezas,
Luego las piezas a la Caja ván.

V   ¡Oh Dios! que el tiempo pase, que las Rosas
una a una abandonen el Rosal,
que el blanco Velo de la Infancia ceda
al Triste Luto de la triste Edad.

VI   Oh dicha de mi amor siempre constante;
la Luna asoma en el Palmar su faz;
Vendrá la noche en que esa misma Luna
ha de buscarme y no me encontrará.

VII   Y cuando tú, como la Luna, vuelvas
con pies de plata y no me encuentres ya,
derrama el Vaso que jamás mi boca
en Noche alguna volverá a gustar.

VIII   ¡Oh dicha de mi amor! yo estaré quieto,
tendido en tierra de una larga Paz,
durmiendo el sueño que no tiene sueños,
ni aurora, ni inquietud, ni despertar.

Borges, Jorge Guillermo. 'Rubáiyát'. *Proa* 1.5 (1924): 55–7.

RUBÁIYÁT

(Castellanizadas del inglés de Fitzgerald por Jorje Borges.)

I
Ya levantan sus tiendas las estrellas
del agredido campo nocturnal.
Con Flechas de Oro el Cazador de Oriente
acribilla la Torre del Sultán.

II
Suena el Clarin del Gallo, en la Taberna
dice una voz:—Hermanos despertad!
¡Si se seca la Copa de Vida
ya nunca más se volverá a llenar!

III
Y aquellos que esperaban
de la Taberna fuera en el Portál
Breve es el Plazo, gritan si partimos
ya no podremos retornar jamás!

IV
Con el Año que empieza, verdemente
el prado torna a su florida Edad,
de sus tibias cenizas los Deseos
a repetir las Súplicas vendrán.

V
El Iram I sus Rosas se perdieron
en la blanca extensión del Arenal,
pero aún la Vid nos brinda sus Rubies
i junto al Agua hay un Verjél de Paz.

VI
David rezando calla, más la Flauta
del Ruiseñor alegre en su cantar
dice a la Rosa: Vino, rojo Vino
tu pálida Mejilla encenderá.

VII
¡Llenad la Copa, en el ardiente Estío
quemad el Manto de invernal Pesar!
El Tiempo es Ave que fugaz se aleja
Ya el Ave alerta sobre el ala está!

VIII
Rosas a miles nacen cada Día
i a miles mueren cuando el Sol se va
El mismo Mes que nos regala Rosas
arrebata a Jamshyd I a Kaikobad.

IX
Ven con el viejo Omar I no lamentes
porque Jamshyd se fuera I Kaikobád
deja que llame Rustrum a las armas
o grite Jatim vamos a yantar!

X
Sobre el verte Tapete que separa
el campo en Flor de árido Arenal

¿Quién al almo distingue del Esclavo
quién codicia la Fama del Sultán?

XI
Bajo el verde Dosel de un Libro amigo,
un Bota de Vino, blanco pan
tu a mi lado cantando I el Desierto
fuera de veras el Jardin de Alláh.

XII
Unos buscan la Gloria de este Mundo
otros buscan la Gloria Celestiál
Venga el Dinero en mano I vaya el Resto,
deja el Tambor lejano retumbar.

XIII
En el Jardin, desatan sus corolas
los florídos Rosales y nos dán
el aureo Polen I aromado Incienso
que las Brisas esparcen al pasar.

XIV
Las terrenales Ansias realizadas
Sombra de Polvo son I nada más!
como la Nieve en el Desierto brillan
un Instante fugaz . . . .

XV
Oro atesores, despilfarres Oro.
La Tumba os mide con Criterio Igual
El barro de tu Cuerpo es siempre Barro
¡Y el barro de la Tierra abonará!

XVI
En este Albergue en ruinas cuyas Puertas
son Noches I son Dias ¡cuánto Afán!
¡Cuánto fiero Señor por breves Horas
detuvo el Paso I se volvió a marchar!

XVII
¡Los Patios de Jamshyd! donde su gozo
ardiera un día—albergan el chacal,
¡Silvestres Asnos pastan a su antojo
donde descansa el Cazador Bohrám!

XVIII
Donde muriera el Paladin, las Rosas
como teñidas por su Sangre están
¿Sueñas acaso de que blanco Pecho
estos Jazmines dicen la Beldad?

Borges, Jorge Guillermo. 'Rubáiyát'. *Proa* 2.6 (1925): 61–8.

RUBÁIYÁT

(Continuación)

XIX
Y este Musgo viviente que tapiza
la Tierra de finísimo Lampás,
se leve a su Blandura, pues quién sabe
de que Cuerpo jentil llegó a brotar.

XX

Llena le Copa que resguarda el Pecho
de torpe Miedo y de infantil Pesar
¡Mañana! dónde me hallaré mañana?
¿cuándo la Luz se apaga, donde vá?

XXI

Cuando noble Varón de claro Empeño
en el Embate quieto del Azar
vació su Copa I se perdió en silencio
entre la Bruma Gris del Mas-Allá.

XXII

Entretanto busquemos la Ventura,
que presto cesa, en el oscuro Umbral
donde la Muerte aguarda; Dime sabes?
¿Ese hondo Lecho para quien será?

XXIII

Gozad la Vida, fenecida pasa
A Nadas de insaciable Eternidad
Polvo de Polvo, sin Amor ni Amada
sin Vino, sin canción y sin soñar.

XXIV

A cuantos se desvelan por las Cosas
de este Mundo o del Mundo que vendrá
un Muezín de la Torre grita: ¡Tontos!
La Recompensa no está aquí ni allá.

XXV

Los Santos y los Sabios que charlaban
de esto I de aquello en tono doctoral
como falsos Profetas se eclipsaron.
Tierra es su Boca, Tierra es su Verdad.

XXVI

Deja charlar al Sabio, nuestras Vidas
Gotas son en la Sed del Arenal.
La Rosa muere I muere su Perfume
esto sabemos, I no indagues más!

XXVII

Cuando Jóven cursé las Academias
del mucho discutir I fué tenaz
mi Empeño de Saber más por la Puerta
de Entrada, la Salida hube de hallar.

XXVIII

Yo sembré de Sapiencia mi Sendero
i el Desencanto solo ví brotar;
como resopla el Viento I corre el Agua
asi la Vida viene, asi se vá.

XXIX

Porqué he venido al Mundo, Quién reesponde?
Agua que corre ciega hasta la Mar?
¡Como el Agua I el Viento que no saben
porqué corren I soplan I se ván!

XXX

Quién al Mundo nos trajo, quién nos lleva?
¿i donde iremos luego: á que Avatár?
Llenad la Copa para ahogar en ella

El Recuerdo de tanta Necedad.

XXXI
Al trono de Saturno en los Espacios
me elevé por el Séptimo Portal
i muchos Nudos desaté a mi Paso
pero no el Nudo del Humano Azar.

XXXII
Hallé una Puerta que no tiene Llave
Un Velo que no puede penetrar;
hoi hablarán un poco de nosotros
i luego, no hablarán.

XXXIII
Entonces a la Altura interrogando
dije: ¿Qué Ley me guía, qué Verdad?
I una Voz infinita respondióme:
Tienes un ciego Instinto I nada más

XXXIV
En la Copa de Arcilla el Labio puse
el Enigma tratando de aclarar
I ella me dijo: Mientras vive, bebe;
la avara Tumba nada te dará.

XXXV
La Arcilla de esta Copa en otro Tiempo
un Bebedor alegre fué quizás
¡O cuanta Boca habrá besado el Barro
que hoi a mis labios de beber les dá.

XXXVI
Recuerdo que una Tarde a un Alfarero
que una Copa moldeaba en el Bazar
la Arcilla dijo musitando apenas:
ten cuidado Hermanito, me haces Mal.

XXXVII
Llenad la Copa que la Vida alegra;
el Tiempo en fuga hacia la Nada vá
Ayer ha muerto, por venir Mañana
con Hoi tan solo es lícito contar.

XXXVIII
Palidecen los Astros, ya la Noche
toca a su Fin. La Caravana! Helás!
se apresta para el Alba de la Nada
¡En Marcha pues, el Paso apresurad!

XXXIX
Porqué estas Ansias que se ajitan ciegas
en pós de un vano inasequible Ideal?
Mejor el Fruto de la fresca Viña
que el Fruto amargo que esas Ansias dán.

XL
Venid hermanos I entonemos presto
de nuevas Bodas la Canción Nupcial,
la estéril Razon dejo I por Esposa
llamo al lecho la Hija de Lagar.

XLI
Arriba, Abajo, de derecha a izquierda
mi Lógica sondó la Realidad.

al Fondo de las Cosas no he llegado
solo del Vaso el Fondo supe hallar.

XLII

Ha tiempo que a la Hora del Ocaso
un Anjel me detuvo en el Umbral
de la oscura Taberna I de sus Labios
el Fruto de la Vid me dió a probar.

XLIII

El Fruto de la Vid que con severa
Elocuencia refuta el Razonar
de todas las Escuelas, Alquimista
Que el Plomo trueca en fúljido Metal.

XLIV

El gran Mahmúd que vence en un instante
las Penas de la triste Humanidad
i con su Fuerza májica nos libra
de torpe Sombra I de más torpe Afan.

XLV

Venid conmigo I que discutan Sabios
del Universo el misterioso Plan;
también el Vino es elocuente I sabio.
i todo Enigma descifrar sabrá.

XLVI

El Mundo es sólo el Cuadro iluminado
que arroja la Linterna del Juglar
cuya Vela es el Sol, I nuestras Vidas,
Sombras que vienen, Sombras que se ván.

XLVII

Y si el Vino que bebes I la dulce
Caricia de las Amada pasarán
como todo en la Vida pasa I muere
¿que más ni menos te podrán quitar?

XLVIII

Bebe conmigo el Fruto de la Viña
mientras arda la Rosa en el Rosal
i cuando el Anjel de la Muerte tienda
a ti su Copa, ríente beberás.

XLIX

El Mundo es un tablero cuyos Cuadros
son Noches I son Dias, I el Azar
a un antojo nos mueve como a Piezas
Luego—las Piezas a la Caja van.

L

La Mano escribe I pasa, I tu Ternura
tus Rezos, tu Saber o tu Piedad
no lograran que vuelva ó que hehaga
ó borre aquello que ya escrito está.

LI

Y esa Copa invertida que sustenta
el Cielo prometido del Korán
en su propia Impotencia rueda, rueda
ajena a todo Bien y a todo Mal.

LII

Del Barro que dió el ser al primer Hombre

ha de formarse el último Mortal,
estaba escrito en la primera Mañana
lo que el postrer Crepúsculo dirá.

LIII

Los astros arrojaron en la Senda
de la Vida, su Sombra I su Pesar
En la Senda las Piedras están listas
donde los Pasos tropezando van.

LIV

Aulle fuera el Derviche sus Plegarias
de la cerrada Puerta en el Umbral
Nunca insensato encontrará la Llave
que el Vino excelso, jeneroso dá

LV

Tú que la Senda hicistes engañosa
donde debí perderme I tropezar,
no afirmes luego que la Culpa es mía
Tuyo es el Mundo, tuya es su Maldad!

LVI

Tú que moldeaste el Vaso de mi Cuerpo
en él vertiendo Sombas I Pesar
tu que el Eden hiciste I la Serpiente:
nuestro Perdon recibe I perdonad!

LVII

Cuando se extinga el Fuego que me anima,
mi cuerpo en rojo Vino lavarás
i en Pámpano silvestre amortajado
que descanse a la Sombra de un Parral.

LVIII

Y mis Cenizas muertas al Ambiente
Fragancia tan sutil arrojarán
que hasta el Creyente absorto en su Plegaria
al grato Dogma de la Vid vendrá.

LIX

Los Idolos que amara tanto tiempo
derrocharon ingratos mi Caudal
ahogaron mi buen nombre en una Copa
i al Barro denigrose mi Verdad.

LX

¡Aymé! que el Tiempo pase, que las Rosas
una a una abandonen el Rosal,
que el blanco Velo de la Infancia ceda
al triste Luto de la triste Edad!

LXI

Oh dicha de mi Amor siempre constate,
La luna asoma en el Palmar su faz
Vendrá la Noche en que esa misma Luna
ha de buscarme I no me encontrará.

LXII

Y cuando tú como la Luna vuelvas
con pies de plata I no me encuentres ya

derrama el Vaso que jamás mi boca
en Noche alguna volverá a gustar.

LXIII

O dicha de mi Amor! yo estaré quieto
tendido en tierra de una larga Paz
durmiendo el Sueño que no tiene sueños
ni auroras, ni inquietud, ni despertar.

Bibliography

For Borges and Kafka, details are only provided for works cited in this book. For bibliographies listing their complete works, see Nicolás Helft, *Jorge Luis Borges: Bibliografía completa* (Buenos Aires; México: Fondo de Cultura Económica, 1997) and Maria Luise Caputo-Mayr and Julius Michael Herz, *Franz Kafka: internationale Bibliographie der Primär- und Sekundärliteratur* (Munich: Saur, 2000).

JORGE LUIS BORGES

(i) Anthologies: Fiction and Poetry

El Aleph. 1949. *Obras completas*. Vol. 1. Buenos Aires: Emecé, 1996. 531–630.

Ficciones. 1944. *Obras completas*. Vol. 1. Buenos Aires: Emecé, 1996. 425–529.

El hacedor. 1960. *Obras completas*. Vol. 2. Buenos Aires: Emecé, 1996. 155–232.

Historia universal de la infamia. 1935. *Obras completas*. Vol. 1. Buenos Aires: Emecé, 1996. 287–345.

El informe de Brodie. 1970. *Obras completas*. Vol. 2. Buenos Aires: Emecé, 1996. 397–454.

El libro de arena. 1975. *Obras completas*. Vol. 3. Buenos Aires: Emecé, 1996. 9–73.

La moneda de hierro. 1976. *Obras completas*. Vol. 3. Buenos Aires: Emecé, 1996. 119–61.

El oro de los tigres. 1972. *Obras completas*. Vol. 2. Buenos Aires: Emecé, 1996. 455–516.

(ii) Anthologies: Non-Fiction

Biblioteca personal: Prólogos. 1988. *Obras completas*. Vol. 4. Buenos Aires: Emecé, 1996; Alianza, 1988. 445–529.

El círculo secreto: Prólogos y notas. Buenos Aires: Emecé, 2003.

Discusión. 1932. *Obras completas*. Vol. 1. Buenos Aires: Emecé, 1996. 173–285.

Evaristo Carriego. 1930. *Obras completas*. Vol. 1. Buenos Aires: Emecé, 1996. 97–172.

Historia de la eternidad. 1936. *Obras completas*. Vol. 1. Buenos Aires: Emecé, 1996. 347–423.

Jorge Luis Borges: A/Z. Madrid: Siruela, 1988.

Jorge Luis Borges en 'El Hogar' (1930–1958). Buenos Aires: Emecé, 2000.

Jorge Luis Borges en 'Sur' (1931–1980). Barcelona: Emecé, 1999.

Otras inquisiciones. 1952. *Obras completas*. Vol. 2. Buenos Aires: Emecé, 1996. 9–153.

Páginas de Jorge Luis Borges. Ed. Alicia Jurado. Buenos Aires: Celtia, 1982.

Prólogos con un prólogo de prólogos. 1975. *Obras completas*. Vol. 4. Buenos Aires: Emecé, 1996. 11–160.

Prólogos de La biblioteca de Babel. Madrid: Alianza, 2001.

El tamaño de mi esperanza. 1925. Buenos Aires: Seix Barral, 1994.

Testimonios de mis libros. Buenos Aires: Revista del Notariado, 1972.

Textos cautivos. 1986. *Obras completas*. Vol. 4. Buenos Aires: Emecé, 1996. 206–443.

Textos recobrados (1919–1929). Buenos Aires: Emecé, 1997.

Textos recobrados (1931–1955). Buenos Aires: Emecé, 2001.

Textos recobrados (1956–1986). Buenos Aires: Emecé, 2003.

This Craft of Verse. Ed. Calin-Andrei Mihailescu. Cambridge: Harvard UP, 2000.

(iii) Uncollected Works

'An Autobiographical Essay'. *The Aleph and Other Stories: 1933–1969*. Trans. and ed. Norman Thomas di Giovanni. London: Jonathan Cape, 1968. 203–60.

'Borges sur Kafka'. *Change International* 3 (1985): 44–5.

'Franz Kafka'. *Franz Kafka: A Centennial Celebration*. Spec. issue of *Newsletter of the Kafka Society of America*. Philadelphia: The Kafka Society of America, 1983. 3.

'Jorge Luis Borges habla del mundo de Kafka'. *La metamorfosis*. Paraná: Orión, 1982. 5–28.

'Kafka, la philosophie, la poésie'. *Change International* 3 (1985): 46.

'El Libro de Job'. *Conferencias de Jorge Luis Borges en el Instituto de Intercambio Cultural y Científico Argentino-Israelí*. N.p.: Instituto de Intercambio Cultural y Científico Argentino-Israelí, 1967. 5–16.

Prologue. *Bartleby*. By Herman Melville. Trans. Jorge Luis Borges. Buenos Aires: Edicom, 1969. 9–13.

Prologue. *El buitre*. By Franz Kafka. Trans. Jorge Luis Borges. Buenos Aires: La Ciudad, 1979. 7–11.

'Una valoración de Kafka por Jorge Luis Borges'. *Clarín: Cultura y nación* 30 June 1983: 1–2.

(iv) Works in Collaboration

Borges, Jorge Luis, and Adolfo Bioy Casares. Prologue. *Los orilleros*. 1955. *Obras completas en colaboración*. Buenos Aires: Emecé, 1979. 199–200.

Borges, Jorge Luis, and Adolfo Bioy Casares. 'La víctima de Tadeo Limardo'. *Seis problemas para don Isidro Parodi*. 1942. *Obras completas en colaboración*. Buenos Aires: Emecé, 1979. 85–104.

Borges, Jorge Luis, and Betina Edelberg. 'El modernismo'. *Leopold Lugones*. 1955. *Obras completas en colaboración*. Buenos Aires: Emecé, 1979. 463–9.

Borges, Jorge Luis, and Margarita Guerrero. 'Martín Fierro y los críticos'. *El Martín Fierro*. 1953. *Obras completas en colaboración*. Buenos Aires: Emecé, 1979. 557–61.

Borges, Jorge Luis, and María Esther Vázquez. 'Nuestro siglo'. *Introducción a la literatura inglesa*. 1965. *Obras completas en colaboración*. Buenos Aires: Emecé, 1979. 850–7.

Borges, Jorge Luis, and Esther Zemborain de Torres. *Introducción a la literatura norteamericana*. Buenos Aires: Columba, 1967.

(v) Translations of Kafka Attributed to Borges
'Ante la ley'. *Jorge Luis Borges en 'El Hogar' (1930–1958)*. Buenos Aires: Emecé, 2000. 108–9.
'Un artista del hambre'. *La metamorfosis*. 1938. Buenos Aires: Losada, 1967. 95–110.
'Un artista del trapecio'. *La metamorfosis*. 1938. Buenos Aires: Losada, 1967. 111–16.
'El buitre'. *La metamorfosis*. 1938. Buenos Aires: Losada, 1967. 121–4.
'Una confusión cotidiana'. *La metamorfosis*. 1938. Buenos Aires: Losada, 1967. 133.
'Conviene distinguir'. *Libro de sueños*. Buenos Aires: Torres Agüero, 1976. 55.
'Una cruza'. *La metamorfosis*. 1938. Buenos Aires: Losada, 1967. 117–20.
'La edificación de la muralla china'. *La metamorfosis*. 1938. Buenos Aires: Losada, 1967. 79–94.
'El escudo de la ciudad'. *La metamorfosis*. 1938. Buenos Aires: Losada, 1967. 125–8.
'La metamorfosis'. *La metamorfosis*. 1938. Buenos Aires: Losada, 1967. 13–78.
'Prometeo'. *La metamorfosis*. 1938. Buenos Aires: Losada, 1967. 129–30.

(vi) Translations of Kafka Attributed to Borges in Collaboration
Borges, Jorge Luis, and Adolfo Bioy Casares, trans. 'Cuatro reflexiones'. *Cuentos breves y extraordinarios*. 1955. Buenos Aires: Losada, 1992. 146.
Borges, Jorge Luis, and Adolfo Bioy Casares, trans. 'Los cuervos y el cielo'. *Libro del cielo y del infierno*. Buenos Aires: Sur, 1960. 52.
Borges, Jorge Luis, and Adolfo Bioy Casares, trans. 'El silencio de las sirenas'. *Cuentos breves y extraordinarios*. 1955. Buenos Aires: Losada, 1992. 81–2.
Borges, Jorge Luis, and Adolfo Bioy Casares, trans. 'La verdad sobre Sancho Panza'. *Cuentos breves y extraordinarios*. 1955. Buenos Aires: Losada, 1992. 132.
Borges, Jorge Luis, Adolfo Bioy Casares, and Silvina Ocampo, trans. 'Josefina la cantora o el pueblo de los ratones'. *Antología de la literatura fantástica*. Buenos Aires: Sudamericana, 1965. 222–38.
Borges, Jorge Luis, and Margarita Guerrero, trans. and eds. 'Un animal soñado por Kafka'. *El libro de los seres imaginarios*. 1967. *Obras completas en colaboración*. Buenos Aires: Emecé, 1979. 575.
Borges, Jorge Luis, and Margarita Guerrero, trans. and eds. 'Odradek'. *El libro de los seres imaginarios*. 1967. *Obras completas en colaboración*. Buenos Aires: Emecé, 1979. 676–7.

(vii) Translations of Borges
Aizenberg, Edna, trans. 'The Book of Job'. *Borges and His Successors: The Borgesian Impact on Literature and the Arts*. Columbia: U of Missouri P, 1990. 267–75.
Allen, Esther, Suzanne Jill Levine, and Eliot Weinberger, trans. *Selected Non-Fictions*. Ed. Eliot Weinberger. New York: Viking, 1999.

Hurley, Andrew, trans. *The Book of Sand*. 1975. *Collected Fictions*. New York: Viking, 1998. 409–85.

Hurley, Andrew. *Fictions*. 1944. *Collected Fictions*. New York: Viking, 1998. 65–179.

Hurley, Andrew. *The Maker*. 1960. *Collected Fictions*. New York: Viking, 1998. 289–327.

Hurley, Andrew. *A Universal History of Iniquity*. 1935. *Collected Fictions*. New York: Viking, 1998. 1–64.

Levine, Suzanne Jill, trans. 'A Profession of Literary Faith'. *On Writing*. London: Penguin, 2010. 67–71.

Simms, Ruth L. C., trans. *Other Inquisitions: 1937–1952*. Austin: U of Texas P, 2000.

Yates, Donald A., and James E. Irby, trans. and eds. *Labyrinths: Selected Stories and Other Writings*. London: Penguin, 2000.

FRANZ KAFKA

(i) Anthologies: Fiction and Non-Fiction

Amerika: Roman. Gesammelte Schriften. Vol. 2. Berlin: Schocken, 1935.

Beschreibung eines Kampfes: Novellen, Skizzen, Aphorismen aus dem Nachlass. Gesammelte Schriften. Vol. 5. Prague: Heinr. Mercy Sohn, 1936.

Drucke zu Lebzeiten. Frankfurt (Main): S. Fischer; New York: Schocken, 1994.

Erzählungen und kleine Prosa. Gesammelte Schriften. Vol. 1. Berlin: Schocken, 1935.

Nachgelassene Schriften und Fragmente I. Ed. M. Pasley. New York: Schocken, 1993.

Nachgelassene Schriften und Fragmente II. Ed. M. Pasley. New York: Schocken, 1992.

Nachgelassene Schriften und Fragmente II. Apparatband. Ed. M. Pasley. Frankfurt (Main): Fischer, 1992.

Der Proceß. Ed. M. Pasley. New York: Schocken, 1990.

Das Schloß. Ed. M. Pasley. New York: Schocken, 1982.

Tagebücher. Eds. H.-G. Koch, M. Müller, and M. Pasley. New York: Schocken, 1990.

Tagebücher (1910–1923). New York: S. Fischer/Schocken, 1948–49.

Tagebücher und Briefe. Gesammelte Schriften. Vol. 6. Prague: Heinr. Mercy Sohn, 1937.

Der Verschollene. Ed. J. Schillemeit. New York: Schocken, 1983.

(ii) Translations of Kafka

Crick, Joyce, trans. *The Metamorphosis and Other Stories*. Oxford: Oxford UP, 2009. 100–40.

Hofmann, Michael, trans. *The Zürau Apohorisms*. 1931. London: Harvill Secker, 2006.

Kaiser, Ernst, and Eithne Wilkins, trans. 'The Eight Octavo Notebooks'. *Wedding Preparations in the Country and Other Posthumous Prose Writings*. London: Secker and Warburg, 1954. 54–156.

Kresh, Joseph, trans. *The Diaries of Franz Kafka, 1910–1913*. Ed. Max Brod. New York: Schocken, 1971.

Muir, Willa, and Edwin Muir, trans. *The Complete Novels*. London: Vintage, 1999.

Muir, Willa, et al., trans. *The Complete Stories*. Ed. Nahum N. Glatzer. New York: Schocken, 1971.

JORGE GUILLERMO BORGES

'El cantar de los cantares'. *Gran guignol* 1.2 (1920): 5–7.

El caudillo. 1921. Buenos Aires: Academia Argentina de Letras, 1989.

Hipoteca naval. Buenos Aires: L. Franzoni, 1897.

'Momentos'. *Nosotros* 7.18 (1913): 147–8.

'Del poema de Omar Jaiyám'. *Gran guignol* 1.1 (1920): 8.

'Rubáiyát'. *Proa* 1.5 (1924): 55–7.

'Rubáiyát'. *Proa* 2.6 (1925): 61–8.

La senda. 1917. Ed. María Julia Rossi. Pittsburgh: U of Pittsburgh, 2015.

CRITICISM ON BORGES AND KAFKA

Aizenberg, Edna. 'Kafka, Borges and Contemporary Latin-American Fiction'. *Newsletter of the Kafka Society of America* 6.1–2 (1982): 4–13.

Azancot, Leopoldo. 'Borges y Kafka'. *Indice* 17.170 (1963): 6.

Belitt, Ben. 'The Enigmatic Predicament: Some Parables of Kafka and Borges'. *Prose for Borges*. Eds. Charles Newman and Mary Kinzie. Evanston: Northwestern UP, 1974. 212–37.

Boegman, Margaret Byrd. 'From Amhoretz to Exegete: The Swerve from Kafka by Borges'. *Critical Essays on Jorge Luis Borges*. Ed. Jaime Alazraki. Boston: G. K. Hall, 1987. 173–91.

Boegman, Margaret Byrd. 'Paradox Gained: Kafka's Reception in English from 1930 to 1949 and his Influence on the Early Fiction of Borges, Beckett, and Nabokov'. Diss. U of California, Los Angeles, 1977. Microfilm.

Brodzki, Bella P. 'Deceptive Revelation: The Parable in Agnon, Kafka, Borges'. Diss. Brown U, 1980. Microfilm.

Caeiro, Oscar. 'Borges, por la huella de Kafka'. *Criterio* 1769 (1977): 416–21.

Chiappini, Julio. *Borges y Kafka*. Rosario: Zeus, 1991.

Cueto, Sergio. 'Un discípulo tardío: El Kafka de Borges'. *Boletín del Centro de Estudios de Teoría y Crítica Literaria* 7 (1999): 34–40.

de Torre, Fernando. 'Notas sobre el laberinto y el centro en algunas obras de F. Kafka y J. L. Borges'. *Iberoromania* 22 (1985): 67–78.

de Torre Borges, Miguel. 'Kafka and Borges on Postcards'. *Variaciones Borges* 7 (1999): 272–4.

de Wald, Rebecca. 'Possible Worlds: Textual Equality in Jorge Luis Borges's (Pseudo)Translations of Virginia Woolf and Franz Kafka'. Diss. U of Glasgow, 2015.

Faye, Jean-Pierre. 'Kafka avec Borges: La narration et sa chose'. *Change International* 3 (1985): 44.

Fló, Juan. 'Jorge Luis Borges traductor de *Die Verwandlung* (fechas, textos, conjectoras)'. *Papeles de trabajo* 1 (1995): 1–36.

García, Carlos. 'Borges y Kafka'. *Fragmentos* 28–9 (2005): 49–59. *The Kafka Project.* Web. 24 Aug. 2010.

Gargatagli, Marietta. '¿Y si La metamorfosis de Borges fuera de Borges?' *El Trujamán: Revista Diaria de Traducción* (2014): np. Web. 10 Nov. 2014.

Geisler, Eberhard. 'Notas introductorias para el estudio de la lectura borgiana de Kafka'. *Actas del octavo congreso de la asociación internacional de hispanistas.* Vol. 1. Providence: Brown UP, 1983. 597–606.

Geisler, Eberhard. 'La paradoja y la metáfora: En torno a la lectura Borgiana de Kafka'. *Revista de Crítica Latinoamericana* 11.24 (1986): 147–71.

Graetzer, Margarita. 'Las paradojas del cosmos en Borges y Kafka'. *Dactylus* 8 (1987): 27–30.

Harman, Theodore Allan. 'New Testament and Modern Parables: Their Relationship and Literary Character, a Reader's Response'. Diss. U of Durham, 1990. Microfilm.

Just, Rainer. 'Kafka und Borges—ein hermeneutische Konfrontation'. Diss. Weinn, 1997.

Kluback, William. 'Our Gentile Guides, Jorge Luis Borges and Franz Kafka'. *Confluencia: Revista Hispanica de Cultura y Literatura* 8.1 (1992): 19–27.

Krenz, David Christoph. 'Metaphors for/in Infinity: The Parables of Kafka, Borges, and Calvino'. Diss. U of Wisconsin–Milwaukee, 1992. Microfilm.

Lages, Susana Kampff. 'Jorge Luis Borges, Franz Kafka e o labirinto da tradição'. *Revista de letras* 33 (1993): 13–21.

Lehman-Srinivasan, Kathryn. 'Revolution in Writing: Borges's Reading of the Expressionists'. Diss. U of Michigan, 1987. Microfilm.

Libuse, Moníková. *Schloß, Aleph, Wunschtorte.* Munich: Hanser, 1990.

Massuh, Gabriela. '"La lotería en Babilonia": Una comparación entre Kafka y Borges'. *Boletín de Literatura Comparada* 7–8 (1982–83): 21–37.

Melero, Nina. 'Los traductores de La Metamorfosis'. *Hieronymus* 12 (2008): 87–92.

Ogden, Thomas H. 'Kafka, Borges, and the Creation of Consciousness, Part I: Kafka—Dark Ironies and the "Gift" of Consciousness'. *The Psychoanalytic Quarterly* 78.2 (2009): 343–67.

Ogden, Thomas H. 'Kafka, Borges, and the Creation of Consciousness, Part II: Borges—A Life of Letters Encompassing Everything and Nothing'. *The Psychoanalytic Quarterly* 78.2 (2009): 369–96.

Olsen, Lance. 'Diagnosing Fantastic Autism: Kafka, Borges, Robbe-Grillet'. *Modern Language Studies* 16.3 (1986): 35–43.

Pestaña Castro, Cristina. 'Intertextualidad de F. Kafka en J. L. Borges'. *Especulo: Revista de estudios literarios* 7 (1997): np. Web. 25 Aug. 2010.

Pestaña Castro, Cristina. 'Quién tradujo por primera vez "La metamorfosis" de Franz Kafka al castellano?' *Especulo: Revista de estudios literarios* 11 (1999): np. Web. 25 Aug. 2010.

Podlubne, Judith. 'Lecturas cruzadas en la revista *Sur*: Mallea y Borges sobre Kafka y Chesterton'. *Anclajes* 9.10 (2005): 119–39. Web. 10 Nov. 2010.

Roger, Sarah. 'Finding Franz Kafka in the Works of Jorge Luis Borges'. *Oxford German Studies* 43 (2014): 140–55.

Roger, Sarah. 'A Metamorphosis? Rewriting in Borges's Translations of Kafka'. *Comparative Critical Studies* 8.1 (2011): 81–94.

Roger-Taillade, Nicole. 'L'oeuvre littéraire et le labyrinthe (*Le Château* de F. Kafka, *L'Aleph* de J. L. Borges, *L'Emploi du Temps* de M. Butor)'. *Littératures* 31 (1994): 124–56.

Ryan, Judith. 'Kafka's "An Imperial Message" in a Comparative Context'. *Approaches to Teaching Kafka's Short Fiction*. Ed. Richard T. Gray. New York: MLA, 1995. 43–52.

Ryan, Judith. 'The Maze of Misreadings: Thoughts on Metaphor in Kafka'. *The Journal of the Kafka Society of America* 2.7 (1983): 38–43.

Sandbank, Shimon. *After Kafka: The Influence of Kafka's Fiction*. Athens: U of Georgia P, 1989.

Sorrentino, Fernando. 'El kafkiano caso de la *Verwandlung* que Borges jamás tradujo'. *Especulo: Revista de estudios literarios* 10 (1998): np. Web. 20 Nov. 2009.

Sorrentino, Fernando. '"La metamorfosis" que Borges jamás tradujo'. *La Nación: Suplemento literario*. 9 Mar. 1997. 4.

Vrhel, František. 'Borges y Praga'. *El siglo de Borges*. Vol. 1. Eds. Alfonso de Toro and Fernando de Toro. Madrid: Iberoamericana; Frankfurt (Main): Vervuert, 1999. 439–49.

Yelin, Julieta. 'Kafka en Argentina'. *Hispanic Review* 78.2 (2010): 251–73.

SECONDARY SOURCES

Amis, Kingsley. 'The Poet and the Lunatics'. 1971. *G. K. Chesterton: A Half Century of Views*. Ed. D. J. Conlon. Oxford: Oxford UP, 1987. 269–73.

Anzieu, Didier. 'El cuerpo y el código en los cuentos de Jorge Luis Borges'. Trans. Antonio Marquet. *Plural: Revista cultural de excelsior* 208 (1989): 20–40.

Anzieu, Didier. Prologue. *The Secret of Borges: A Psychoanalytic Inquiry into his Work*. By Julio Woscoboinik. Trans. Dora Carlisky Pozzi. Lanham: UP of America, 1998. vii–xi.

Balderston, Daniel. *Out of Context: Historical Reference and the Representation of Reality in Borges*. Durham: Duke UP, 1993.

Barnatán, Marcos-Ricardo. *Borges: Biografía total*. Madrid: Temas de Hoy, 1995.

Barnstone, Willis. *With Borges on an Ordinary Evening in Buenos Aires: A Memoir*. Urbana: U of Illinois P, 2000.

Barrenechea, Ana María. *La expresión de la irrealidad en la obra de Jorge Luis Borges*. México, DF: El Colegio de México, 1957.

Barthes, Roland. 'La mort de l'auteur'. 1967. *Le bruissement de la langue*. Paris: Seuil, 1984. 61–7.

Bell-Villada, Gene. *Borges and his Fiction: A Guide to his Mind and Art*. 2nd ed. Austin: U of Texas P, 1999.

Benton, Michael. *Literary Biography: An Introduction*. Oxford: Wiley-Blackwell, 2009.

Bioy Casares, Adolfo. *Borges*. Buenos Aires: Destino, 2006.

Bloom, Harold. *The Anxiety of Influence: A Theory of Poetry*. 2nd ed. Oxford: Oxford UP, 1997.

Bozal, Sela. 'Franz Kafka/Alfred Kubin: *Ein Landarzt*. La parabola sin clave'. *Cuadernos de Filología Alemana* 1 (2009): 73–88, (p. 74). Web. 10 Nov. 2014.

Brod, Max. *Franz Kafka: eine Biographie*. 3rd ed. Berlin: S. Fischer, 1954.

Burgin, Richard. *Conversations with Jorge Luis Borges*. New York: Holt, 1969.

Burton, Robert. *The Anatomy of Melancholy*. 1621. 3 Vols. Vol. 2. London: Folio Society, 2005.

Canto, Estela. *Borges a contraluz*. Madrid: Espasa Calpe, 1989.

Chesterton, Gilbert Keith. *The Man Who Was Thursday: A Nightmare*. 1908. New York: Random House, 2001.

Chiappini, Julio. *Los prólogos de Borges*. Rosario: Zeus, 1991.

Christ, Ronald, Alexander Coleman, and Norman Thomas di Giovanni. 'Borges at NYU: 8 April 1971'. *Prose for Borges*. Eds. Charles Newman and Mary Kinzie. Evanston: Northwestern UP, 1974. 396–411.

de Milleret, Jean. *Entretiens avec Jorge Luis Borges*. Paris: Pierre Belfond, 1967.

Eliot, T. S. 'Tradition and the Individual Talent'. *The Sacred Wood: Essays on Poetry and Criticism*. 2nd ed. London: Methuen, 1928. 47–59.

Escóbar Plata, Dante. *Las obsesiones de Borges*. Buenos Aires: Distal, 1989.

Fiedler, Leslie A. 'Archetype and Signature: A Study of the Relationship Between Biography and Poetry'. *The Sewanee Review* 60.2 (1952): 253–73. *JSTOR*. Web. 28 Oct. 2009.

FitzGerald, Edward. *Rubáiyát of Omar Khayyám*. Ed. Daniel Karlin. Oxford: Oxford UP, 2009.

Freud, Sigmund. *The Psychopathology of Everyday Life*. 1901. *The Basic Writings of Sigmund Freud*. Trans. and ed. A. A. Gill. New York: Random House, 1938. 35–178.

González, Aníbal. *A Companion to Spanish American Modernismo*. Woodbridge: Tamesis, 2007.

Gray, Richard T. et al. *A Franz Kafka Encyclopedia*. Westport: Greenwood, 2005.

Greenberg, Martin. *The Terror of Art: Kafka and Modern Literature*. London: Andre Deutsch, 1971.

Greenberg, Moshe. 'Job'. *The Literary Guide to the Bible*. Eds. Robert Alter and Frank Kermode. London: Fontana, 1997. 283–304.

Griffin, Clive. 'Philosophy and Fiction'. *The Cambridge Companion to Jorge Luis Borges*. Cambridge: Cambridge UP, 2013. 5–15.

Hawes, James. *Excavating Kafka*. London: Quercus, 2008.

Hayman, Ronald. *K: A Biography of Kafka*. London: Weidenfeld and Nicolson, 1981.

Heath, Stephen, trans. and ed. 'The Death of the Author'. *Image Music Text*. By Roland Barthes. London: Fontana, 1977. 142–8.

Heller, Erich. *Kafka*. London: Fontana, 1974.

Hoffman, Frederick J. 'Escape From Father'. *The Kafka Problem*. Ed. Angel Flores. London: New Directions, 1946. 214–46.

Humphreys Roberts, G., and Richard Winston, trans. *Franz Kafka: A Biography*. By Max Brod. 1937. New York: Da Capo, 1995.

Jakobson, Roman. 'What Is Poetry?' 1934. *Semiotics of Art: Prague School Contributions*. Trans. Michael Heim. Eds. Ladislav Matejka and Irwin R. Titunik. Cambridge: MIT, 1976. 164–75.

Jefferson, Ann. *Biography and the Question of Literature in France*. Oxford: Oxford UP, 2007.

Jrade, Cathy L. 'Modernist Poetry'. *The Cambridge History of Latin American Literature*. Eds. Roberto González-Echevarría and Enrique Pupo-Walker. Cambridge: Cambridge UP, 2008. 7–68. *Cambridge Histories Online*. Web. 18 Oct. 2010.

Jurado, Alicia. Prologue. *El caudillo*. By Jorge Guillermo Borges. Buenos Aires: Academia Argentina de Letras, 1989. 11–23.

'Kafkaesque', *Oxford English Reference Dictionary*. Eds. Judy Pearsall and Bill Trumble. Oxford: Oxford UP, 2002.

Kancyper, Luis. *Jorge Luis Borges, o el laberinto de Narciso*. Buenos Aires: Paidos, 1989.

Kancyper, Luis. *Jorge Luis Borges, o la pasión de la amistad: Estudio psicoanalítico*. Buenos Aires: Lumen, 2003.

Karlin, Daniel. Introduction. *Rubáiyát of Omar Khayyám*. By Edward FitzGerald. Oxford: Oxford UP, 2009. xi–xlviii.

Kociancich, Vlady. 'Retrato de un padre: El hacedor secreto de un gran poeta'. *Clarín: Cultura y nación* 22 Aug. 1999: 5–6.

Koelb, Clayton. 'Critical Editions II: Will the Real Franz Kafka Please Stand Up?' *A Companion to the Works of Franz Kafka*. Ed. James Rolleston. Rochester: Camden House, 2002. 27–33.

Kristal, Efraín. *Invisible Work: Borges and Translation*. Nashville: Vanderbilt UP, 2002.

Kristeva, Julia. 'Le mot, le dialogue et le romain'. 1967. *Semeiotike: Recherces pour une sémanalyse*. Paris: Seuil, 1969. 82–112.

Landy, Francis. 'The Song of Songs'. *The Literary Guide to the Bible*. Eds. Robert Alter and Frank Kermode. London: Fontana, 1997. 305–19.

Martínez Estrada, Ezequiel. *En torno a Kafka, y otros ensayos*. Barcelona: Seix Barral, 1967.

Merrell, Floyd. *Unthinking Thinking: Jorge Luis Borges, Mathematics, and the New Physics*. West Lafayette: Purdue UP, 1991.

'La metamorfosis'. [Translator Unknown.] By Franz Kafka. *Revista de Occidente* 8–9 (1925): 33–79 and 273–306.

Michaels, Jennifer E. 'Psychoanalysis, Literature and Sociology'. *Sexual Revolutions: Psychoanalysis, History and the Father*. Ed. Gottfried Heuer. London: Routledge, 2011. 155–67.

Murray, Jack. *The Landscapes of Alienation: Ideological Subversion in Kafka, Céline, and Onetti*. Stanford: Stanford UP, 1991.

Neider, Charles. *The Frozen Sea: A Study of Franz Kafka*. New York: Russell & Russell, 1962.

'Nightmare'. Def. 2. *Shorter Oxford English Dictionary*. Vol. 2. 6th ed. Oxford: Oxford UP, 2007.

Novillo-Corvalán, Patricia. 'James Joyce, author of "Funes el memorioso"'. *Variaciones Borges* 25 (2008): 60–81.

Nuño, Juan. *La filosofía de Borges*. México, DF: Fondo de Cultura Económica, 1986.

Ortelli, Roberto A. 'Letras argentinas: *El Caudillo*, novela por Jorge Borges'. *Nosotros* 17.166 (1923): 403–7.

Pagés Larraya, Antonio. '*El caudillo*: Una novela del padre de Borges'. *Repertorio Latinoamericano* 2nd ser. 5.36 (1979): 3–6.

'Parable'. *Shorter Oxford English Dictionary*. Vol. 2. 6th ed. Oxford: Oxford UP, 2007.

Pascal, Roy. 'Kafka's Parables: Ways Out of the Dead End'. *The World of Franz Kafka*. Ed. J. P. Stern. London: Weidenfeld and Nicholson, 1980. 112–19.

Pasley, Malcolm. Notes. *The Transformation and Other Stories: Works Published in Kafka's Lifetime*. By Franz Kafka. London: Penguin, 1992. ix–xii.

Pawel, Ernst. *The Nightmare of Reason: A Life of Franz Kafka*. London: Collins Harvill, 1988.

Politzer, Heinz. *Franz Kafka: Parable and Paradox*. Ithaca: Cornell UP, 1962.

Pozzi, Dora C. trans. *The Secret of Borges: A Psychoanalytic Inquiry Into His Work*. By Julio Woscoboinik. Lanham: UP of America, 1998.

Reid, Alastair. 'Kafka: The Writer's Writer'. *Journal of the Kafka Society of America* 2.7 (1983): 20–7.

Robertson, Ritchie. *Kafka: A Very Short Introduction*. Oxford: Oxford UP, 2004.

Rodríguez Monegal, Emir. *Jorge Luis Borges: A Literary Biography*. New York: E.P. Dutton, 1978.

Roger, Sarah. 'Critics and Their Precursors: Theories of Influence in T. S. Eliot, Jorge Luis Borges, and Harold Bloom'. *Bloomsbury Adaptations*. Eds. E. H. Wright and Paul Edwards. Newcastle: Cambridge Scholars, 2014. 2–15.

Roger, Sarah. 'Translation, Identity, and Jorge Luis Borges'. *The Limits of Literary Translation: Expanding Frontiers in Iberian Languages*. Kassel: Reichenberger, 2012. 57–71.

Salas, Horacio. *Borges: Una biografía*. Buenos Aires: Planeta, 1994.

Shaw, Donald. *Borges: Fictions*. London: Grant and Cutler, 1976.

Sokel, Walter H. *The Myth of Power and the Self: Essays on Franz Kafka*. Detroit: Wayne State UP, 2002.

Stach, Reiner. *Kafka: The Decisive Years*. Trans. Shelley Frisch. London: Harcourt, 2005.

Stach, Reiner. *Kafka: The Years of Insight*. Trans. Shelley Frisch. Princeton: Princeton UP, 2013.

Standish, Peter. ' "El Congreso" in the Works of J. L. Borges'. *Hispanic Review* 55.3 (1987): 347–59. *JSTOR*. Web. 7 Nov. 2009.

'Subordination'. *Oxford English Dictionary Online*. Oxford UP, 2009. Web. 10 Oct. 2009.

Teitelboim, Volodia. *Los dos Borges: Vida, sueños, enigmas*. México, DF: Hermes, 1996.

Thorlby, Anthony. *Kafka: A Study*. London: Heinemann, 1972.

Vaccaro, Alejandro. *Georgie (1899–1930): Una vida de Jorge Luis Borges*. Buenos Aires: Proa-Alberto Casares, 1996.

Venegas, José Luis. 'Eliot, Borges, Tradition, and Irony'. *Symposium: A Quarterly Journal in Modern Literatures* 59.4 (2006): 237–55. *Literature Online*. Web. 29 Dec. 2009.

Williamson, Edwin. *Borges, A Life*. London: Viking, 2004.

Williamson, Edwin. 'Borges in Context: The Autobiographical Dimension'. *The Cambridge Companion to Jorge Luis Borges*. Ed. Edwin Williamson. Cambridge: Cambridge UP, 2013. 201–25.

Wilson, Jason. *Jorge Luis Borges*. London: Reaktion, 2006.

Wimsatt, W. K., and Monroe C. Beardsley. 'The Intentional Fallacy'. 1974. *Praising It New: The Best of the New Criticism*. Ed. Garrick Davis. Athens: Swallow-Ohio UP, 2008. 102–16.

Woodall, James. *The Man in the Mirror of the Book: A Life of Jorge Luis Borges*. London: Hodder and Stoughton, 1996.

Woods, Michelle. *Kafka Translated: How Translators Have Shaped Our Reading of Kafka*. New York: Bloomsbury, 2014.

Woscoboinik, Julio. *El alma de 'El Aleph': Nuevos aportes a la indagación psicoanalítica de la obra de Jorge Luis Borges*. Buenos Aires: Nuevohacer, 1996.

Woscoboinik, Julio. *El secreto de Borges: Indagación psicoanalítica de su obra*. Buenos Aires: Trieb, 1988.

Zito Lema, Vicente. 'Jorge Luis Borges y su ultimo libro: "El Congreso" que yo soñé (1973)'. *El otro Borges: Entrevistas (1960–1986)*. Ed. Fernando Mateo. Buenos Aires: Equis, 1997. 38–48.

Index